HOW TO RAISE A BRIGHTER CHILD
IS MY BABY ALL RIGHT?
Written with Virginia Apgar, M.D.

Effective Parenting

A Practical and Loving Guide to Making Child Care Easier and Happier for Today's Parents *Joan Beck*

Simon and Schuster · New York

1 2 3 4 5 6 7 8 9 10
Library of Congress Cataloging in Publication Data
Beck, Joan Wagner, date.
    Effective parenting.
    Includes index.
    1. Children—Management.   I. Title.
HQ769.B3458   649'.1   76-10820
ISBN 0–671–22299–6

Contents

Preface

This is a book for people who want to be good parents, who choose deliberately to have children—in an age when fathering and mothering are optional lifestyles and not the inevitable consequence of sex or an expectation of society. It is for the new generation of men and women who care intelligently and lovingly about the quality of life they provide for their children and who, for the most part, enjoy creating a family and home along with their involvement in the world outside.

Raising children is one of the most difficult, challenging, demanding, expensive undertakings in which a woman and a man ever become involved. It can also carry far greater rewards than any other endeavor. New research about genetics, prenatal development, mental growth, behavior modification, education and child psychology all promise that these rewards can increase in the near future for parents willing to spend the requisite effort.

This is not a detailed instruction manual about babies, full of advice on formula and rashes; good books like that are easy to obtain. It is a collection of practical answers to the questions most frequently raised by parents in the course of caring for their children, and it does provide tested techniques for handling dozens of problems parents often encounter: How can you manage a happy three-week vacation with two preschoolers in tow? What should you tell your youngsters about sex, Santa Claus, bullies, talking to strangers, the death of a pet? How can you cope with a reading problem, a hospitalized youngster, a four-year-old's birthday party, a two-and-a-half-year-old's bedtime tantrum, a thumb-sucker? What's the easiest, happiest way to handle toilet training, to start a three-year-old in nursery school, to survive a winter sick-in, to avoid a hassle over music lessons, to save money on baby-sitting?

Some of the answers come from reports of new research about children in the fields of medicine, psychology, education, biology and the arts. Some are compendiums of conclusions from mothers whose offspring have just grown through particular stages in child development and who therefore have had practical experience on how problems can be prevented or minimized. There's even some advice from on-scene grandmothers, relatively rare people these days, since increasingly women whose children are grown are finding jobs of their own outside the home. Much of the information in this book was compiled during a dozen years of writing the nationally syndicated column for parents, "You and Your Child," in reporting news about pediatrics, child psychology and education for the *Chicago Tribune*, and in finding answers to the questions asked in thousands of letters from fathers and mothers.

No book on child care should be considered an infallible recipe for turning out an ideal, raised-to-order child. Children differ too much one from another to benefit from precisely the same parenting techniques. Fathers and mothers vary, too, in the child-care styles that are comfortable for them. Research in medicine and psychology shows conclusively that babies are born with innate differences in temperament and learning style that determine to some degree how they react to their environment and to their parents' care. Fathers and mothers must learn to take these differences into account.

The key to using any child-care book is to choose the ideas and suggestions that seem appropriate for your particular youngsters and then to observe carefully the effect of the actions you are taking. You should continue to use those techniques which are helping them to develop into happy, creative, intelligent, self-disciplining, thoughtful, loving human beings. You should discard any methods which seem to be producing nagging conflict between you and your children, or guilt feelings on your part, or undesirable behavior on their part. Because the suggestions and ideas in this book have been tested by so many hundreds of thousands of newspaper readers, you will probably find that most of them are helpful and successful with your children.

Despite the increasing and highly beneficial involvement of fathers in child care, this book continues the traditional use of "she" or "you" to mean a "parent" of either sex, because women still carry out by far the greater amount of parenting. So, for convenience, the pronoun "he" is generally used for "child" although without any sexist intent.

In preparing this book, thanks are due to the Chicago Tribune–New York News Syndicate, Inc., for permission to use material from the column, "You and Your Child"; to Herbert Alexander and Sol Immerman of Simon and Schuster for their tactful prodding and encouragement; to the American Academy of Pediatrics for research data and other information; to scores of experts in pediatrics, psychology, education and related fields who made their knowledge and research available to me; and to hundreds of parents who shared their child-care experiences with readers of my column. I also wish to thank my husband, Ernest W. Beck, for his help and encouragement; my parents, Roscoe and Mildred Wagner, for showing me from the beginning what good parents are like; and my children, Christopher and Melinda, for teaching me how rewarding becoming a parent can be.

1. Love Comes First

So, how do you begin?

You start by loving, by caring and by responding to a need. Turning yourself into a parent is a major metamorphosis, a milestone that marks the point of no return between youth and adulthood. Becoming the mother or father of a new baby is more miraculous and more mundane, more exciting and more exasperating, more difficult and more instinctively natural than you can possibly imagine until it happens to you. After having a child, you will never be the same again.

Although your firstborn is a toothless, wrinkled, squalling seven pounds or so of almost total helplessness, you find him uniquely beautiful—unlike all of the other toothless, wrinkled newborns in the hospital nursery. Although the day before he was born you did not know whether your offspring would be a boy or a girl, the day after his birth, he seems so familiar you feel you must have known all along it would be this particular child. Even when you have had your baby for less than 24 hours and have gotten along quite well without him for 20 or 23 or 28 years, you know you will never again be totally happy should anything ever happen to him.

Now you must learn to become a parent to this newborn

infant, as he grows and changes from baby to toddler to kindergartner to pre-teen to adolescent to adult. For his physical health and safety will depend on your care for a long time to come and his emotional well-being and mental development will reflect the quality of his early life for as long as he lives.

You start by loving. Loving a child won't solve all of his problems. But unless he is loved, nothing else will ever help enough.

So you begin with love. The first time you see your newborn baby, you hold him gently, closely, warmly, and you can feel your love for him begin to grow. You feel awkward, tentative, strange, uneasy, of course. That's normal, as it is whenever you start out on any new job or sport or activity. But then comes the first payoff for being a parent: Your baby begins to love you back—with a fist curled tightly around your finger or an intent, cross-eyed kind of stare into your eyes or a sigh of relaxation as he trustfully molds his small body just a little against you.

Loving your baby isn't just a sentimental idea. Psychologists and other behavioral scientists who have studied new mothers and new babies carefully conclude that the love between mother and baby that starts so surely and grows so quickly must have some kind of genetic basis, that it must be an ancient, instinctive interaction requisite for the survival of the species. Psychologists call the phenomenon of mother-baby, baby-mother love "attachment" and know that it sets a pattern for all love to come in the newborn's life.

Just as your love will gradually come to shape your baby's life, your baby's love for you will also begin to change yours. Much of what you learn about child care you will learn from your infant himself as he responds to you by crying or by cuddling close or by soothing at your touch. In a few weeks, he'll be smiling just at the sound of your voice or the sight of your face (he comes genetically programmed, research shows, to respond more to the human face than to any other sight or picture or visual pattern). He'll wiggle all over with total joy when you approach to pick him up. Soon he'll crawl after you as fast as he can maneuver his uncoordinated body when you leave his room; then he'll take his first tottering steps to throw himself into your arms with a laugh of triumph.

Love between parent and child serves many other unsentimental purposes. A baby has a tangible, urgent need for love. A lack of caring can result in stunted emotional growth, or in certain drastic cases the inability to survive for more than a few months, as medical and historical research has clearly proven. Love provides a growing child with a secure home base from which he can safely explore the world—the enticements on the other side of the room at first when he's learning to creep and toddle, then nursery school or kindergarten, camp, college, marriage. And love gives a margin for error, for mistakes parents make in love seldom do any lasting damage to a growing child.

Along with love comes responding to your baby's needs. No matter how much you love your newborn child, you will find that much of the inevitable work connected with him is mindless and menial. It also seems unending. You have to forget the five-day week, the eight-hour day, the 60-minute lunch and the 15-minute coffee break for a while. And most devastating to your morale and efficiency, you probably have to forgo the eight-hour sleep as well. Without love, you couldn't—wouldn't—do it all.

It is almost unbearably difficult at times, particularly for a new mother who has been a successful career woman or a busy co-ed, to gear herself to the shut-in, slow-paced life with baby, to curb her instincts to be quick, efficient and productive while she rocks placidly as the baby nurses for a contented twenty minutes five or six times a day. Or wants to be lullabied to sleep when dinner guests are coming in half an hour. Or misses his mouth with two out of three spoonfuls of cereal. Or takes fifty minutes to toddle two blocks to the store. Or insists on zipping his jacket all by himself when he can't. But with love and understanding of a young child's real needs, you do learn to make these adjustments in your lifestyle for a few years, even if they never come easy.

The physical handling of a new infant looks relatively simple when you watch it in the hospital nursery. But like a golf swing or a tennis serve, this ease is deceptive, for the skills can only be mastered with considerable practice.

A new baby isn't as fragile as he looks; he won't break. But he does scream, wiggle, jerk, arch his back and flop in ways that make him awkward to hold, especially in the weeks right after his birth. He can't help his uncoordinated movements and he needs to be handled firmly and securely, yet with great gentleness.

Long before his birth, during the second, third and fourth months of pregnancy, an unborn infant has plenty of room to stretch, exercise and develop his growing muscles. He moves around in the watery environment of his mother's womb, at the end of his umbilical cord, as gracefully, easily and weight-lessly as an astronaut in outer space.

But during the last weeks before birth, a baby's increasing size cramps him and traps him in awkward positions. After birth it takes many weeks before he gains firm control over his muscles and can make his arms and legs and head obey his conscious intentions. A newborn infant also must learn to cope with gravity for the first time. His flailing arms and legs no longer encounter the confining, protective walls of the uterus and he sometimes seems to startle and scare himself into screaming by his own random movements. This is why it's easier to pick him up if you wrap him securely in a receiving blanket first and why you can sometimes soothe him by putting your warm, adult hand gently on his abdomen or back.

The initial problems of baby care are complicated by the fact that neither mother nor infant are in top form physically during the first weeks of a newborn's life. It takes about six weeks for a woman's body to make the hormonal and other physical adjustments that occur in the shift from a pregnant to a nonpregnant state. And this period is often marked by unexpected emotional upsets, uncharacteristic touchiness and unanticipated fatigue.

The traditional psychological explanation for what is called "baby blues" or "postpartum depression" is that the new mother is insecure in her role, jealous of the new rival for her husband's attention and unhappy about giving up her former occupations. All of these factors probably do contribute to the uneasy adjustment period. But most of the post-baby blues is due to hormonal imbalances, somewhat similar to those occurring over a longer time span at adolescence and at other periods during a woman's life. Her fatigue also has physical origins, resulting from the demands that advanced pregnancy, labor, birth and 24-hour-a-day baby care put on her body.

A newborn child is also in a state of physical disequilibrium as his body gradually adjusts to life outside the womb. His breathing is noisy, sometimes irregular. His digestive system, in particular, is immature. He spits up part of the feedings you've so carefully given him. He has trouble getting rid of the air he inevitably swallows along with the milk. Even the activity of his bowels may seem to scare him and set him screaming.

No matter how efficiently and lovingly you care for him, a new baby almost always spends at least two hours every day in fussy, inconsolable crying. Usually this unhappy period comes in the early or late evening, the most difficult time for the weary adults who have to cope with it. Careful research by behavioral scientists and physicians shows that such crying occurs even in babies born into the most ideal of circumstances, to experienced mothers who have coped well with previous children and who are happily settled in a maternal role, and to families where there are no unusual tensions or emotional disturbances. Most physicians now attribute these crying jags to the immature digestive and nervous systems of the newborn infant, particularly because the problem ends so predictably when the baby is about three months old, regardless of any changes in his environment.

The shakedown period for learning to live with a newborn baby usually takes about three to four weeks, sometimes longer, depending on the temperament of your infant, his weight at birth, his sleep patterns and a range of family circumstances. But gradually you begin to get a little more sleep at night, to feel less worn out and frantic. You become more skilled and relaxed in the routine of caring for your baby's physical needs. The baby begins to smile, to respond to your sight and touch. His behavior becomes more predictable and his waking and sleeping periods begin to fall into a pattern so that you can start to plan the rest of your daily activities. Now your baby is an accepted member of a functioning family unit.

Along with love and physical care, it's time to think about what else your baby needs to grow up well and how you can best provide it for him. It can be summed up like this:

· Your child needs to be treated like an expanding intelligence and a fellow human being rather than as an invalid or a pet or a possession. He shouldn't be kept constantly in bed when he's awake, even when he's too young to sit up. And he shouldn't be imprisoned in a playpen when he's bored with it.

· A young child needs freedom and challenge to explore an expanding environment with safety and encouragement. This means constant and unobstructive supervision, as he grows out of his crib, playpen, playroom and back yard and into the wider world. Parents should understand that such freedom to explore, to touch, to handle, to investigate, to learn is essential for optimum development, because it is often inconvenient and time-consuming to provide.

· A young child needs the emotional security of an adult who is usually present, especially when he's frightened or hurt or sick or lonely or bored or eager to share a new discovery with someone he loves. If he can't count on his mother to be with him when he needs her—and children don't get frightened or bored or hurt or sick or lonely or eager to share on schedule or at adult convenience—then he needs a reliable mother substitute who will be there consistently.

· A young child needs social experiences appropriate for his age with a few other adults and youngsters, with unobtrusive guidance to help him enjoy these contacts and develop social skills.

· Your child needs parents and a home environment that will give him opportunity for maximum mental development, especially during the crucial first six years of his life when his brain is growing fastest and much of his adult level of intelligence is being stabilized. So much of a youngster's mental development occurs before age six and the quality of his early learning is so important that what benefit he gets from later schooling depends on these to a great degree. A youngster who receives little more than custodial care during the critical first few years of his life will not be as bright or as eager to learn as he might have been, nor will his functional intelligence be as high. No amount of schooling later on will entirely make up for what he did not receive in the way of stimulating parenting when he needed it most.

· A youngster should have instant and constant feedback for his efforts to learn to talk. As a baby, he needs an adult who will pay attention to his babbling and respond to it. As a toddler, he should have a parent who reacts with joy and pride to his first words and encourages him to keep on trying to form more by responding to what he can say. When a child is a preschooler, his mind grows best when a parent answers his thousand daily "Why's" in a friendly and interesting way that stimulates a thousand more. He also profits enormously when a parent has time and patience to introduce him to words in written form or to a second language used on a casual, everyday basis.

· Your child needs to be kept safe and well nourished so he will grow up in optimum good health. He must be protected unobtrusively from dangers until he can be taught to recognize and cope with hazards himself. He must be fed a nutritionally sound diet and helped to learn healthful eating habits for himself. He must have regular medical checkups and routine immunizations.

· Your child needs to have fun, to learn to laugh at himself, to enjoy others, to discover a happiness in living, to develop the ability to keep problems in perspective.

None of this is easy to provide as constantly as a baby or a toddler or a small child needs it. It can only be done by an adult whose efforts are motivated by personal, individual love. Raising a child is one of the most difficult, expensive, time-consuming undertakings in which a woman and a man ever become involved. It can also carry far greater rewards than any other endeavor. The aim of this book is to offer suggestions, new research and effective techniques from experienced parents, physicians and experts in human behavior to make the going easier and happier.

2. How to Pick a Pediatrician

Two expectant mothers were discussing which pediatrician to select for their imminent heirs.

"Don't get Dr. X," warned one almost-due mother. "He makes you keep on sterilizing bottles forever. Dr. Y says you can quit that routine in three months."

Deciding on a pediatrician is too often done casually, as if one were choosing a shoe style or a detergent. You owe it to your baby and to your own peace of mind to give serious thought to the type of doctor to whom you will entrust your child's health for the next dozen or more years.

Unless you already have a beloved family doctor, you'll probably choose a child-care specialist for your baby. Actually there's a shortage of general practitioners and a slight over-supply of pediatricians, according to a recent medical survey—a trend that may increase with the drastic drop in births during the 1970s.

You should, of course, begin by phoning your local medical association to check the academic background and professional qualifications of a physician you are considering. But you should ask other questions, too, preferably of the doctor him-self in a get-acquainted visit before your baby is even born.

21

How does he feel about making house calls when your child is sick? Many pediatricians today consider house calls as obsolete as leeches and refuse to go unless it's a dire emergency. They make the point—correctly—that modern office or hospital equipment is necessary to make an accurate diagnosis or give adequate treatment and it's therefore better for an ailing youngster to be brought to the office or to the nearest hospital emergency room.

But there is a clear and present danger that a sick child in a doctor's waiting room may have an undiagnosed contagious disease that could spread to other youngsters who are there for routine checkups—or what's much worse, to a waiting mother who happens to be in the early months of pregnancy. Several contagious diseases can cause severe birth defects in an unborn child if the mother is infected in early pregnancy. So it is essential that a physician who rules out house calls make adequate provision for protecting his small patients and their mothers from such hazards in his waiting room.

How does the physician you are considering handle calls about petty problems? First-time mothers have dozens of questions that don't require a full-scale office visit. The best-loved pediatricians hold a daily worried-mother's hour when you can feel free to telephone about minor matters. Whether the doctor charges for the call isn't important; his attitude toward you as you develop maternal skills does count.

How much does the physician like to tell his patients' parents? When your child is sick, do you want a short layman's lecture on the progress and prognosis of the illness? Or are you happier with a doctor who says, "Now, don't you worry about this. Let me do the worrying. That's why you are paying me."

What hospital staff appointments does the doctor hold? Should your youngster require quick hospitalization, you'll want to know your physician can have him admitted to a good hospital near your home. Some suburban parents prefer a pediatrician with staff privileges in a big-city children's hospital, too, where he can keep up with medical developments and take your offspring in case of an illness too complicated for small local hospital facilities.

What is the doctor's attitude toward a hospitalized child? The trend is now away from the traditional practice of limiting visiting hours for parents and letting a small patient cry out his fears and misery among strangers, and toward encouraging a mother to participate in the care of her hospitalized offspring. But often you need strong support from your physician to make the necessary arrangements at a hospital which is reluctant to work with parents for the good of their child. You should make sure the physician will support you should it ever become necessary.

Do you agree with the doctor's pet theories? If you're positive you want to breast-feed your infant, for example, you won't be very happy with a pediatrician who thinks nursing is a lot of unnecessary nonsense when bottles work just as well.

It's easy for an insecure, first-time parent to feel intimidated about asking questions like these of a physician to whom she is considering entrusting her baby's health. But you will be dependent on this doctor's wisdom and help during what may well be some of the most worrisome times of your life—and it's important that you choose him in advance with all of the consumer-wisdom you can muster.

3. Is Your Baby an "Easy" or a "Difficult" Child?

Some babies are "easy" almost from birth. Some are "difficult." And a "difficult" baby can happen to any mother, regardless of how calm, efficient, experienced and loving she is.

Mothers who have had more than one child, or who have compared offspring with other parents, have long accepted this fact. But physicians and psychologists are only now beginning to pinpoint these innate differences and the ways in which they affect a child's behavior, and to give parents some help in adapting their child-care techniques to cope better with each particular, individual youngster.

Newborn babies show marked differences in behavior and temperament, even from birth, many experts now emphasize. No one fully understands the precise origin of these differences but they are probably due in part to inherited factors and in some degree to the prenatal environment of the infant. "Difficult" babies can be born to parents who are relatively relaxed and calm, and high-strung, excitable mothers can have unusually placid infants, for reasons that can't yet be determined.

Many of the kinds of behavior that make up a baby's temperament are evident in the first few days of life. As early as the second or third month, infants can be rated in nine categories of temperament which will influence the course of their behavior, according to Dr. Stella Chess, of New York University School of Medicine. Dr. Chess and her associates have been conducting a long-term study of individual differences in babies and children. Dr. Chess's categories, as reported in the *Journal of Pediatrics*, are these:

1. Amount of motor activity.

2. Predictability of cycles of hunger, sleep-and-wakefulness and elimination.

3. Approach or withdrawal in response to new stimuli, such as a new food, a new toy, or a new person.

4. Speed and ease of adaptability of behavior in response to a change in the environment.

5. Intensity of reactions.

6. Level of stimulation required for baby to respond.

7. Child's general mood—cheerful and friendly or unpleasant and crying.

8. Distractibility.

9. Attention span and degree of persistence in the face of obstacles.

A parent who takes these temperament factors into consideration will do a much more effective job of child rearing, suggests Dr. Chess. For example, a toddler with a low degree of distractibility and a low activity level can rather easily be persuaded to sit quietly on a toilet seat during training, while a youngster who resists new experiences and has a high activity level will begin objecting loudly and forcibly in half the time.

The second youngster will be much harder to toilet-train, notes Dr. Chess. But the reason is the child's temperament—not the mother's attitude, or methods, or skill, or any psychological factors of anxiety or hostility.

These differences in temperament must always be considered in caring for a child, Dr. Chess emphasizes. Because of such differences, no single set of child-care rules will work optimally well with every youngster, she explains.

The type of baby most likely to become a behavior problem is the one who is extremely irregular in his biological functions, withdraws from new stimuli, has a negative mood, reacts intensely and adapts slowly to change. A parent whose infant comes with this set of characteristics can cope most effectively with him by being unusually firm, patient, consistent and tolerant, suggests Dr. Chess. If the parent reacts to such a difficult youngster by being inconsistent, impatient and punishing, the child is almost sure to become a behavior problem.

One of the easiest types of children to raise is the kind who is regular in his bodily functioning, responds happily to new stimuli, adapts quickly to change and has a generally positive mood. Such a youngster is usually a joy to raise, although he may develop behavior problems if the demands of friends or school conflict too sharply with home standards.

One pediatrician who does work with parents to determine the kind of temperament with which their child is born is Dr. William B. Carey, of Media, Pennsylvania. Dr. Carey uses a seventy-question scale filled out by the mother as a guide to her baby's innate style of reacting to the world around him. Questions probe the baby's reactions to sleeping, eating, being bathed, diapering, visits to the doctor, illness, people, new experiences.

For example, Dr. Carey asks whether a baby "generally takes milk at about the same time" each day. Or "sometimes the same, sometimes at different times." Or whether his hunger is "quite unpredictable."

Another question explores what a baby does when he doesn't want to eat any more—whether he clamps his mouth closed, spits out the food or bats at the spoon, or whether he turns his head away or lets the food drool out of his mouth, or whether his response tends to vary.

In Dr. Carey's study of 101 babies, 11 were rated as "difficult," 41 as "easy" and 49 as in between. The difficult babies included approximately the same number of boys and girls. None was known to be brain-injured (although seven of the 11 had been delivered by cesarean section).

There was no significant differences in temperament between boy and girl babies as rated by Dr. Carey's scale, with one exception. The boy babies were generally rated as being more persistent than the girls. It is not clear whether this is a biased observation by the mothers, a peculiarity of this particular sampling of babies, or a valid observation on human nature, Dr. Carey told a conference of the American Academy of Pediatrics.

How do parents manage to live with a "difficult" baby? There is no easy answer, according to Dr. Carey. He emphasized that the parents of these babies seem to be no different from other fathers and mothers. But he said they must be unusually firm, patient, consistent and tolerant in dealing with their difficult child lest a destructive interaction develop that could result in lifelong behavior problems. He stressed that with careful handling, the difficult child's behavior will gradually ease and be less of a problem.

4. Colic and Its Causes

True or false: When an infant has colic, it's usually because his mother is anxious or unhappy about having a new baby or because there's too much tension in the home.

True, say most articles about colic written for doctors or for parents, which usually blame colic on the baby's home environment and particularly on tensions and guilt feelings in the mother. If the mother calms down, accepts her femininity and her maternal role, her baby's digestive mechanism will no longer reflect her tensions and will function smoothly and painlessly, the accepted theory goes.

Considerable new research indicates a different answer. Mothers of colicky babies may indeed be less confident about handling their infants and temporarily may enjoy them less. But this is clearly the result of the frustrations and problems in caring for a colicky youngster, not the cause, according to research presented to the American Orthopsychiatric Association by Dr. Benjamin A. Shaver.

Infantile colic is one of the most common and distressing problems parents of a new baby face, said Dr. Shaver. It usually begins about the third week of life, for no obvious reason. Despite all the remedies a pediatrician can suggest, it tends to persist until the infant is three or four months old, when it subsides, for no apparent reason.

Usually a colicky infant seems healthy and happy most of the day. But late in the afternoon, or perhaps after his 6 P.M. feeding, he begins to fuss and cry. His mother's gentlest comforting doesn't help. She tries to feed him again, but he turns away from breast or bottle. She tries to burp him and he does bring up an air bubble. But his discomfort continues and he pulls his knees up to his chest in pain and keeps on crying.

The longer the baby cries, the more miserable and useless his mother feels. She and her husband take turns in rocking the infant and walking the floor with him. She pats him, sings to him, puts him in his crib, picks him up again. At last, by 11 P.M. or midnight, the baby falls asleep in exhaustion and so do his frantic parents.

Nothing the pediatrician suggests helps: a change in formula, a sedative, an antispasmodic drug, gentle heat on the baby's abdomen, more burping, different nipples or feeding techniques, a more relaxed routine during the day or more isolation from family bustle in the evening.

"The most helpful treatment for colic," noted Dr. Shaver, "is the reassurance that the symptoms will abate when the infant is three or four months of age. The fact that the condition is not interminable is often enough to keep the parents holding on for a few weeks.

"We do not know why colic begins at age three weeks and why it stops at age three or four months," emphasized Dr. Shaver. If it were due primarily to a mother's anxiety and insecurity, it should logically start as soon as the baby comes home from the hospital—and be most common in firstborn children, he said. But this is not the case.

In the course of his research, studies were made of 57 mothers during the last six months of pregnancy and first six months after their babies were born. A psychiatrist, psychologist, social worker, obstetrician, pediatrician and infant observer compiled details about each woman's life history, personality, current life, problems and feelings about pregnancy—and about her baby after birth. Comparisons were then made between the mothers whose babies had colic and those whose infants didn't. No differences were found between the two groups—in amount and quality of caring for the infants, in sensitivity, amount of stimulation, feelings, anxieties, moods, sense of humor, maturity, responsiveness, or success as wife or mother or homemaker. There also were no differences in family stresses, financial insecurities, illnesses or other problems.

Dr. Jack L. Paradise, of the Children's Hospital of Pittsburgh, agreed when he presented his findings to the American Academy of Pediatrics. His study involved 146 normal newborn infants and their mothers and does not show any significant relationship between colic and a mother's feelings, attitudes toward her infant or problems in the home.

"Of the 101 babies with mild, moderate or severe colic, more than half cried exclusively or predominately between the hours of 6 P.M. and midnight," noted Dr. Paradise.

Mothers in the study took a 550-item test designed to measure their personality and psychological stability. But no differences in the incidence of colic in their offspring were found in comparing the "cheerful, nonworrying mothers" with those rated "most anxious" on the test.

Dr. Paradise did find that the mothers with the highest intelligence and most education had babies with more colic than others. Fathers of about one fourth of the infants were physicians receiving postgraduate training; colic was about twice as frequent in their offspring as in those of other parents. But the better-educated mothers may simply have been more likely to ask for medical help, Dr. Paradise suggested.

No conclusive evidence links any factor in the mother—or the order of birth in the babies—with colic in an infant, emphasized Dr. Paradise. Doctors should make this quite clear to parents, he urged. For unwarranted assumptions in the past have led to much unnecessary "self-blame, frustration and heightened anxiety" among mothers with colicky babies.

Dr. Carl A. Holmes, a physician in Phoenix, Arizona, took a somewhat different view of infants who suffer from colic in an article in *Clinical Pediatrics*. A baby with colic may drive his whole family crazy for the first three months of his life, Dr. Holmes noted, but after that he will grow up to make his parents proud and happy. For a colicky baby will be brighter, more enthusiastic, more energetic, active and talkative than noncolicky individuals, both as a child and as an adult, Dr. Holmes argued.

The basic cause of colic is an overactive nervous system, according to Dr. Holmes. Because gas tends to accumulate in the intestines and the baby's immature digestive system cannot expel it effectively, the baby suffers from abdominal pains which he interprets as hunger and fights with tense, hard crying. Colic disappears when the baby's body matures enough to pass the gas rapidly and completely.

Parents may indeed be the cause of colic, Dr. Holmes noted —but only because they have passed on to the baby an inherited tendency to have a high-strung nervous system. Such an infant is unusually active long before he is born, just as he will be unusually active for the rest of his life, Dr. Holmes said.

Because a colicky baby often acts as if he were hungry, his mother tends to feed him more than she would otherwise. Because the milk appears to satisfy the infant for only a short period, his mother typically asks the doctor to change his formula. The new formula does seem to help for a few days. But then the colic recurs. The mother requests still another formula, which helps only briefly. The cycle continues, said Dr. Holmes, until the infant outgrows the colic, at which point the mother usually says, "We finally found a formula that would agree with the baby."

A colicky baby usually "rolls over, sits, creeps, pulls to his feet and walks much earlier than the noncolicky baby," according to Dr. Holmes. "He often talks earlier and better."

Because a baby with colic may not sleep more than just two or three short naps during the day and isn't content to lie in bed unstimulated, he is unusually demanding of his mother's time and attention. This attention won't spoil the infant, and his mother should be encouraged to cuddle and play with him, Dr. Holmes advised.

Colic can be treated in several ways, according to Dr. Holmes. In its mildest form, it can be relieved simply by feeding the infant more often, he said. Gas pains can be eased by pressure and warmth; he recommended that a colicky infant be trained to sleep on his stomach and that a hot-water bottle half filled with warm (not hot) water be placed under him.

Holding a baby over the shoulder or knees of the parent often encourages sleep, according to Dr. Holmes. The baby may wake up and cry when put to bed—not because he has been spoiled, but simply because he's uncomfortable in bed.

Although it doesn't help to change the formula of a colicky infant, it can be useful to remove any added sugar in his milk, according to Dr. Holmes. Adding cereal to the baby's diet also seems to counteract colic, but other solid foods don't, he said. He recommended putting one teaspoonful of cereal in each bottle, using cross-cut holes in the nipple.

For severe colic, Dr. Holmes prescribed drugs, usually a mixture of barbiturates—two quick-acting, one intermediate, and one slow-acting. Paregoric, he said, is not effective.

5. How Bad Are Baby Habits?

If your baby sucks his thumb—or bites his lip or grinds his teeth or bangs his head or rocks his body in a rhythmic pattern—does it mean he's emotionally insecure or that you are doing something wrong as a parent?

Not at all, says Dr. Harvey Kravitz, of Northwestern University School of Medicine. These habits, begun early in the first year of your baby's life, are signs he's healthy and normal, and probably not retarded or brain-injured.

Dr. Kravitz's conclusions result from more than ten years of research on these common baby habits and have been reported at an annual conference of the American Academy of Pediatrics. The research, done with Dr. John J. Boehm, Director of Newborn Services at Evanston Hospital, Evanston, Illinois, involved minute-by-minute observations by nurses of more than 200 infants from the time of birth. A majority were of normal weight and in good health. But groups of prematures and babies with obvious birth defects and illnesses were included.

In addition, 200 normal infants, 12 babies with cerebral palsy and 22 children with Down's syndrome (mongolism) were studied for the first year of their lives with the help of monthly reports from mothers.

Almost all of the normal, healthy newborn babies managed to suck their thumb or some other part of their hands at least three times within the first two hours after birth, Dr. Kravitz discovered. The median time it took these infants to put thumb into mouth was 54 minutes.

The prematures and those born with respiratory distress or other illnesses took somewhat longer to start sucking on some part of a hand. The median ages for these groups were between 22 and 30 hours, although the slowest did not manage to get his thumb into his mouth for three weeks.

But among the retarded babies, those with Down's syndrome did not suck a thumb or part of a hand until a median age of five months, and nine of these children had not done so by their first birthday. Only one fourth of the infants with cerebral palsy had sucked their thumb by the time they were one year old.

It takes a normal newborn baby much longer to discover his feet and what he can do with them than it does his hands, Dr. Kravitz's research showed. The normal infants he observed began rhythmically kicking their feet with joyful excitement and often waving their arms at the same time by the median age of 2.7 months. Only two of the normal babies failed to experiment with rhythmic kicking by their first birthday. But most of the babies with Down's syndrome or cerebral palsy were not able to do so by that age.

About four months after they started kicking for fun, the normal babies discovered the delights of sucking their toes, with 83 percent of the babies picking up the habit. Dr. Kravitz considers this activity "neurologically important" as a milestone in the baby's discoveries about the lower part of his body. Only two of the mongoloid infants and one of those with cerebral palsy sucked their toes at all by age one.

Sucking or biting of the lip began at a median age of 5.3 months for normal babies and was done by 93 percent of these youngsters, according to Dr. Kravitz. But only one of the mongoloid infants and two of those with cerebral palsy were able to experiment with this activity before their first birthday.

Four other baby habits that parents are likely to associate with emotional problems or retardation—body rocking, head rolling, head banging and tooth grinding—also appear normally in healthy babies, Dr. Kravitz's research shows. But almost none of the mongoloid babies or those with cerebral palsy experimented with any of these activities before their first birthday.

Body rocking began at a median age of 6.1 months in the normal infants and was done by 91 percent of them. Slightly more than half the normal children ground their teeth, starting at the median age of 10.5 months. Ten percent of the normal infants were observed to roll their heads rhythmically before their first birthday and 7 percent banged their heads.

Dr. Kravitz described head-banging babies as quiet, relaxed infants who find comfort in this activity, even if done so often they have a bump on their head. "These rhythmic patterns are a part of infant development and are initially a discovery of self," explained the pediatrician. "The baby is discovering himself through rhythmic patterns. These habits do not indicate disturbance in the mother-child relationship.

"The earlier these common habits begin, the more normal the baby is," according to Dr. Kravitz. "Babies who are slow will pick up these activities at a slower rate and may not do until the second or third year of life what other babies do during the first.

"These habits do not necessarily persist," Dr. Kravitz pointed out. "A baby may do one of these things for a while, but then give it up—perhaps even before his mother has noticed it. Other babies will persist, and some of these habits may last a lifetime. Many adults suck a part of their hand. If you go to a basketball game, you often see kids hanging their feet over a railing and kicking rhythmically. There is no special significance in persistence."

Of all baby habits, thumb-sucking worries parents most. Three decades ago mothers were told to tie a baby's arms to the sides of the crib to keep his thumb out of his mouth. A child's fingers were painted with vile-tasting solutions. Unbending cardboard sleeves were devised to hold thumbs out of sucking range.

Next came the psychological theories that sucking is a basic infant instinct and must be gratified before a child could grow successfully into the next stage of development. According to these theories, children past toddler age who still sucked a thumb had had insufficient sucking opportunity as infants, had been weaned too soon or were emotionally neglected by their mothers. Parents were warned not to discourage thumb-sucking, not to nag, not even to suggest a thumb didn't belong in the mouth.

The spunky mother who argued back that Molly had been breast-fed for eight months and had a bedtime bottle until age two and only sucks her thumb when she is being cuddled or feels particularly happy was apt to be told she was too close emotionally to her child to assess her behavior correctly.

But there is vindication now for thumb-suckers' mothers in the results of three massive studies reported by research psychologist Martin Heinstein. The greatest amounts of thumb-sucking observed in three large samples of representative children occurred among those who had been breast-fed by mothers with happy marriages and stable homes and who were judged to be more emotionally healthy than average. Girls and boys who sucked their thumbs as preschoolers had fewer behavior problems than other youngsters, the three studies show.

But prolonged thumb-sucking does worry dentists and orthodontists. Orthodontists, who deal with the damage done to children's mouths by their thumbs, turn emphatic thumbs down on the habit, at least after a child reaches the age of three or four.

Damage to teeth and jaw from thumb-sucking is not limited to protruding upper front teeth, orthodontists warn. Less obvious, but equally serious, is malocclusion of the molars caused by pressure of the cheeks against the thin upper jaw as the thumb is sucked.

Normally the upper molars bite slightly outside of the lower molars. But if the upper molars rest slightly inside the lower teeth, it may be evidence that a child's mouth is being mis-shaped by thumb-sucking.

Today, the consensus on thumb-sucking is this: It is a harmless, even soothingly helpful, habit in infants or toddlers. Parents should see that a baby does get plenty of opportunity to suck (although some doctors prefer that a baby use a pacifier rather than his thumb). But the habit should not persist after age three or four and certainly not after age five.

What can a parent do if a child doesn't give up thumb-sucking normally?

First, you can try to discover when and why your child is most apt to suck his thumb. You may find it's when he's feeling particularly happy, cuddly, sleepy or bored—or possibly when he's frustrated or upset. Sometimes you can stop the habit simply by seeing that your child has plenty to do with his hands during the times he would usually put his thumb into his mouth: crayons and paper to use while he's watching television, a cuddly animal to take to bed, a mother's hand to hold while she's reading to him, a later bedtime so he won't lie awake long with nothing to do.

Sometimes a child can understand why it's important to break the habit and will stop voluntarily. It is usually more effective if the explanation is delivered authoritatively by the orthodontist or dentist.

Some orthodontists feel that if the habit can be licked first at night, it can more easily be stopped during the day. They recommend that parents tie golf-club mitts over the child's hands at bedtime. These are loose, not uncomfortable, and cannot be untied by the youngster. Yet they do help remind him to keep his fingers out of his mouth and help to change his habit patterns.

6. How You Can Help Your Baby Learn

A baby is capable of genuine learning from the day he is born.

Yet until just a few years ago, an infant's great need for opportunities to learn had generally been overlooked in the emphasis on physical care and emotional development. Now, however, research in many universities and medical centers is demonstrating how much infants even a few weeks old can learn when they are given the opportunity—and how important this learning is to future mental development. Educators, physicians, psychologists and even biologists are now recommending new learning techniques to parents. And mothers and fathers who are using these ideas and suggestions are finding a delightful and rewarding new dimension to child care. It's much more satisfying and rewarding to help a youngster learn to use his brain than to use the bathroom, parents are discovering; it's much more interesting and challenging to nourish his mind than to fill his stomach.

One way to understand the importance of early learning is to think of your baby's brain as a miniaturized, ten-billion-unit computer of astounding complexity and efficiency—a comparison frequently used by experts in child development. But like any super computer, your baby's brain must be stocked with an incredible amount of information before you can expect much intelligent output. And the more information with which his brain is filled, the more intelligent will be its behavior.

Your baby programs his brain by sending to it a vast number of information messages from all of his sensory organs—by looking, listening, touching, smelling and tasting.

But this sensory stimulation does more than just file information away in your baby's nerve cells. It also causes his brain to grow in size, increases the amount of several essential chemical substances in his brain and promotes the development of more interconnecting links between brain cells, scientists now conclude on the basis of thousands of studies with animals.

You can't just bombard your baby with things to look at, listen to, touch, taste and smell, however. To be effective, the sensory input has to be appropriate for the state of your baby's growing brain, must be a match for his mental development. Much research is now underway to pinpoint precisely what kinds of stimuli are most effective for children of every age level.

But as you get to know your own infant better in the weeks after you bring him home from the hospital, you can tell from his reactions what sensory stimulation is best for him. You'll learn to recognize when he is enjoying the stimuli you are providing, when he is being mentally malnourished, or when he's tuning out from an overload.

When a young infant sees or hears or touches something interesting, his whole body often seems to come to attention, a kind of behavior physicians call "alerting." You'll sometimes see your baby act this way when he recognizes that you have come to his cribside to pick him up, or when his eyes are focusing on a bright design or when he is making a discovery about what his hands can do.

When your baby is old enough to reach out and grasp with his hands and, later on, to move about independently, you can tell what stimuli are effective simply by what he pays attention to. Because his need for fresh sensory information is so acute, he'll try to touch almost everything he can get his hands on, to put things into his mouth whenever possible, to gain for himself as much sensory data as he can.

What intrigues a child most is something that is "discrepant," some recent research at Harvard University suggests. A youngster will pay the most attention to an object that is somewhat different than anything with which he is familiar, but not too much different. He will get bored quickly with what is familiar and he will tend to tune out or ignore any object which is totally unlike anything he already knows. This phenomenon suggests what Dr. Jean Piaget, the Swiss expert on early childhood learning, means when he concludes that the more things a child has seen and heard, the more new things he wants to experience, and the greater the variety of environmental stimuli with which he has coped, the greater is his capacity for coping.

This urgent need for fresh sensory stimulation is what drives a toddler to insistent exploration and a preschooler to fuss and complain with honesty, "I don't have anything to do." It explains why a child can be bored with his Christmas presents the day after Christmas and why it is often possible to distract a youngster from crying by offering a new activity.

When a baby has been fed, has dry diapers, isn't physically uncomfortable and is still fussing or crying, it's likely he's suffering from mental hunger. His need for stimuli to feed his fast-growing brain is just as acute as his drive for food to nourish his developing body. This explains why you can often comfort a crying baby just by picking him up and giving him something different to look at or touch. Or by carrying him with you around the house or out of doors. Or by singing to him. Or by rocking him. Or by giving him a change of toys.

When an infant is being bombarded with more sensory stimuli than he can handle, he often reacts by scrunching his eyes shut and going to sleep with what seems to be almost conscious deliberation. A toddler may scream, even have a tantrum or go to sleep. A preschooler may hold his ears or run away, complain that "there are too many people in here," or demand that you "shut up that bad noise."

A parent's best guide to how much mental stimulation a child needs is to make available a rich amount and watch his youngster's reactions carefully. As in providing your youngster with food, your aim is to give him all the sound nourishment his body and his brain need for optimal development. You want to give him all the nutrients he needs to reach his individual physical potential, but not force-feed him in hopes of rearing a super-athlete. So, you should be providing all the mental nutrients his brain needs to reach optimum intellectual growth, but not push him beyond his stage of development in hopes of producing a genius.

Along with the new research in the development of the brain, educators, psychologists and physicians have begun to formulate guidelines for parents to help them give their children a good mental start in life. For example:

Your baby needs interesting things to look at. Even newborn infants in hospital nurseries can focus their eyes on shapes at specific distances from their eyes and they do so with obvious enjoyment if they are not sleepy, hungry or uncomfortable. They prefer complicated patterns, like bull's-eyes and diagonals to solid colors, and they pay more attention to new designs than to ones they've seen before. By the age of four months, babies can focus on a moving object and follow it with their eyes at varying distances as well as an adult. By one year, vision is adequate for reading.

Yet, too often, babies are kept in bassinets or cribs lined with solid-color bumpers, where they have nothing to look at but the ceiling and their own hands and toes. Even outdoors in a buggy, babies are buried deep inside with their view of the sky partially obscured by the hood.

You can add to your baby's visual stimulation by giving him as many interesting things to see as possible. You can tape bright pictures to the walls of his room and change them often. You can hang a bright mobile over his crib and put a variety of objects on it. (Dr. Burton White, of Harvard University, uses a stabile, with colorful toys and an unbreakable mirror fastened over the crib within easy reach of the baby. He also substitutes printed bedding and bumpers to enrich an infant's visual environment.)

Just picking your baby up and holding him on your shoulder so that he gets a different perspective on the world around him gives him some mental stimulation, research done at Stanford University shows. One reason why a baby often stops crying when he's picked up is that this new view of things provides him with some of the mental activity he is craving.

It helps if you can sometimes carry your baby about with you from room to room when you are doing housework. You can call his attention to different objects in your house and outside your window. Or you can put him in a playpen in the kitchen so he can watch you work. (It's when a playpen is used frequently to fence off an active creeping or toddling child that it begins to curtail development.)

Propping your baby up in an inclined infant's seat in a safe spot gives him a more stimulating view of the world than he gets from a crib. When he's able to hold up his head, you can buy or make a contemporary version of a cradle board—a canvas sling that holds him on your back or astride your hip— so you can tote him around with you while your own hands are free.

A baby needs tactile experiences, too. A sense of touch is one of the basic ways a baby learns—from the first days of life when he begins to associate the sensory stimuli of being cuddled close against his mother as he is fed. Gradually he links this tactile information with the visual impressions of his mother and with the sound of her voice.

It does help to give your baby interesting textures to touch. Because he learns so much from the tactile sensations of his lips and mouth, a baby also feels an instinctive urge to learn by putting everything he can pick up into his mouth. So you will have to make sure that any objects he can hold or reach are too big to go into his mouth or you will have to supervise his handling of them to prevent any possible dangers from choking.

For example, you can give your baby swatches of fabric like satin or burlap to feel, smooth wooden toys, an ice cube, a warm hot-water bottle, foam-rubber blocks, a flower or a leaf, a fuzzy stuffed animal, a piece of sandpaper or crinkly tissue paper. You can hold a friendly kitten while he strokes it. You can let him crawl outside on the grass on a dry summer day, or touch a drift of clean, white snow.

Giving a young baby objects to play with and interesting things to touch helps him with another major learning task during the early months of life—coordinating hands and eyes. It takes weeks of practice and random batting with the fists before a baby develops the ability to reach out accurately and grasp. But research shows that the more interesting things a baby has to look at, the sooner he develops this essential ability. And the more objects he can grasp and handle for himself, the more he is able to learn on his own, the more content and less fussy he is, and the more time he spends alert and learning during the day, according to careful studies.

His great need to touch often gets a baby into trouble with the adults who are caring for him, because they often misinterpret his insistent urge to handle everything he can reach in his environment as being naughty instead of understanding that he is trying to satisfy a compelling mental hunger. But as a child grows and learns, he gradually comes to depend more upon seeing and less on touching. He comes to know from experience how an object will feel just from looking at it, and he no longer feels he must touch it to recognize it. But even as a toddler and a preschooler, a child still wants to verify his visual impressions sometimes by touching—just as adults do in a china shop or at a fabric counter.

Besides visual and tactile stimuli, a baby needs opportunity to listen—to music, to sounds of all kinds, and particularly to language. Learning about spoken words begins in the earliest weeks of life, so you should begin talking to your infant from the very first time you hold him. If you vary your tone as you cuddle him, feed him, say "Good morning," bathe him and tuck him into bed at night, he'll begin to absorb the idea that sounds have meanings. You can begin showing your infant objects and telling him their names—"ball," "block," "spoon" —as early as the first few months of life. Researchers who have tried this techniques with their own children report that the youngsters begin to talk much earlier than the average age, and that being able to talk makes them happier and less likely to cry and whine to make their needs known.

It helps, too, to respond to your baby's attempts to communicate with you. Even in the first few weeks of life you can detect by his cries whether he is hurt, hungry, colicky or bored. If you respond, it will encourage him to further efforts at making meaningful sounds. When your baby begins to babble, talk back to him as if you were having a conversation, speech experts recommend. Babies spend endless hours practicing vowels, consonants, syllables—but all this effort needs to be rewarded by your happy response. According to linguists, an infant makes all the basic sounds of all the languages on earth at this stage in his life. But unless he hears these sounds in his environment, he soon loses his ability to make them and retains only those used in his native language. That's why it is so difficult for an adult to learn to speak a foreign language without an accent.

In addition to spoken words, you should also give your baby

happy opportunities to experience a variety of other sounds: bells, music boxes, records, lullabies, songs, rattles, radio music, the clink of a spoon against a glass of water, the honk of a car horn, the ticking of a clock.

Just how much a baby can respond to music is pointed up by the work of Dr. Shinichi Suzuki, the Japanese teacher who has trained thousands of young Japanese violinists. Suzuki musical training begins as soon after birth as possible. A baby's mother is instructed to start by playing on a phonograph a recording by a fine musician of one piece of classical music, such as a Beethoven quartet or a Tchaikovsky serenade. The same recording is played for the baby to hear every day.

After about five months, reports Suzuki, the baby will clearly recognize this music and will be able to differentiate it from other recordings—to which he will also respond with obvious enjoyment. This very early exposure to music helps condition a child so that by the time he has reached the age of two and a half he is ready to begin playing the violin by ear.

A baby also learns through movement. When he moves about, it generates a great number and variety of sensory impulses, which feed information into his brain and become an important basis of knowledge about the world. Movements help a child learn about gravity, about eye-hand coordination, about distances, about his body and its relationship to the environment.

Encouraging a baby to move, to reach, to grasp, to touch, to make eyes and hands work together can speed up his development markedly, research shows. You can help by giving your infant bright, attractive objects to reach for and by suspending bells and other objects on elastic ribbon over his crib. (Several fascinating new types of crib toys are now available for this purpose, too.) You can free him from constricting clothing and from a confining bassinet as much as possible within health and safety limits.

It helps to put your baby on his stomach on a pad in the

playpen or on the floor where he can move arms and legs freely—long before he is able to push himself up on hands and knees to creep. When he does begin to move forward on his own, you can encourage him by putting attractive objects just in front of him to lure him on. You can give him as much freedom as safety permits to crawl about and explore.

The comparison that opened this chapter which pictured a baby's brain as a ten-billion-unit computer which must be programmed with a great variety of sensory input is a useful simile. But it gives only a limited picture of the complex ways in which young children go about learning.

During the first 24 months of life, when a baby changes from a near-helpless newborn into a walking, thinking, exploring, curious two-year-old, he actually uses at least 25 learning techniques, according to Dr. Lois B. Murphy, former director of developmental studies at the Menninger Foundation, in an article in *Children*, a journal for professionals in child-care work. By looking for these learning strategies in your baby, you can discover ways to give him enriched opportunities to learn.

In addition to using all of his senses and instinctive reflexes, such as sucking, to learn, a baby soon discovers how to combine two things to cause a happening, according to Dr. Murphy. He finds out that he can produce a clatter by banging a spoon against the high-chair tray or that he can pull the stuffing out of his crib bumper.

A baby learns from pain and discovers how to avoid unpleasant stimuli whenever possible. He also learns what he enjoys, developing his own preferences in foods, colors, people, playthings and play, Dr. Murphy observed.

All during these early months, a baby learns how to love and be loved. He notes and remembers how to evoke the rewards he wants, how to make his mother smile, his brother laugh and his father play "horsey."

A baby also uses trial and error as a learning stratagem,

growing out of his previous learning through his senses, his motor skills, curiosity and delight in making things happen, according to Dr. Murphy. A toddler may be sitting on the floor engrossed in trying to fit together a six-piece wooden inlaid puzzle. His mother sees his struggles and tries to help by taking one of the pieces out of the toddler's hand to show him where it should go. Suddenly, in frustration and rage, the toddler tips the puzzle over, throws the pieces against the wall and starts to cry. It's his only way of trying to tell his mother that she can help him best when he is using this learning technique by not interfering with his efforts.

A baby also learns through contagion, explained Dr. Murphy. The offspring of a tense and anxious mother catches her tenseness, possibly through skin and muscle sensations and facial expressions, Dr. Murphy suggested. A relaxed and cheerful mother can help her youngster learn to be calm and happy.

Learning by participation is a strategy in which parents can help a child directly. This kind of learning occurs when a mother holds a baby's hands to wave bye-bye or to play pat-a-cake.

Learning by imitation takes place when a baby notes and copies the activities of those about him. Learning by identification is a more complicated kind of imitation, in which the child imagines that he actually is the individual he is imitating.

A baby also learns by coping with frustration, by discovering that sometimes he must wait for what he wants, or to accept a substitute instead. A mother can often help her baby adapt to new situations and frustrations by skillful cuddling, soothing or ways of introducing new experiences that make it easy for him to accept changes, suggested Dr. Murphy.

A baby learns, too, to be comforted, to understand that hurts and discomforts are only temporary and what he must do to evoke the comforting he wants.

Learning to amuse himself, to realize that he can do satisfying things by himself and to initiate these activities is another strategy a baby develops before age two. So is learning to fear the right things. A baby is born with the instinct to be afraid and anxious, pointed out Dr. Murphy. But he must learn *what* to fear.

Although a newborn infant can express anger quite forcibly, a baby has to discover how to use his anger and how to show it to get the response he wants from those around him. Unless he is neglected or mistreated, he usually finds out, too, how to get rid of his angry feelings without hurting himself.

If a baby grows up in a good environment, with good parenting, he learns to trust the world and to go about future learning eagerly and enthusiastically.

And even during the first two years of life, a baby learns to unlearn, to give up babyish activities as he becomes a child, Dr. Murphy pointed out. Sometimes he accepts the changes eagerly; at other times he needs the tactful, understanding help of his parents to smooth the way.

Once you understand your baby's urgent needs for mental stimulation and a wide variety of learning experiences, you'll discover many effective and happy ways to supply them. Your best guide is your baby himself. As you get to know him and to understand his temperament, you'll be able to tell when he is fascinated by something he is hearing or seeing or touching or doing—and when he's too sleepy or hungry or uncomfortable or indifferent to care. You'll learn when you are crowding too many stimuli into his life—and when he's bored and wants more.

What's most important is to remember that your baby is not a witless invalid who needs to be kept in bed even when he's awake and alert. He is an active, learning, growing, curious human being whose need for sensory stimuli is greater during the first few years of life than it will ever be again.

7. How to Help Your Baby Avoid a Summer of Discontent

Keeping a baby comfortable and happy in summer's heat is both a loving art and a gentle skill. Success is largely a matter of common sense and cornstarch, sponge baths and shade, fresh air and unflappability.

Usually, the summer complaints that trouble a baby are of four varieties. Your baby may have an itchy skin problem. He may be too hot. His stomach may be upset. And he may be bored. Regardless of why he's uncomfortable, you can be sure he'll share his miseries with you.

As in most problems with children, hot-weather troubles are easier to prevent than they are to remedy. For example:

You should reassess your baby's routines and clothing as summer weather starts, to make sure he isn't getting too warm. Putting an infant down to nap in a baby carriage in the sun while he's wearing plastic pants and lying on a waterproof mattress cover can make him feel like a vegetable being boiled in a plastic pouch. It's also an open invitation to prickly heat and diaper rash.

Your infant will be less fussy—and nap longer—if you can

49

find a cool corner or shady spot for him, where the air is circulating freely but not blowing directly on him.

Once he's past the earliest weeks of infancy, a baby needs little more clothing than you do during the heat waves of July and August. Diapers alone may be enough. But most infants—like most adults—are somewhat more comfortable wearing a light shirt or top that helps to absorb perspiration.

If you can, let your baby go without waterproof diaper coverings during the hottest part of summer days, especially if his rear is reddening or sore. Diaper rash from bacterial action on urine-soaked skin and diapers blooms with greater speed in hot weather. Once these small red pimples and patches of itchy red skin start to spread, it can take long, careful effort to clear it up.

If you change your infant's diapers as soon as they are soaked or soiled, if you clean and dry and powder the area carefully at every change, and if you skip the plastic pants as often as possible, you can usually prevent most of this major cause of summer discomfort.

Prickly heat is another summer complaint that afflicts a baby who is overdressed or overheated, leaving him itchy, irritable and irritating. These slightly raised, pinpoint pink spots usually start around the neck and shoulders and in folds of the skin where perspiration accumulates. Often, tiny blisters develop, dry up and leave a tan-looking rash.

Preventing prickly heat involves keeping your baby clean and dry and cool. It helps to make sure he isn't overdressed, to give him frequent sponge baths in tepid water on simmering days, and to powder him lightly with cornstarch, making sure it doesn't cake in the creases of his skin.

Because you haven't had your youngster very long, you can't be sure whether he'll turn out to be the type who sunburns easily or tans without difficulty. You can be sure, however, that his tender, new skin will burn more easily the first summer of his life than it ever will again. An infant too little to sit up needs to be angled carefully so that no sun shines directly in his face. A baby old enough to sit up or crawl should wear a wide-brimmed hat when he's in the sun, to protect his eyes and the tender skin on his thin-haired head. Sunny-hazy days and nearby water with its reflected glare are extra hazards you'll need to guard against.

Just as your appetite diminishes in hot weather, so will your baby's. Don't try to make him eat when he doesn't want to. And try to avoid making any major changes in his diet or weaning him during hot weather. You should also be extra careful about what goes into your baby's mouth. The intestinal disturbances that used to be fatal to many babies are now better controlled and treated. But a baby is still especially susceptible to infections and diarrhea his first summer of life and needs your scrupulous protection.

Do offer your baby cool water to drink (sterilize it if he's still tiny) several times a day. He may refuse it. But he may also be thirsty and unable to tell you except by fussing.

Even if your baby is cool, comfortable and well fed, he may still be fussy and demanding. That's usually a sign that he needs more mental stimulation than he's getting. You'll save your time and energy and make him much happier in the long run if you make just as careful effort to satisfy the needs of his brain for nourishment as you do the needs of his body.

8. SLEEPING PROBLEMS OF BABIES AND YOUNG CHILDREN

SLEEP PROBLEMS, STAGE I

Once, goes a science-fiction story, by some celestial slip-up a baby named Alexander was born an eon or two too soon. His parents were average, good, loving, twentieth-century folk. But Alexander was a vastly superior product of future evolution.

Although he was mentally a genius, Alexander was as dependent upon his parents after birth as ordinary infants. But he never needed to sleep. And he made demands upon his hapless father and mother continually, day and night.

Many parents who know the story suspect that they, too, have drawn an Alexander, especially in the long, dark, cold hours between midnight and dawn. For the most distressing fact of nonfiction life-with-a-new-baby is this: Although a month-old infant sleeps an average of 17 hours a day, his longest daily sleep period is only about 5½ hours. Because he's born not knowing night from day, it's rare that this 5½-hour sleep stretch comes when his parents want most to sleep, too.

Some fortunate parents have infants who can be changed,

fed, burped, patted and put back to bed when they awaken at night. If they don't go back to sleep, these babies at least lie quietly and contentedly enough for their weary parents to rest.

Other fathers and mothers bring home from the hospital raucous alarm clocks that go off urgently and unpredictably three or four times every night. Instead of being comforted and lulled by a feeding, such a baby may react with symptoms of obvious distress, pulling up his legs in crampy pain and screaming himself hoarse. A few of these extra-difficult infants never sleep longer than two consecutive hours out of any 24-hour period during the first few weeks of life.

It used to be customary to blame the parents when their infant had problems with sleeping, to say that their tensions, fears, anxieties and conscious or subconscious rejection of the baby triggered his difficulties. But careful research in recent years fails to substantiate this theory.

Newer studies suggest that, like Alexander, difficult babies simply come with an innate temperament that makes it hard for them to adjust to life-with-parents. They tend to be irritable, demanding and irregular in eating and eliminating as well as in sleep.

Why is it sometimes so difficult to teach a baby to sleep through the night?

First, very young infants do need one or two nighttime feedings during the early weeks of life. These babies enjoy the warmth of the mother who answers their cries in the dark. They appreciate the dry diaper, the comforting milk and the loving attention. And it's remarkably easy for them to drift into the habit of expecting this attention and nourishment and to demand it with increasingly loud wails when it isn't immediately forthcoming.

Another reason is that tiny babies are restless sleepers. They wake up and cry, or move around or experiment with making noises quite often in the night. If no one responds and it's dark and quiet and they are reasonably warm and not too wet or hungry, they usually drift back to sleep without anyone's even being aware that they were awake. Gradually they begin to sleep more soundly and to awaken less.

But a conscientious mother who forces herself to sleep lightly and listen for her baby's cries may hear these half-awake sounds other parents miss. If she gets up, changes, feeds and cuddles her baby, it's easy for him to come to expect this kind of attention in the middle of the night, to make a habit of waking up for it, to adjust his intake of food to need it, and to demand it with increasing determination as his right.

Some pediatricians—and some nurses in newborn sections of hospitals—tell new mothers to try to discontinue the 2 A.M. feeding within the first few weeks of life, before it becomes a fixed habit. With some infants this is quite easy, especially in families where the baby comes with an undemanding, adaptable, placid kind of temperament and the mother is a relaxed, experienced, nonworrying sort. About 12 percent of infants are already skipping the post-midnight nourishment when they come home from the hospital. Half of all girls are ready to give up the 2 A.M. feeding at about 4½ weeks of age; half of all boys do so by 6½ weeks, according to a report from the University of Colorado School of Medicine.

All but 3 percent of babies are skipping that post-midnight meal by the age of four months, according to the Colorado study. By then, they are increasing their intake of food during the day and no longer need the nighttime calories. They are awake longer during the day and more ready to sleep at night. They tend to be less restless and noisy at night. And their exhausted parents—by now quite sure the baby will survive, but not sure they themselves will—are less ready to jump up at every cry.

For one of those extra-difficult babies, however, nothing much seems to work, especially if he seems to have colic. Your pediatrician may try changing the baby's formula if he's bottle-fed. Or he may prescribe a mild sedative. Or add more solid foods to his 6 or 10 P.M. feedings (although studies show this usually doesn't help).

Some parents try sending for a grandmother (so they can at least get a little sleep themselves). Or sending a grandmother back home (on the theory she may be generating tensions). They try making the bedroom warmer or cooler. They add or subtract covers. They change the baby's diapers more or less often. They turn a night light, a radio, a loud-ticking clock on or off. They get a pacifier, a teething ring, nipples for bottles with larger or smaller holes.

Walking the floor sometimes helps a screaming infant. So does rocking. One father discovered his infant would go peacefully to sleep in the car. ("We felt like idiots driving around at 2 A.M., but you get desperate enough to do anything," he said.)

Alexander's parents finally found an answer. They simply sat by permissively while their infant genius discovered how to transport himself into another time dimension.

Time does solve the infant sleep problem. Even the most demanding of the difficult babies did give up 2 A.M. feedings and start sleeping through the night sometime between the ages of eight and fifteen months, the Colorado research reports.

SLEEP PROBLEMS, STAGE II

Most parents get two or three months' respite after the seven-feedings-a-day, walking-the-floor-at-night stage before another round of sleep problems begins.

Like first-round sleep difficulties, Stage II usually starts with physical factors you can't ignore. Typically, a baby who has finally learned to sleep an 8- to 11-hour stretch at night, with perhaps one feeding about 10 P.M., suddenly starts waking up at night, crying or fussing in obvious discomfort.

You may discover that his nose is blocked with a stuffy cold;

he can't breathe easily and is a bit frightened about it. Sometimes the crying is triggered by painful teething. Occasionally, ammonia forming in wet diapers during the long night hurts his sensitive, rash-reddened skin.

You have no choice but to use all your willpower to prop your eyelids open and comfort your baby as best you can—with dry diapers, a lullaby, rocking, warm milk, a pacifier or just your loving presence. Eventually he goes back to sleep. Usually, in a few days, the initial cause of the night wakefulness has disappeared. The cold has cleared up; the tooth is through the gums; the diaper rash has gone.

But the habit of waking at night and being loved, comforted, fed or played with by a parent is now well established. Even the most easy-going, adaptable baby isn't going to give up the pleasure of your company without considerable angry protest. And he is likely to begin expecting the same kind of comforting attention when you put him in his crib for naps and at his usual bedtime, too.

The solution, according to most doctors—and neighbors who live out of hearing range—is to let the baby cry it out, after you have checked him for sticking pins and other legitimate sources of complaint. Theoretically he'll scream twenty to thirty minutes the first night, ten the second, still less the third night, fuss only briefly a night or two more, and thereafter be re-established in a tolerable sleep pattern.

In most cases this works. But there are super-determined infants who will scream for much longer, or even until they vomit. And there are parents (count me among them) who are simply unable to let a child scream uncomforted, even when they are advised to do so by a physician.

If you don't want to have an outright battle of wills over the matter—and it is the art of parenting to find better methods of teaching and discipline than a showdown fight—there are other approaches you can try.

You can begin to increase your child's intake of food

during the day, so he won't be so likely to get hungry in the middle of the night. You can be slower to respond to his wakefulness at night. Instead of feeding him when he wakes up, you can simply pat him briefly, say a few reassuring words and leave without making it a social occasion. Some babies are weaned away from a nighttime feeding by a mother who offers them only a bottle of water with a quiet word. You can also increase your baby's physical activity during the day, so he will be more likely to sleep soundly at night. And you may need to check with your physician to make sure your baby doesn't have a respiratory difficulty or allergy that needs to be relieved to help him sleep more soundly.

It helps to remember that sleep problems at this age are almost never caused by emotional problems. They are simply patterns of behavior a baby has chanced into and out of which he can usually be nudged by gentle, persistent planning by parents.

It helps, too, to keep your baby out of his crib at times he isn't supposed to be sleeping so that he associates sleep with his crib. (He urgently needs more sensory stimuli than he can get abed anyway, at this age.) A night light may help, if it doesn't cast scary shadows. So, sometimes, may a ticking clock, a soft radio program, a special blanket and/or a stuffed animal.

Bedtime routines begin to crystallize into rituals during the second half of your baby's first year. Most parents encourage them at first, because they help make the transition from waking to sleeping easier. But once your baby adopts a routine and a set of props, he'll cling to them fiercely until he's three or four. So make sure the patterns you start at this age are ones you can tolerate for a long time and that the animal or blanket that becomes his security is machine-washable.

Most doctors, psychologists and psychiatrists caution parents not to take a baby at this age into their own bed when he cries at night on grounds that are Freudian and sexual. They warn about the dangers of emotional problems and note that once started, this habit is particularly difficult to break. But the desperately weary parents who resort to it at 3 or 4 A.M. usually find that it works, even with the most difficult sleep problems of all.

A pediatrician—in the minority—suggests that this practice may not be all wrong, that in the United States we are forcing independence upon our babies at an uncommonly early age by insisting they spend the long, dark night alone. Parents comfort a small child by holding, touching and other physical contact during the day, and nothing is wrong with using the same techniques at night in bed, some psychologists have concluded.

Said one father, who had just had seven and a half consecutive hours of sleep for the first time in months, "The experts are always trying to sell parents on natural childbirth and natural methods of feeding. What's so wrong with a way of sleeping that is natural in so many other cultures?"

More parents than usually will admit it have reached the same practical conclusion. They discover that taking a young child into bed with them is the only way they can get much sleep when he's teething or suffering from an earache or having bad dreams, and they decide that the inconvenience and crowding is easier to bear than the constant getting up.

Who is right? There is no good evidence to support one side of the issue to the discredit of the other, according to a recent study done by a Harvard University researcher. What passes now for informed scientific conclusions or folk wisdom probably was based originally on climate and convenience, the study suggested.

In a sampling of 68 societies in hot climates, where the temperature doesn't drop below 68 degrees at night, it was found that a majority of mothers sleep with their babies and young children in beds separate from their husbands. But in 27 societies in cold climates, where the temperature goes below freezing at night, husband and wife customarily sleep together in the same bed with the child in a separate crib, cradle board or sleeping bag. These people explained that the couple welcomed each other's body heat, but believed the baby kept warmer if separately covered, the study said.

In societies in which young children do sleep with one or both parents, there is no evidence of the two harmful effects usually attributed to the custom, the Harvard study observed. These are the possibilities of smothering the youngster physically and of distorting his emotional attitudes about sex.

SLEEP PROBLEMS, STAGE III

From the age of two on, every human being considers it his inalienable right to fight bedtime. And he usually wins the great game of bedtimemanship because he makes up most of the rules.

Sleep problems, Stage III, aren't entirely the fault of children. Most youngsters from toddlerhood on want and need less sleep than is convenient for their busy parents.

Children of the same age vary enormously in the amount of sleep they get and apparently need. For example a study of two-and-a-half-year-olds showed that they average almost 13 hours of sleep out of every 24, with about 11 hours of it at night. But individual moppets ranged from 8 to 17 hours of total sleep. Some dozed off for less than 8 hours at night; others logged more than 14 hours of sack time nightly.

Most children give up a morning nap between the ages of one and two. Some youngsters don't nap at all after age three, although others can be persuaded to nap until almost age six. During these transition stages, even the most skilled parent inevitably tries to put a child to bed before he's sleepy.

Young children don't go right to sleep when they are put to bed, regardless of their age and despite the fact that they are often genuinely tired. It takes about 20 minutes, on the average, for a preschooler to fall asleep at nap time and as much as an hour every night, studies show. Research also confirms a common parental observation: When a child becomes too tired, it's often harder to get him to sleep than usual, and he tends to sleep less when he does doze off.

Quite early in life, most youngsters develop a big repertoire of bedtime games to fill the time between the hour their parents set as curfew and the minute they actually fall asleep. Here are some that parents are most likely to encounter:

Guess Again is the first bedtime game a youngster discovers, often by the age of six months. He simply cries when you put him to bed and your move is to find a way to make him stop without letting him get up again. You check his diaper. You bubble him. You turn on a night light. You shut his door. You open it. You rock him. You sing to him. You give him a bottle. After every try he cries.

The game lasts as long as you're willing to play—or until your offspring falls asleep in exhaustion. Unless you refuse to start playing, there's no way you can win.

Me Master You Slave is a verbal version of Guess Again, with a somewhat older youngster calling a variety of signals for the parent to obey—potty, drink of water, light, no light, door open, door shut, story, kiss. Object of the game is to reassure the child and remind the parent that the youngster is still firmly in command and has no intention of going to sleep until ready.

As in poker, successful strategy lies in recognizing a bluff and calling it.

Play It Again, Sam is another version of Me Master in which the child insists you read him a bedtime story again and again, without skipping a page or a word. What makes it exciting for the child is to pretend to fall asleep about the third time around and to watch you tiptoeing out of the room through eyelids 99 percent closed, only to call, "More, Mommy," just as you reach the door.

A youngster who has imaginative parents can have even more fun with *Diagnosis*. He has only to whimper, "It hurts," or "I don't feel good" to trigger a flurry of sleep-postponing activity. A child who plays an expert game of Diagnosis against the right kind of worry-prone parents can get himself rocked, patted, examined for signs of rash, comforted and forgiven for all his day's small misdeeds. Should he overplay his hand to the point where his mother starts after the cough medicine or the nose drops, all he has to do is pretend to be asleep when she returns. There isn't one parent in a thousand who would wake him up.

Switch Players is a strategy a youngster tries when his bluff is about to be called in any of the games above. He simply cries for a substitute player—father, visiting aunt or uncle, grandmother, grandfather, even older brother or sister. Then the game starts all over again. Switch Players is particularly successful when a husband and wife are competing for a child's affections or when either feels guilty about neglecting the youngster. It's also surefire when a visiting grandmother thinks her daughter-in-law is being too strict with her adorable grandchild.

Where the Wild Things Are usually starts out with a child voicing the traditional There's-a-lion-in-the-closet. Then, depending on his age, how much of what kind of television he watches, and whether he has a bent toward science fiction, it can develop into such imaginative ploys as There's-a-black-widow-spider-on-the-rug and I-thought-I-saw-a-flying-saucer-outside-the-window. Many youngsters also find *Wild Things* plays well when they want parental attention in the middle of the night; fathers and mothers are quick to assume their child has had a nightmare and to give him loving comfort.

Oh, What a Good Boy Am I is one of several variations children develop on the basic game of *Stall*, which is played not in the bedroom itself but elsewhere in the house, often as a preliminary to other bedroom type games. In Oh, What a

Good Boy, the child suddenly remembers at bedtime that he forgot to put away his tricycle or clean out the hamster's cage or write a thank-you note to Aunt Kate for a birthday present received two months earlier. He counts on your caring more about the putting away or the cleaning out than about a prompt bedtime. He's right, usually, but at least you get a consolation prize of a thank-you note or a clean cage.

Daddy You Promised is another variation on Stall, particularly useful to a child in a family where the father has been away on a business trip or has gotten home late or is feeling guilty about playing so much golf on weekends. Beginning with "Daddy, you promised to tell me a story," this game can be escalated into a more sophisticated version like, "Daddy, you said you'd explain to me later what that bad man in Washington was doing on the TV news; now it's later."

Most youngsters begin to play nighttime games of *Thirty Questions* within a week or two of learning to say the word "Why?" They quickly realize that their parents like to credit them with an enthusiasm for learning and usually won't shush them in annoyance for at least several minutes. Some preschoolers so enjoy framing sticky questions that they scarcely wait for an answer; others prefer letting a father or mother talk on until there's a pause for breath and then inserting an angelic, "Why?" And well before age five, most youngsters discover that if their questions are about religion or sex— "Where is God?" or "Where do babies come from?"—even the weariest parent will take a stab at answering for fear of losing a vital communication line with his offspring on an important subject.

What strategies can a parent use against bedtimemanship?

For dawdling and other nonviolent forms of resistance: Try a piggyback ride to bed on Daddy's shoulder. Or a race with a kitchen timer. Or a countdown game ("Ten is for taking off your shoes, nine is for socks . . ." down to "one," which can be a small surprise under a pillow). A bedtime story. A clock of his own with a deadline marked in crayon on the face. A phonograph in his room with a special record.

For lions and tigers and bears in his room: Give your youngster a flashlight to keep by his bed and turn on to dissolve his fears.

For demands for drinks: Offer your small-fry water before he starts to bed. Then say firmly and cheerfully, "No," to subsequent requests—and don't give in.

For insistence on going to the bathroom: Do give in and make the trip as brief and businesslike as possible.

For me-do-it-all-by-myselfness, which has you screaming internally with impatience while your offspring gets ready for bed in slow motion: Keep small jobs like mending or correspondence handy to do while you wait.

For bedtime talkativeness: Twist your child's gambit to accomplish ends that are more important than a few extra minutes of sleep by using the opportunity to establish a clear channel of communication. Your child will be unusually receptive to what you say at bedtime, for he is eager to keep you by his bedside. It's your best chance of the day to talk over his day and his problems (but not to scold), to field his questions and to enjoy each other.

If your child persistently fights bedtime with unabated energy, it may be a sign you should reassess the amount of sleep you're expecting him to get. Children's sleep needs change so quickly during the first few years of life that such reevaluation is necessary every two or three months.

9. QUESTIONS PARENTS ASK ABOUT THE EATING PROBLEMS OF BABIES AND YOUNG CHILDREN

How can you tell if your baby is getting the right amount of milk?

Despite great advances in the science of infant nutrition, the voice on the other end of the pediatrician's phone is still most likely to be a new mother with a problem in feeding her baby. Most of these difficulties aren't serious from a medical standpoint, but they can worry a weary parent enough to steal some of the pleasure out of having a new baby.

An infant may have a minor feeding problem if he spits up or vomits frequently. Other symptoms of feeding difficulties include any of these: diarrhea, constipation, bulky stools with excessive fat, irritable crying, abdominal discomfort, failure to gain weight or excessive increase in weight.

Most of these difficulties can be easily eliminated. To help pinpoint the problem, these quick questions and answers can be useful. If the solution isn't readily apparent, or if you think your baby's formula needs changing, you should check with your doctor:

· Are you feeding your baby too often because you think he's hungry every time he cries? This common mistake forces an infant into the habit of taking less and less formula at more and more frequent intervals. This won't hurt him; but it *is* hard on his parents. Because a baby's stomach tends to empty slowly, you should keep an interval of at least two and one half to three hours between feedings, physicians emphasize.

· Do you place the nipple far enough into your baby's mouth? An infant's swallowing abilities aren't completely developed until a few months after birth, doctors explain. So he can't manage food placed on the front part of his tongue, and his attempts to swallow may just push it out again.

· Are the holes in the nipple the proper size? Milk should drip slowly when you turn the bottle upside down.

· Are you holding your infant properly when you feed him? He can't take a bottle comfortably if he's lying down flat or propped with a pillow. You should support him in a half-sitting position, at about a 45-degree angle.

· Do you ever let him suck on an empty bottle? Formula should fill the nipple end of the bottle throughout the feeding and you should leave one-half to one ounce of milk in the bottle at the end of the feeding to prevent him from swallowing air.

· Could your baby be getting too much formula? Indications of this kind of problem include spitting up, vomiting, diarrhea, frequent large stools and excessive weight gain for the baby's age. If you suspect that this might be the problem, you should check with your doctor rather than just try to cut down on the amount of milk your baby takes. Your physician may suggest you try giving him more solid foods.

· Is your infant getting enough formula? If he is fussy, underweight and/or constipated, he may not be. Your doctor will probably solve this difficulty by increasing the calorie content of the formula and advising bigger feedings at more frequent intervals.

· Is your baby getting the right formula? Sometimes adjustments in the precise proportion of nutrients have to be made by your doctor to fit your infant's needs and digestive system.

· Could your baby's feeding problems be a reflection of tensions and anxieties in your family? Many physicians attribute symptoms like irritability, vomiting and failure to gain weight to marital conflicts, domestic disputes and other tensions in the home.

If you're nursing your baby and have a question or problem you can get personal advice from the La Leche League, 9616 Minneapolis Avenue, Franklin Park, Illinois 60131 (Phone: 312–455–7730), or from a local chapter of La Leche League near your home. The La Leche League is an international organization of mothers formed to encourage breast-feeding. Experienced mothers are available to answer calls or letters from mothers with nursing questions or problems, and from prospective mothers seeking information about breast-feeding.

When can you stop making formula and put your baby on regular milk?

Despite all the medical and nutritional knowledge available today, pediatricians don't always have clear-cut, scientific reasons for all of their directions to mothers about feeding tiny babies—as mothers discover when they start comparing notes. A survey made through the Mayo Well Child Clinic in Rochester, Minnesota, and reported in the American Journal of the Diseases of Children shows that most of the doctors queried recommended switching to cow's milk when a baby is three or four months old. But a few of the physicians favored postponing the change-over until the age of six months or-even nine to twelve months. Two of the doctors (the survey included ten Mayo Clinic staff physicians, fifteen pediatric residents, seven Rochester physicians and seventeen members or examiners of the American Academy of Pediatrics) put newborn infants on straight cow's milk and reported no difficulties.

At what age can you stop sterilizing your baby's bottles?

Usually you can stop sterilizing when formula is no longer used and the baby is getting milk poured directly from the dairy container into the baby bottle, the Mayo Clinic doctors advised. There's no point in sterilizing bottles and nipples when a baby is getting unsterilized food and putting toys and other unsterilized objects in his mouth, some of the doctors commented.

At what age should you begin giving your baby solid food?

If you've compared notes with other mothers, you know that pediatricians are by no means agreed on the answer to this question. Your doctor may wait until your infant is six, eight or ten weeks old to add cereal and strained vegetables to his diet, while your neighbor's physician starts her child with cereal at three weeks. A third physician in your community may warn that early introduction of cereals and meats may increase the likelihood of allergy in a susceptible infant.

Yet despite these concerns, the age at which infants get their first solid food has been steadily lowered in past years. No doctor today advocates going back to the practice earlier this century of keeping a baby on a milk-only diet until almost his first birthday. But many doctors do question what benefits are gained by introducing solids into a baby's diet before the age of three months.

According to a study made by researchers at Pennsylvania State University, adding solids to a baby's diet does not cut down the number of daily feedings the infant needs. In fact, the study indicated that babies who get both solids and milk took more feedings per day than those on milk alone. About one third of the infants were getting seven feedings per day at the age of three weeks. At five weeks, 20 percent of the bottle-only babies wanted seven feedings, while 29 percent of the solids-and-milk group had seven mealtimes.

A baby who is fed solids along with milk does receive more

nutrients—particularly iron and thiamine—than the bottle-only infant. He doesn't consume more calories, however, for he tends to cut down on the amount of milk he drinks. And these nutrients aren't necessary for a baby younger than three months.

Some babies don't like solid foods, although most of them enjoy fruits, the Pennsylvania State University study showed. Many infants refuse strained vegetables, and at least 10 percent of the babies suffered an allergic reaction to some of the solid foods they were fed.

There's no evidence that babies benefit from an early introduction to solid foods, according to this study. And there's no evidence that introducing solid foods helps a baby sleep longer at night.

You should, however, begin giving your baby foods he can chew by about the age of six months. A baby finds it particularly easy to learn to chew just after he loses the infantile tongue-thrust reflex and no longer pushes food placed on the front of his tongue out of his mouth. Some studies show that if a child does not have an opportunity to begin eating solid foods during this particular stage in development, it may be more difficult later on.

What about teaching a child to drink milk from a cup? What's the best age?

Six months of age is also a good time to introduce a baby to liquids in a cup, whether or not he is fed breast milk or a formula. It's easier if you give him an unbreakable cup to play with first, then add just a small amount of liquid. Some babies enjoy drinking from a cup so much that they progress from breast-feeding directly to drinking from a cup at about nine months of age without ever taking milk from a bottle. Other babies enjoy a bottle so much, especially at bedtime, that they cling to it until the age of two, two and a half or three.

If your baby is still drinking some of his milk from a bottle at age three, there's no harm in it. It isn't worth making a family scene. Usually he will give it up easily when the last bottle breaks or is "lost." Or, if he has a stuffy nose some day, you can suggest casually that he might be more comfortable having his nightcap milk from a cup rather than a bottle. Or you can simply suggest that because he is getting so grown up, he probably isn't interested in such a baby habit any more.

When should a child learn to feed himself?

The easiest age to get a youngster started on using a spoon to feed himself is about eleven to fifteen months of age, when most babies try to wrestle the spoon away from a parent and use it themselves. At this age a baby makes such a mess of trying to get food into his mouth that it's a temptation for a parent to wrestle the spoon back and insist on doing the job herself. But there's a danger, then, that the baby will lose interest in learning and won't try to feed himself when his mother decides she is ready for him to learn. Most youngsters are interested in feeding themselves small bits of finger food starting even earlier than eleven months of age and should be encouraged to do so, even if they seem to be playing with the food. Youngsters aren't ready to learn much about table manners or the correct way to hold utensils until about age three or later.

What can you do about a finicky eater?

You may feel better about your youngster's eating habits if you note these points from a report by the American Academy of Pediatrics' committee on nutrition:

· Children of the same age and sex vary extremely in how much food they eat. You can't judge how much your youngster should consume by the amount your neighbor's child eats or by any standard calorie chart.

· Food intake varies in amount during most of childhood, and in addition, many youngsters also shift from being big eaters to being small eaters, or vice versa, as they develop. Only about one third of the children stayed in the same "big eater," "medium eater" or "small eater" classification during their preschool, primary school and teen-age years, a recent study shows.

· Boys and girls differ considerably in how much they eat and at what age they eat most. Girls reach their peak intake of food—about 2,500 calories a day—between thirteen and sixteen. Boys consume 3,500 calories per day during their top eating years of fifteen to eighteen.

· Don't expect your child to show a regular day-to-day relationship between how many calories he uses up in a day and how much he feels like eating. It is not a sign of illness when a youngster plays hard all day and then has no appetite. Fatigue itself is likely to interfere with appetite.

· The desire for food tends to drop sharply during hot weather, according to the report of the nutrition committee.

· Don't be surprised or alarmed if your child has what you consider to be irrational food preferences. Emotional and cultural factors play an important part in determining the eating habits of almost every individual and society, notes the report.

"Although we tend to think of food taboos in relation to strange and seemingly irrational practices of primitive societies, such taboos are actually common in our society, too," says the report. "For example, we eat live oysters, but not live shrimp. At breakfast, Americans are likely to have an appetite for ham and eggs, but not for roast pork. In view of such irrational practices, the child who craves ice cream for breakfast need not be considered by his parents to be ill or perverse; he may be merely less regimented by culture than are the adult members of society."

· Family squabbles and emotional upsets also reduce a child's appetite, other nutrition experts point out. He also will eat less during stages in his development when he is not growing rapidly.

· The time-honored rule that a child must clean his plate at every meal has long been challenged by physicians, particularly when a child has no voice in the size of his servings. Hazards of overfeeding a baby or a child are increasingly being stressed by doctors today. Overeating in early childhood sets a psycho-logical pattern which is difficult to break. It also stimulates the body to produce an excessive number of fat cells, recent studies show; these cells remain in the body for the rest of a lifetime and although they can be reduced in size, they don't decrease in number, making weight-loss programs relatively unsuccess-ful.

Studies show that the overweight baby tends to become the overweight child and the overweight adult. You may consider your plump toddler attractive, but you won't feel the same way about your tubby school child or chubby teen.

What do you do with a child of five who will not eat and who will absolutely not taste anything new? Should he be forced, if that is possible, to eat, even if he gags? He gets no extras at meals, but he does get small afternoon and bedtime snacks. Denying these does no good because he would rather do with-out than eat something he has decided he doesn't want.

Unless you've lived with a persnickety eater, it's impossible to imagine how stubborn and determined a few of them are. (Some doctors speculate that these problems may originate in undetected allergies or in the fact that foods actually taste different to some individuals.) It does no good to try to force such a child to eat; an adult simply can't win a battle with a child over food.

If your child is eating a reasonably balanced diet daily and is healthy and growing, there's nothing to gain and much to lose by trying to force him to eat. If you are worried that your youngster is not eating enough of the essential nutrients, keep a list of what he does eat for several days and discuss it with your doctor. He may prescribe a vitamin supplement. You may also be able to find some forms of a valuable food your child will accept. For example, youngsters will often eat raw spinach, peas, carrots, cabbage or cauliflower, but not these same vegetables in cooked form.

Some families help solve the problem of finicky eating by insisting that each person sample at least one bite of each dish served. Others enjoy introducing their children to exotic foreign dishes at home and in restaurants. Occasionally, lessons in simple cooking help a reluctant eater expand his food horizons.

Many a child who won't eat certain foods at home will at least try them when he's having lunch or dinner at a friend's house, at camp or in other special social situations.

Some parents may feel that efforts such as these to make food appealing to a finicky eater mean catering too much to his fussiness. But the key to the problem is to help him learn to enjoy the foods he's refusing—and it can't be done by coercion.

How can you get a reluctant eater to have breakfast before he starts to school?

Trying to persuade or coax or cajole or lecture or threaten a youngster into eating a nourishing breakfast before the school bus beeps can be one of a mother's most frustrating problems. Yet it seems impossible to let a reluctant or rebellious eater off with just a snitch of toast and a sip of orange juice to sustain him until noon, when he might or might not eat the school lunch or what's packed in his lunchbox.

An unorthodox way out of the breakfast impasse has been demonstrated by public-school nurses in Cleveland. So successful has the Cleveland plan been that it has been reported in *The American Journal of Nursing.*

Cleveland's 65 school nurses tackled the breakfast problem when they noted that large numbers of youngsters were reporting to the school nurse about 10 A.M., complaining vaguely of headache or stomachache. Questioned by a nurse, these children would usually admit they had either eaten no breakfast or an inadequate one.

To avoid a head-on, eat-this-because-it's-good-for-you battle and still win over the juvenile breakfast resisters, the Cleveland nurses started by tossing out the juice-egg-toast-milk tradition. Then they built up their own program based on premises such as these:

1. Anything eaten for breakfast is better than nothing—even a candy bar and a cola drink, or a bologna sandwich and apple pie (two breakfasts reported by Cleveland pupils).

2. Cold foods are just as nutritious as warm foods.

3. Dozens of good, balanced breakfasts can be built by ignoring most conventional breakfast foods completely. These can give a child just as much nourishing sustenance for a busy morning.

To help the children plan well-balanced breakfasts they would eat without argument, the Cleveland school nurses taught them that a good morning meal should contain "magic energy," "quick energy," and "lasting energy." "Magic energy" is contained in foods such as orange juice, tangerines, grapefruit, strawberries, milk, carrots, cantaloupe, tomato juice and apricots, pupils were told. It provides vitamins and minerals that cannot be seen or tasted. "Quick energy" means foods such as cereal, grits, toast, sweet rolls, doughnuts and milk, which give a person pep for a quick getaway but are used up in a hurry. "Lasting energy" comes from eggs, meat, fish, cheese, peanut butter and milk, the protein foods that can power up a child for a long morning of study, games and fun.

On their own, the children drew up menus they would enjoy in the morning: Apple pie, cheese and milk. Cocoa, doughnut, peanut butter and crackers and orange. Tuna-fish sandwich, strawberries and milk. Hot dog, milk and orange juice. Grapefruit, bologna sandwich and milk.

Follow-up classes helped the youngsters improve and widen their selection of foods. And many mothers told school nurses that they would much prefer spending ten minutes frying a hamburger in the morning than thirty minutes arguing about an uneaten egg.

How important is it for parents and children to eat all of their evening meals together? Is it really so bad to let the children eat alone and maybe watch their favorite cartoon in the TV room while Mom and Dad eat in peace? How should you manage when a father comes home and wants to relax and read his mail before dinner but the children are hungry earlier?

This problem is common in families with a commuter father, and no dogmatic answer is possible. It helps to keep in mind the goals that family meals should accomplish: (1) seeing that everyone is adequately nourished; (2) helping the children learn pleasant manners so thoroughly that they become automatic; and (3) making meals a happy time of family sharing and love.

If family dinnertimes just aren't working out because a commuter father doesn't arrive home until 7 P.M., exhausted and needing to unwind, while the youngsters have been whining with hunger since 5:30 P.M., it's only sensible to look for alternate ways to accomplish the same goals.

Sometimes small children can learn to wait contentedly for a late dinner if you give them a substantial snack about 3:30 P.M. But often there's no workable alternative except to feed the family in two shifts for a few years.

This accomplishes the first goal rather easily; but it makes the second and third aim more difficult to attain. It would help if you would sit down with your children while they eat, rather than letting them watch television, so you could encourage the good manners and conversation, in a relaxed nonpressuring way. You should also try to make family meals on weekends special occasions for happy talk. And the children should have a regular daily time to talk and play with their father.

10. Is Your Baby Developing Normally?

"Shouldn't my son be able to sit up by now?"

"When does a baby say her first word?"

"My boy is fourteen months old and still hasn't started to walk. Is something wrong with him?"

"Is my baby developing normally?"

Such questions are frequently asked—of doctors, nurses, grandmothers, next-door neighbors and writers of child-care columns and books. It's important that parents know the answers for two reasons. Usually, information about the ages at which children normally reach what physicians call "developmental milestones" gives parents reassurance that their youngster is progressing well. But should a child's development be delayed for some reason, such information provides parents with an early warning signal to advise them they should discuss the situation with their doctor.

Normal, healthy children vary considerably in the ages at which they first begin to achieve specific physical abilities, learn to talk and acquire social skills. A child's growth is not a continuous upward curve, but a series of plateaus and spurts. So parents should not be alarmed if their baby or toddler or preschooler lags a little behind a neighbor's child in some areas of development or progresses at a somewhat different rate or with a different learning style than an older brother or sister, or if he isn't learning new skills precisely on some arbitrary schedule.

In assessing how well a child is growing, most physicians use one of several developmental screening tests. These are intended to pick out the youngsters who show some signs of possible physical and/or mental retardation and who should be given further testing to pinpoint possible problems. One of the newest and best of such screening tests is the Denver Developmental Screening Scale, developed by Dr. William K. Frankenburg and Dr. Josiah B. Dodds at the University of Colorado School of Medicine. The Denver Scale is unique and particularly helpful because it gives four different ages for each test item, showing when 25, 50, 75 and 90 percent of children develop each ability. The test was standardized on more than one thousand normal Denver youngsters, a cross section of the city's population.

Because an accurate scale of development can be helpful and reassuring to parents, here is a sampling of items from the Denver Developmental Screening Scale. You needn't worry if your child fails to perform only one or two of the skills at the age when 90 percent of youngsters can. But if he seems behind in more than that, it's wise to discuss his development with your doctor so that more diagnostic tests can be made. Early diagnosis of a problem can mean more effective treatment.

Motor abilities

Lifts head when lying face down on a flat surface so that face makes a 90-degree angle with the surface:
   —25 percent by 1.3 months
   —50 percent by 2.2 months
   —75 percent by 2.6 months
   —90 percent by 3.2 months

Holds head steady when supported in a sitting position:
—25 percent by 1.5 months
—50 percent by 2.9 months
—75 percent by 3.6 months
—90 percent by 4.2 months

Rolls over, back to stomach or stomach to back:
—25 percent by 2.3 months
—50 percent by 2.8 months
—75 percent by 3.8 months
—90 percent by 4.7 months

Can be pulled to a sitting position without head lagging behind:
—25 percent by 3 months
—50 percent by 4.2 months
—75 percent by 5.2 months
—90 percent by 7.7 months

Sits alone without support for at least five seconds:
—25 percent at 4.8 months
—50 percent at 5.5 months
—75 percent by 6.5 months
—90 percent by 7.8 months

Stands for at least five seconds holding onto a solid object:
—25 percent at 5 months
—50 percent at 5.8 months
—75 percent at 8.5 months
—90 percent at 10 months

Pulls himself to standing position without help:
—25 percent by 6 months
—50 percent by 7.6 months
—75 percent by 9.5 months
—90 percent by 10 months

Walks holding onto furniture:
—25 percent by 7.3 months
—50 percent by 9.2 months
—75 percent by 10.2 months
—90 percent by 12.7 months

Walks well:
—25 percent by 11.3 months
—50 percent by 12.1 months
—75 percent by 13.5 months
—90 percent by 14.3 months

Walks up steps:
—25 percent by 14 months
—50 percent by 17 months
—75 percent by 21 months
—90 percent by 22 months

Kicks ball forward:
—25 percent by 15 months
—50 percent by 20 months
—75 percent by 22.3 months
—90 percent by 2 years

Throws ball overhand:
—25 percent by 14.9 months
—50 percent by 19.8 months
—75 percent by 22.8 months
—90 percent by 2.6 years

Pedals tricycle:
—25 percent by 21 months
—50 percent by 23.9 months
—75 percent by 2.8 years
—90 percent by 3 years

Balances on one foot for five seconds:
- —25 percent by 2.6 years
- —50 percent by 3.2 years
- —75 percent by 3.9 years
- —90 percent by 4.3 years

Personal and social skills

Smiles spontaneously, without stimulus:
- —25 percent by 1.4 months
- —50 percent by 1.9 months
- —75 percent by 3 months
- —90 percent by 5 months

Feeds self a cracker:
- —25 percent by 4.7 months
- —50 percent by 5.3 months
- —75 percent by 6.2 months
- —90 percent by 8 months

Plays pat-a-cake, moving arms and hands by himself:
- —25 percent by 7 months
- —50 percent by 9.1 months
- —75 percent by 9.8 months
- —90 percent by 13 months

Plays ball, by tossing or rolling ball back to another player:
- —25 percent by 9.7 months
- —50 percent by 11.6 months
- —75 percent by 13.5 months
- —90 percent by 16 months

Drinks from a cup without spilling much:
- —25 percent by 10 months
- —50 percent by 11.7 months
- —75 percent by 14.4 months
- —90 percent by 16.5 months

Uses spoon to get food to mouth without spilling much:
—25 percent by 13.3 months
—50 percent by 14.4 months
—75 percent by 18 months
—90 percent by 23.5 months

Takes off coat, shoes, socks or pants:
—25 percent by 13.7 months
—50 percent by 15.8 months
—75 percent by 19.2 months
—90 percent by 21.9 months

Puts on shoes without tying:
—25 percent by 20.1 months
—50 percent by 22.3 months
—75 percent by 2.6 months
—90 percent by 3 years

Washes and dries hands:
—25 percent by 19 months
—50 percent by 23 months
—75 percent by 2.5 years
—90 percent by 3.2 years

Plays cooperative games, like tag:
—25 percent by 20 months
—50 percent by 2 years
—75 percent by 3 years
—90 percent by 3.5 years

Buttons one article of clothing:
—25 percent by 2.6 years
—50 percent by 3 years
—75 percent by 3.7 years
—90 percent by 4.2 years

Dresses self with supervision:
- —25 percent by 2.2 years
- —50 percent by 2.7 years
- —75 percent by 3.1 years
- —90 percent by 3.5 years

Dresses without supervision, except for back buttons and tying shoes:
- —25 percent by 2.6 years
- —50 percent by 3.6 years
- —75 percent by 4.1 years
- —90 percent by 5 years

Language

Laughs:
- —25 percent by 1.4 months
- —50 percent by 2 months
- —75 percent by 2.6 months
- —90 percent by 3.3 months

Turns toward a voice from behind:
- —25 percent by 3.8 months
- —50 percent by 5.6 months
- —75 percent by 7.3 months
- —90 percent by 8.3 months

Says "mama" or "dada," not necessarily associating the sound with a parent:
- —25 percent by 5.6 months
- —50 percent by 6.9 months
- —75 percent by 8.7 months
- —90 percent by 10 months

Imitates speech sounds:
- —25 percent by 5.7 months
- —50 percent by 7 months
- —75 percent by 9.2 months
- —90 percent by 11.2 months

Says "dada" and "mama" to mean the parent:
  —25 percent by 9.2 months
  —50 percent by 10.1 months
  —75 percent by 11.9 months
  —90 percent by 13.3 months

Uses three words besides "mama" and "dada":
  —25 percent by 11.8 months
  —50 percent by 12.8 months
  —75 percent by 15 months
  —90 percent by 20.5 months

Combines two different words to make meaningful phrase (like "Want milk" but not counting a single-idea combination like "Thank you"):
  —25 percent by 14 months
  —50 percent by 19.6 months
  —75 percent by 22 months
  —90 percent by 2.3 years

Names a single picture, like cat, apple, duck, dog or horse:
  —25 percent by 15.9 months
  —50 percent by 20.3 months
  —75 percent by 2.1 years
  —90 percent by 2.5 years

Uses plurals:
  —25 percent by 20 months
  —50 percent by 2.3 years
  —75 percent by 2.8 years
  —90 percent by 3.2 years

Gives first and last name:
  —25 percent by 2 years
  —50 percent by 2.7 years
  —75 percent by 3.2 years
  —90 percent by 3.8 years

Comprehends four prepositions (by placing block under, on, in front of, or behind another object):
    —25 percent by 2.7 years
    —50 percent by 3.1 years
    —75 percent by 3.4 years
    —90 percent by 4.5 years

Recognizes three colors:
    —25 percent by 2.7 years
    —50 percent by 3 years
    —75 percent by 3.7 years
    —90 percent by 4.9 years

Small muscle activity and coordination

Brings hands together in front of chest:
    —25 percent by 1.3 months
    —50 percent by 2.2 months
    —75 percent by 3 months
    —90 percent by 3.7 months

Reaches out for an object on table when held by mother:
    —25 percent by 2.9 months
    —50 percent by 3.6 months
    —75 percent by 4.5 months
    —90 percent by 5 months

Picks up block or toy in each hand at the same time:
    —25 percent by 5.1 months
    —50 percent by 6.1 months
    —75 percent by 7 months
    —90 percent by 7.5 months

Transfers cube or small block from one hand to the other:
    —25 percent by 4.7 months
    —50 percent by 5.6 months
    —75 percent by 6.6 months
    —90 percent by 7.5 months

Picks up raisin using thumb and fingers in opposition:
—25 percent by 7.1 months
—50 percent by 8.3 months
—75 percent by 9.1 months
—90 percent by 10.6 months

Grasps raisin efficiently with thumb and index finger:
—25 percent by 9.4 months
—50 percent by 10.7 months
—75 percent by 12.3 months
—90 percent by 14.7 months

Scribbles spontaneously when given paper and pencil:
—25 percent by 11.9 months
—50 percent by 13.3 months
—75 percent by 15.8 months
—90 percent by 2.1 years

Builds tower of four blocks:
—25 percent by 15.5 months
—50 percent by 17.9 months
—75 percent by 20.5 months
—90 percent by 2.2 years

Builds tower of eight blocks:
—25 percent by 21 months
—50 percent by 23.8 months
—75 percent by 2.4 years
—90 percent by 3.4 years

Copies a drawing of a circle:
—25 percent by 2.2 years
—50 percent by 2.6 years
—75 percent by 2.9 years
—90 percent by 3.3 years

Copies a drawing of a square:
  —25 percent by 4.1 years
  —50 percent by 4.7 years
  —75 percent by 5.5 years
  —90 percent by 6 years

Draws a man, showing three parts of the body:
  —25 percent by 3.3 years
  —50 percent by 4 years
  —75 percent by 4.7 years
  —90 percent by 5.2 years

Draws a man, using six body parts:
  —25 percent by 4.6 years
  —50 percent by 4.8 years
  —75 percent by 5.4 years
  —90 percent by 6 years

11. How to Make Baby-sitters Pay Off

If you have a baby, a toddler or a preschooler, one of the greatest favors you can do for him is to hire a sitter and treat yourself to an occasional break. Your child will have a better mother for it.

Using sitters in unusual ways to help yourself over the humps—physical and emotional—can do surprisingly much to ease the battle fatigue of young motherhood. A mother who is on 24-hour-a-day duty with a new baby or chasing an energetic toddler—or both—needs more than an occasional Saturday night off. Skimp elsewhere on your budget if you have to, but try using sitters in ways like these:

• Hire a high-school girl an afternoon a week to wheel the baby's carriage or walk your toddler to the park. Use the hour and a half for your favorite indulgence: a guilt-free nap, a book, a leisurely soak in a perfumed tub, an experiment with an intriguing new recipe, an uninterrupted phone call for adult talk, some time for a hobby.

• If your moppet is an energetic male, find a reliable teen-age boy to act as a camp-counselor type of sitter after school. He can teach your offspring to pitch and catch, chase after his tricycle, push the swings and referee the arguments with play-mates. Come 5:30 P.M., your runabout should be more calm and you more collected to face the daily bedtime bath-bed bedlam.

· Before an important party, schedule your sitter sixty to ninety minutes early. She can feed the children and get them ready for bed while you bathe and dress in unaccustomed leisure. It's worth the extra tab for the sitter to start off for the evening with an aura of perfume rather than Pablum.

· When the party's at your house, a sitter behind the scenes can save your sanity by supervising the children's dinner-and-bed routine. Better yet, she might take them out to the nearest hamburger stand for a supper treat while you concentrate on being hostess.

· When circumstances beyond your control box you into taking two or more youngsters at a time for medical checkups, dental appointments or extended shopping trips, add a sitter to your entourage. You can concentrate on accomplishing your mission with one child at a time, while she minds the tag-alongs.

· For your child's birthday party, the best present you can give yourself is a sitter. She'll more than earn her keep just by mopping up spills and keeping the cake from being squashed into the carpet.

· If you're feeling submerged completely in the pre-five world without a shred of personality to call your own, schedule a sitter on a regular basis (even just two afternoons a month) to give you time to continue or develop an interest strictly your own. Whether you take piano lessons, lock yourself in the bedroom to sew or watercolor, go to a concert or browse in antique stores, it gives you an oasis of time you need.

Some mothers even use their sitter time to volunteer for work in the nearest hospital. Even though they make beds and tote trays, they find it a tonic that helps them to be brighter, better mothers.

THE BABY-SITTER COOPERATIVE

If you're short of cash for sitters, or you feel guilty spending money to give yourself a little time off, you may want to check into the possibility of organizing a baby-sitter cooperative in your area.

"There is a stage in family life when baby-sitting cooperatives are the very greatest thing that could happen in a neighborhood," says a suburban mother. "You get experienced sitters, mostly young mothers whose children are the same age as yours. You can leave a sick child, or a baby or a whole houseful of youngsters with confidence that the sitter knows as much about child care as you do, and furthermore, that she is current in her knowledge.

"The children know the sitter, for she is usually the mother of a friend in the neighborhood," continues the mother. "Sitters are available during the day, when it's impossible to get teen-agers. You can drop your child off at another mother's house or have her come to yours. Or your youngster can walk home from school with a friend and just go to the sitter's house or have lunch there. Because you can pay for the help in points, you don't feel like you are asking for a favor or imposing.

"You really are freer to go and you do go out more often because you don't have to pay the sitter. And I think it's good for small children. They get used to going into other people's homes and playing with other youngsters. Many of them look forward to 'being sitted.' "

For a baby-sitter cooperative to work, however, a carefully considered organization needs to be established with rules each family understands and supports. From 15 to 30 families is the most workable size; that's large enough to provide a good pool of potential sitters, yet not too big to make accounting complicated. Typically, a successful sitter coop rules that members live within a certain geographical area so transportation isn't a burden.

Each member serves as secretary (or bookkeeper) for a term of one month, keeping track of hours each member sits and for whom. In some groups the secretary is responsible for obtaining the sitters, provided request is made at least three days in advance. In others, members phone the secretary for a list of available sitters, then make their own arrangements.

Some cooperatives use a point system, with sitters earning one point for every 15 minutes of sitting time before midnight and extra points after midnight, or during mealtimes or for extra children outside the family for whom she sits. Other groups keep records in terms of hours, with time and a half after midnight or for extra duty. Husbands may do the baby-sitting, if it's agreeable to the family requesting the sitter.

During the daytime, sitting by cooperative members is usually done in the home of the sitter. Evenings, the sitter usually comes to the sittee's home.

Other rules cover last-minute cancellations (the canceling family is usually billed a minimum number of points or hours); sending substitutes; and what the sittee family must provide (coffee, pillow and blanket for late nights, the usual information about where the couple can be reached, first aid information, medical data, candles and matches or flashlight in case of power failure, and emergency phone number).

All successful sitter cooperatives set a maximum on the amount of time or points a member family may owe. Usually it's about 25 hours, although some cooperatives allow extra hours to build up during the last three months of pregnancy or in other special situations. Some groups allow a payoff in cash rather than baby-sitting time, especially when a member family is transferred out of town with little notice.

Some cooperatives operate only during weekdays, especially if the group is small. Teen-agers or older women are hired for weekends. This avoids creating problems on occasions like New Year's Eve or nights when there is a party a large number of cooperative members want to attend. Unless the families occasionally use teen-age sitters or older women, it can be difficult to find a sitter when the cooperative can't provide one.

12. OUTGROWING A BABY-SITTER

When does your child outgrow a baby-sitter?

Like most questions about children, there's no one definite answer that fits every youngster, every family, every circumstance. And like most stages in a child's development, ability to get along without a sitter grows gradually, in small steps, and with occasional backsliding.

How soon you can do without a baby-sitter depends not only on your child's age, but also on his maturity, the safety of your neighborhood, the nearness of reliable neighbors, how far and how long you'll be away, and whether your offspring is pleased or frightened about being on his own.

You can begin by leaving your child alone in the house for a short time during the day while you visit a neighbor. Age seven—certainly eight—is usually not too young, provided (a) your offspring isn't the kind who is just waiting for a chance to make mischief; (b) you don't leave him in charge of younger children; (c) your home safety precautions are adequate; (d) he knows where to find you if he gets uneasy; and (e) you really do stay away just a few minutes.

If your child begs you not to leave him, comes running after you, gets into trouble while you're away or is unusually clinging when you return, he's not ready to be without a sitter even for a short time. You'll need to give him several more months to mature before you try again.

Most nine-year-olds—and some mature eights in safe communities with nearby neighbors—are old enough to stay at home alone during the day for an hour or two. Here, again, your child should know where to reach you, be trained not to admit a stranger to the house, understand how to use the telephone in an emergency, know where to find a helpful neighbor and be happy about the idea of staying alone.

If you're going to be away for longer than an hour or two, or during mealtimes, you'll probably still require a sitter, even in the daytime, for a nine-year-old. He's apt to be tempted to use the stove without supervision, or grow bored and restless.

By age eleven, a boy or girl usually feels grown-up enough and is responsible enough to be left alone without a sitter for an hour or so in the early evening—provided you are not going far away and he knows he can easily reach you by phone. If you return to find him uneasy, with all the lights in the house ablaze, or discover he's ignored your rules about bedtime or snacking, you'll know he's not yet quite mature enough for this step.

A twelve-year-old is usually reliable and mature enough to stay alone in the evening and to sit with younger brothers and sisters with whom he gets along well. In fact, he'll probably feel more secure if he has a younger child for company. The first few times you leave him sitterless, though, it helps to make sure a friendly, reliable neighbor will be home all evening whom your youngster will feel free to phone if he gets uneasy.

It's sometimes harder for a parent to make this last transition away from baby-sitters than it is for youngsters. One mother hired a thirteen-year-old to stay with her children on the recommendation of a friend. When the girl arrived to sit, the mother's oldest child took one horrified look at her and yelped, "She's not going to baby-sit with me! She's in my class at school!"

13. How to Get the Most Fun for Your Toy Dollars

Buying toys for children is a lot like playing baseball. You strike out far more often than you get a hit. In fact, a good batting average is about the same: .300.

How can you avoid buying toys that your child plays with once and rarely again? Or that break so quickly you can scarcely remember them when you get the bill for them the following month? What toys will give your youngster the most play value per dollar of cost?

Here are some toy-buying suggestions compiled from interviews with mothers, children and preschool teachers and from material prepared for parents by the Illinois Montessori Society:

You should begin by shopping for toys with the interests, readiness and needs of your particular youngster in mind—not by basing your choices on an age group, a TV commercial or a memory of your own past childhood. In evaluating a toy purchase, you should think through exactly what your youngster will be doing with it. Wind-up-and-watch gadgets usually hold small-fry interest for only a short time, while toys that engage a child's active creativity—like blocks or a baby doll—may be enjoyed for years.

You should consider whether your youngster can successfully use the toy you are considering. Usually a child gets the most pleasure and use from a plaything that challenges him to some degree, but not so much that he is constantly frustrated.

Age levels suggested on many toy and game packages are often unrealistically high, particularly for children from mentally stimulating homes. Montessori teachers point out that if a youngster is shown how to handle delicate materials carefully, he usually can do so, even at a surprisingly young age.

You shouldn't buy a toy your child can't use without instructions from you—unless you are prepared to give him the patient, tactful kind of help he will need. Too many parents, for example, expect a five-year-old to play for hours with a dump truck, although he has never seen one in operation.

"Don't let the toy increase your child's dependence," advises the Illinois Montessori Society. "Avoid toys which require too many verbal directions (this does not rule out games which child and parent can play together).

"Choose toys that are self-correcting, that have a built-in control of error (such as an inlaid wooden puzzle). Remember, the child isn't embarrassed if the toy tells him he made a mistake, but he may be if the parent has to tell him so."

You should make sure the toy you are considering is fun to play with—and that it gives your youngster something new to learn. "The fun value increases the learning value and vice versa," notes the Illinois Montessori Society. "A child can't learn from a toy he doesn't use."

You should also check to see how durable and well made the plaything is. Will it last long enough with reasonable handling to serve the purpose for which it is intended? Is it aesthetic rather than over-gimmicked and garish? Is the design good or does it detract and distract from the purpose of the toy? Do the parts that are supposed to move really work? Are your youngster's fingers strong and skilled enough to do what the toy requires?

Do you have room for the toy now? Big road-racing sets, indoor croquet, electric-train layouts and large-size building blocks come with built-in problems if your home is small. Do you have storage space for the toy you're considering? Is the container adequate? Does it have lots of little pieces that will be easily lost? Can your youngster care for it and put it away himself?

In choosing toys, you should consider the overall balance of playthings your child possesses. He needs toys to encourage him to use both large and small muscles, to provide indoor and outdoor activity, to develop eye-hand coordination, to suggest restful activity, to stimulate creativity and to teach new skills. He should have toys that provide him with comfort and companionship, that help him develop new concepts, that give him opportunities to play with other youngsters and with adults.

"Don't let your child's toy collection overemphasize one type of activity, though the emphasis may change from one period to another," advises the Illinois Montessori Society. "For instance, the toddler is in an active stage and will need toys that require a lot of large muscle manipulation, whereas the pre-teen is ready for more quiet, intricate activities."

You should learn to know the manufacturers that produce good toys. There are several companies which are more interested in marketing low-key, aesthetic playthings children really use than in flashy gimmicks that can be oversold via TV commercials.

You can often find excellent "toys" in places other than toy stores and toy counters. One wise and understanding grandfather, for example, bought his grandson, six, an adult safe with a combination lock because he realized how often the boy was frustrated and upset when his small treasures were disturbed by three younger children. The six-year-old was delighted.

Most youngsters would rather have "real" objects than toy replicas—and usually the real equipment is easier to manipulate than the toy copies. You can find excellent gifts for children in a hardware store, lumber yard, florist shop, art-supply store, stationery store, drug store, camera store, pet shop, biological supply house—and book store. When the Illinois Montessori Society surveyed parents to learn what toys their children used and enjoyed most, many of the items listed were not toys at all. Included on the list were kitchen tools such as a cheese grater with turning handle, a peeler and a cheese slicer.

Other top play-value-per-dollar toys included a child-sized sink and cupboard, an indoor slide, a rope swing, a jumbo inflatable ball, several varieties of blocks, wooden puzzles, wooden shape-sorting boxes, colored pencils, reading and phonics materials, dominoes and easy board games.

Here are some specific suggestions for toys, grouped loosely by ages. Some of the listings are suitable for more than one age group, and you'll need to study your own youngster carefully to make the best choices.

BIRTH TO ONE YEAR

Researchers now know that a baby has an urgent need to hear a great variety of sounds and to look at, touch and manipulate many different types of objects. As toy designers and manufacturers become familiar with new findings in the field of early childhood development, they are beginning to produce more appropriate toys for babies than have been available in the past. Some appropriate playthings include these:

Bright mobiles to hang over an infant's crib and the place where his diapers are changed (you should switch the objects on the mobile occasionally to give the baby new visual experiences)

Soft, rag-type dolls (with eyes that can't be twisted off)

Washable stuffed animals with pleasant textures (and unremovable eyes)

Wooden touch toys

Phonograph records—of simple songs, lullabies or even classics with clear melody and rhythm (there's a talking toy, shaped like a plastic ball, that fastens inside a crib or playpen and plays soft voices or sounds when a baby turns it on by pushing against its unbreakable mirror face; it can be operated by a baby as young as six months)

Leakproof heavy plastic fish tank that fits inside or just outside playpen or crib and safely holds bright, live goldfish for baby to watch

Crib bar that fits across baby's bed and holds changeable pictures in see-through plastic packets, sealed-in sequins and paper flowers, sound makers and interesting textures for infant to reach out and touch

Foam-rubber blocks

Soft, textured ball

Rubber-rimmed, unbreakable mirror

Blocks with bells inside

Crib gym

Sponge toys, floating animals, boats and pouring utensils for bathtub

Small nest of unbreakable bowls

Roly-poly push-over toys that pop back up to standing position

Look-through tubular toys with marbles, mirrors or other moving parts inside

Nesting blocks

Small kitchen pot with wooden block inside

Rocking horse

Easy fit-together wooden toys (for a child almost one year old)

Stacking cone with wooden rings that fit around a central core

Books—to begin reading aloud at least by the time a baby is ten months old, including picture books that show familiar objects, books that have built-in sound effects, simple stories, and books that involve the sense of touch, for example, by having sandpaper whiskers on a picture of a man's face or cotton on a bunny's tail to feel

ONE TO THREE YEARS

Toddlers have an urgent need for active toys, wheeled play-things to push and pull, toys that help them use their developing skills at manipulating objects and play materials which help them learn concepts such as "into," "out of," "behind," "in front of," "bigger than," "on top of." They need toys for imitative play and playthings for outdoor fun. Here are some possibilities:

Baby-type dolls (for both boys and girls)
Simple equipment to use with dolls, especially for two-and-a-half- and three-year-olds. Doll bed, doll carriage and bedding for dolls are good.
Toys to love, such as soft, cuddly, feel-good-to-touch stuffed animals (washable if possible)
Blocks—foam rubber, large-size cardboard, cubes or wooden kindergarten blocks
Push or pull toys (especially for one- to two-year-olds)
Rocking horse
Balls of every variety
Inlaid wooden or hard-rubber puzzles (after age one and a half)
Nesting blocks, bowls, barrels or eggs
Inlaid form board containing simple geometric shapes
Bathtub toys
Slide

Sled

Wagon

Tricycle

Trucks, especially sturdy wooden or metal ones of large size

Housekeeping toys, especially for two-and-a-half- to three-year-olds (as sturdy and realistic as possible)

Garden tools

Swing (indoor varieties as well as outdoor type)

Paper and pencil, finger paints, crayons or washable felt-tipped pens (especially for two- and three-year-olds)

Flashlight (for ages two to three)

Lock box made of wood with doors secured by different types of fasteners

Giant magnifying glass on legs (for two- to three-year-olds)

Take-apart trucks and toys

Giant magnet

Unstructured playhouse

Counting toys and number puzzles (after age two)

Farm layouts with animals

Large wooden beads to string or fasten together

Simple lotto-type games

Simple phonograph with children's records or classics with a clear melody

Books

THREE TO SIX YEARS

These are the peak years for toys, when play is an important part of a child's life, providing him with important stimuli for learning and for physical and emotional growth. Toys lure a child into active physical play that helps his body grow. They intrigue his mind and help him become more creative. And they help him discover a little more of the world around him on his own. Here are some good choices:

Blocks—well-made kindergarten type, in as large an assortment as possible (you might begin with a starter set and add to it for birthdays and Christmases as necessary). Also, simple fit-together construction materials of wood and plastic

Block sets or farm layouts using animals

Hollow wooden blocks in sizes for outdoor play. Or blocks can be home-made, using milk cartons of assorted sizes, which have been cleaned, thoroughly dried and covered with foil or contact paper in bright colors

Dolls, with doll clothes (simple enough for small fingers to manage)

Doll house with furnishings

Doll carriage

Unstructured playhouse that can also serve as pretend store, firehouse, jail, space ship, school or whatever imagination dictates

Props for imitating adults at work, such as cash register, play money, doctor and nurse kits

Housekeeping equipment (buy the real thing in small sizes if possible)

Carpenter tools (again, the real thing if possible)

Gardening tools

Trucks, construction toys, trains and cars (for girls as well as boys)

Large-scale ride-'em toys

Art and craft materials—crayons, finger paints, colored pencils, marking pens with felt tips, washable ink, chalk, paper of all kinds, small pads of colored paper. Invest in a stand-up easel if you can afford it.

Musical equipment—drums, tamborines, cymbals, triangles, bells, xylophone

Phonograph and records or tape player with tapes (those easy for preschoolers to operate themselves)

Props for pretending, such as boxes full of clean, discarded clothes and hats, masks

Toys for loving, such as cuddly stuffed animals and baby dolls
Easy board games
Lotto-type games
Games that teach numbers, such as dice, puzzles, dominoes, number rods and telling-time games
Inlaid puzzles (be sure they are not too easy for this age group)
Pegboard
Kaleidoscope
Flannel board with cutout numbers, letters and designs
Magnifying glass or wooden stool with large-size magnifier
Magnets
Indoor swing that fits in door frame
Cushion-type trampoline for indoor use
Wheelbarrow
Wagon
Scooter
Tricycle
Ice skates
Flashlight
Sled
Outdoor play equipment such as slide, swings, climbing bars
Books—no child has too many

IDEAS FROM NON-TOY STORES

"Teach the young with real things," the French philosopher Jean Jacques Rousseau counseled more than two centuries ago. His advice is still worth considering when applied to choosing gifts and playthings for children. "Real things" have a special aura for most youngsters. Chances are, if they're carefully chosen, "real things" are also better made, longer lasting, less likely to be frustrating for small hands to use and no more expensive than the general run of toys. Here are some possibilities:

Tickets for a short round-trip train ride, or a helicopter flight over a city

Bird feeder with starter supplies

Overnight bag or colorful tote for a youngster old enough to start "sleeping over" at Grandmother's house or with a friend

A batch of threaded bolts and nuts in the largest sizes available in a hardware store to make a marvelous matching and manipulating game for a preschooler

The smallest hammer and the biggest nails in the hardware store to combine with soft lumber pieces for youngsters aged four and older

Tickets to a professional sporting event, children's theater performance, youth symphony, ice show or circus

Bulbs, ready to bloom, in a pretty dish, or a terrarium

Real art supplies, chosen for the child's interests and abilities. Possibilities include oil paints, canvas board, water colors, sketch pads, stand-up easel, poster paints, mosaics, leathers, jewelry makings, felt pens

Bicycle and tricycle trimmings, such as speedometer, fancy handlebars, saddlebags, horn, light, special seat

Stationery-store supplies, such as autograph book, personalized notepaper, maps, globe, fancy seals and stickers, desk accessories, stapler

Coin folders, perhaps with a few rolls of pennies and nickels from the bank for a starter

Stamp book and assortment of inexpensive stamps

Hobby supplies

Put-together models

Sewing materials from a fabric house, such as bright pieces of felt, fabric to make doll bedding or a length of interesting cloth for an easy-to-make skirt or shirt

Real working microscope with starter slides from a biological supply house

Real working stethoscope, combined with a drugstore assortment of cotton balls, tongue depressors and bandages, for a boy or girl who wants to play doctor

Guitar, recorder, zither or band-type instrument in which a youngster has expressed some interest. (It's best to acquire it on a three-month rental basis, if possible, before buying anything expensive outright)

Rubber stamp that prints the child's name or signature
Book plates with a child's name
Inexpensive tape recorder with blank tapes
Inexpensive transistor radio

14. TRAVELING WITH CHILDREN

Nothing indicates the privileged status of the American male as clearly as the fact that it is he who gets to drive the car when a family goes on vacation. It's Mother who has to cope with the kids.

The basic problem is that no normal child is constitutionally able to sit still for more than ten miles, even at tollway speed. His attention span is too short. His need for fresh stimuli is too great. And trying to travel with two or three youngsters doesn't just double or triple the difficulty. It squares it—or cubes it.

So a mother not only has to navigate, but also to wipe the sticky fingers, pry the gum off the door handles, referee between the rival siblings, change the dirty diapers, answer the aren't-we-almost-there questions, satisfy demands for food and drink and bathroom stops, and keep the sound level below one hundred decibels—all presumably while keeping her seat belt fastened and seeing that the children do, too.

The secret of traveling happily with children is to start off with your expectations firmly in line with reality—to remind yourself that you are going for a change of scenery, a fresh outlook and new experiences with your children. You are not

—repeat, not—looking for rest or grownup recreation. It also helps to start out prepared to be entertainment committee, food committee, bathroom detail and clean-up crew. And even if it makes your car look like a traveling junkyard, you'll need plenty of props.

TAKING A TRIP WITH A BABY

How far and how happily you can travel with a baby depends on how much gypsy is in your soul and how much of a stick-in-the-rut conformist your infant is.

If you don't mind seeing the country laundromats first, with sticky fingers in your hair and spit-up on your shoulder, and if your offspring isn't the kind who protests at 110 decibels about variations in his routine, traveling is worth a try. At worst, the experience will make you content to be back home again.

The basic problem is how to provide food, water, sleep, clean diapers, comforting contact and entertainment for your infant—without refrigeration or running water—and still arrive without looking like you've just stepped out of a dirty clothes hamper.

If you're planning a long trip, consider going by jet. Its single great advantage: speed. But there are disadvantages, too. The baby equipment you need to tote strains your luggage space. Your struggles to feed and diaper and amuse and soothe a fussy infant must all be carried on in public. You can manage to nurse a breast-fed infant without other passengers being aware of what you're doing, but you'll feel the lack of privacy and find it difficult to relax. And you can seldom count on any kind of help from a stewardess; on most jet flights, she's too busy serving meals to help tend your baby.

In an auto, a fussing infant is a private affair. If he spits up on your shoulder you won't feel quite so conspicuous. And you can have more survival gear handy.

You can travel easiest and lightest with a breast-fed baby. But you will need to take along sterilized bottles and sterile water (variations in drinking water can upset a tiny baby), especially for a long, hot car trip.

Next easiest to tote along is the baby accustomed to a pre-mixed, pre-sterilized formula that comes in ready-to-serve bottles. All you do at feeding time is attach a sterile nipple. You won't even have to heat the formula on a warm day, unless your baby is especially finicky; in that case, get a bottle warmer that works via your car's cigarette lighter.

You can also manage an evaporated-milk formula without refrigeration. Premix sterilized water and sugar in correct proportions in as many sterilized bottles as you'll need for the trip. Then open a small can of evaporated milk and add the proper amount just before each feeding, discarding whatever is left.

If your baby gets another type of formula, you can pack along an extra bottle in an insulated bag or two in an ice chest in your car. Otherwise, ask your doctor if you can switch your offspring to an easier-to-manage mix. But do it at least two weeks before departure. Your baby's food should be familiar to him, even if his surroundings aren't.

If your baby is eating canned fruits, vegetables and meats, take along his favorites. But open a fresh jar for each feeding and discard what's left. This may not be economical, but it's the only way that's safe without refrigeration. Teething biscuits can also be useful en route, not only as food but as entertainment, if you don't mind the mess.

Disposable diapers, a can of powder or oil in a plastic container, and plastic bags to hold the soiled diapers until you reach the next litter container take easy care of that end of the baby business. Premoistened paper towelettes in individual packets are neat and handy for cleanups in the car. Or you can stow your own dampened cotton balls in a plastic bag to sponge your baby's sticky fingers and diaper area en route. The baby powder, or cornstarch in a small shaker, is also a guard against prickly heat, an ever-present possibility, especially during a hot car trip.

If your baby is still sleeping in a bassinet, wedge it into the back seat of your car, parallel to the car's length. This is the safest place for your baby to ride, helps protect him against drafts and gives him a familiar bed to sleep in, wherever you stay at night.

If your baby is old enough to sit up, you'll need a safe car seat or harness arrangement. It's hard to keep a fidgety youngster anchored for a long trip, but if you insist on using this safety precaution right from the start of his life, he'll accept it with less fussing than if you give in sometimes and let him roam around the car. A baby sitting on his mother's lap on the passenger side of the front seat is exceptionally vulnerable to injury in a car accident or sudden stop. He isn't safe, either, if he's strapped into a seat belt with his mother; a crash or quick stop can squeeze him dangerously between her body and the restraining belt.

Your infant will need his favorite blanket and stuffed animal, of course, no matter how you travel. It helps, too, to have a handy cache of fascinating objects to distract him from fussing and supply some of his urgent needs for sensory stimulation. Possibilities: cuddly stuffed animals, teething rings, unbreakable mirror with rubber rim, large wooden beads, hand puppet you can work for him, sponge-rubber blocks, soft ball, handkerchief for playing peekaboo, soft doll, simple musical toys.

A canvas sling or baby backpack makes it much easier to sight-see with a baby when you're vacationing. It shifts most of his weight onto your back and hips, leaves your hands free.

TODDLERS IN TRANSIT

The terrible two's are terrible travelers. Of all children parents are tempted to take on vacation, toddlers are the most likely to wiggle, to squirm, to fuss, to get carsick, to try to crawl onto the driver's lap, to relapse on toilet training just as the hostess motions you to a table in a crowded restaurant, to throw a shoe out the car window when you're going 70 m.p.h. on a no-turn tollway.

But if traveling with your toddler is inevitable, here are suggestions that may help you relax and enjoy it:

Stock your car (or hand luggage, if you're going by train or plane) with small surprises to help your moppet forget, temporarily at least, how much he wants to wiggle and fuss. Good choices at this age include hand or finger puppets, magic slate, drawing paper, picture books, storybooks, small stacking toys, inlaid wooden puzzles with large pieces, flannel board with cutouts.

Plan to pause for play breaks every hour or two, if you go by car. It's physically impossible for a toddler to sit still any longer than that. Cache a few props—ball, balloons, a beanbag —in the car to encourage your child to run off some of his wiggle during these stops. Or find a village park or deserted schoolground with play equipment you can help him use for a few minutes.

Carry a store of food to refuel your toddler en route, for his appetite will probably be capricious and he'll insist he's hungry before you've gone 20 miles. Apples, bananas, pears, seedless grapes and oranges are best, as they don't raise a thirst like crackers or cookies.

You will need a vacuum jug of something nonsweet for your toddler to drink. But the more he drinks, the more often you'll have to find a gas station, and it's hard to keep a straight face as you tell the attendant to "fill it up" just 45 miles from the last rest stop.

Try to work it so your trip doesn't come in the middle of your toddler's toilet training. It's easier to cope with a child in diapers than a half-trained moppet in training pants when you're away from your own bathroom. If you've almost conquered the problem and can't bear to let your toddler back-slide, you'll probably have to truck along the potty or potty seat he's used to, even if it makes you feel like you're traveling third class in Bulgaria.

Take along another assortment of distractions to give your toddler something to do until the waitress comes when you stop for meals. Better yet, plan for one parent to secure the table and place the order, while the other paces your toddler up and down outside until food is actually on the table.

Your toddler will almost surely sleep in the car, even if it's just during the last ten minutes before you check into a motel, so you'll have to wake him up to put him to bed. You'll need to take along his favorite blanket, a pillow and a cuddly toy.

Unless you have an exceptionally good youngster or are unusually hardhearted, put some books and crossword puzzles in your luggage for yourself. You'll want them for those long summer evenings when your tired toddler refuses to go to sleep in a strange bedroom or stay with a strange sitter.

CARBOUND WITH A PRESCHOOLER

Traveling with a preschooler can be a delight or a disaster, an experience that either makes you glad to be a parent or agree with the father who said every child should be sealed in a barrel and fed through the bunghole until he's grown up.

Much depends on how well you prepare ahead of time and how skillful you are as the entertainment committee. A three-to six-year-old is more fun and easier to travel with than a baby or toddler. But you still can't vacation with him on adult terms. You have to expect a child to act childish most of the time wherever he is and plan accordingly.

Talk about and play-act out ahead of time what's going to happen when you travel. Most preschoolers have no idea that going on vacation means sitting still for long periods—on plane, or train, in car and restaurant. Discuss this with your child, tell him you know it may be difficult at times, and plan together ways to make it easier.

You should also explain ahead of time where you'll find bathrooms for him to use en route. Some preschoolers are uneasy away from familiar facilities and worry about having an accident. Others enjoy variations in restrooms so much that you'll be maneuvered into making several dry runs.

Let your child pack along as many of his possessions as he can fit into a shoebox or small traveling bag, plus his favorite blanket if he still feels the need for it. Let the choice of playthings be his, but rule out anything that is sharp, breakable, has more than ten pieces, is sticky or melts. Having favorite belongings handy also helps ward off the uneasiness many preschoolers feel when they are put to bed at night in an unfamiliar motel.

Here are a few other ploys parents find helpful:

For restlessness on a long trip, arrange some sort of flat surface your child can use for drawing or simple handicraft projects. A clipboard works. So does a bed table with hinged legs. Or a breadboard to which paper can be anchored with masking tape. Or you can make a handy work table by removing the top from a cardboard carton, cutting out semicircles on two opposite sides and fitting it over your child's lap so it rests on the car seat on either side of him. Along with paper, take pencils, washable marking pens, flannel board with cutouts.

For hunger on the highway when it's 50 miles to the next tollway stop, carry a supply of light snacks for your preschooler. Fruits like apples and seedless grapes, gum, hard candy and raisins are the best basics, along with an iced, insulated jug of water or apple juice.

For a child who continually asks, "Are we almost there?" but isn't old enough to read a map or tell time, try finding an answer he can understand. You might explain you'll get to

Grandmother's house "after we've had lunch and you have had a little nap," or "we'll sleep in a motel tonight and tomorrow we'll get to the ocean just before it's time for lunch." Some preschoolers enjoy having a simple time line to mark the important events of a journey; you simply put a series of knots in a cord to mark each meal, each play break, each major sight-seeing stop, each overnight stay on your way. A dab of different-colored paint for each type of event can make it easier for your preschooler to keep track of your progress.

For fighting in the back seat, call a play break. A good place is a schoolyard with swings, a small-town park, or anywhere your offspring can run and stretch safely. A game of tag or catch or an active round of "Simon Says" can work off some of the fighter spirit.

For desperate moments, try reading a storybook—either an old favorite or one of several new books you've checked out of your library for the trip. Or suggest that your car-captive offspring draw a picture to illustrate a book he knows and enjoys.

For more desperate moments, have a grab bag with small, tissued-wrapped surprises. Let your offspring pull one out at specified times, or when you most need a few minutes of comparative quiet. A good grab bag might include miniature autos or dolls, magnet with paper clips, compass, sticky-paper strips, song book, magnifying glass, kaleidoscope, magic slate, finger puppets.

Our own preschoolers have gotten the happiest car mileage out of a kaleidoscope, a deck of magnetic cards (for Spit, War and other simple games), paper dolls with lace-on clothes, read-aloud books, magnet and travel bingo (you can find several types in a toy store).

Our biggest mistakes have been puzzles with too many loose pieces and crayons that melted when inadvertently left under the car's rear window during lunch.

For most desperate moments on a long trip, turn your preschooler loose in a dime store once a day to choose one toy on his own. Set a limit on price and time for browsing. With the stretch and the new distraction, he should be easier to travel with, at least for a while.

For fidgeting in restaurants while waiting for the waitress, prime yourself in advance with a book to read quietly aloud until the food arrives. Or avoid the hassle by planning to picnic in a roadside park, at least for lunch; your preschooler needs as much respite from having to sit still and be quiet as you can give him.

For routine emergencies, which are most common at this age, add these to your own survival kit: pre-moistened paper towels or damp washcloths in a plastic bag for inevitable cleanups. Sweaters for overly air-conditioned dining rooms. Sunburn cream. Car-sickness preventatives. Litter bags. Sun glasses. First aid equipment. Insect repellent.

THE GOLDEN AGE OF FAMILY TRAVEL

Between a preschooler's fidgets and a teen's preoccupations come the golden years for family travel. With six- to fourteen-year-olds, you can go farther, pack less, be more flexible about bedtimes and mealtimes and relax more than with the five-and-unders. And school-agers are still enthusiastic and excited about sharing vacations with parents.

It isn't all back-seat songfests and sunsets over the ocean, of course. Drive 2,476 miles through the Western plains and deserts to show your offspring the geologic splendors of the Grand Canyon. What impresses your son? "Gee, Dad, did you see how far down I could spit?"

Brave the summer heat of Washington, D.C., so your children can stand in awe and admiration before our nation's historical glory (and write better themes in next year's social studies). What thrills them most? That they've finally discovered how to make their bubble gum bubble.

Shell out $1,896.53 for a ten-day trek to New Orleans. Are your children excited about the food, the jazz, the French quarter, the bayou tour? No, but they are mightily intrigued by the vibrating bed in the motel that jiggles when you put in a quarter.

The Smoky Mountains aren't self-guiding nature trails through the botanical delights of old forests, but fudge spread out on a marble-topped table in a Gatlinburg store window. Springfield, Illinois, isn't mid-1850's Lincolniana, but the place where Billy fell off the post in the parking lot and cut his knee and we had to take him to the hospital for three stitches. Colorado is where Mommy was always yelling at Daddy to keep-your-eye-on-the-road-and-stop-looking-over-the-edge-or-you'll-kill-us-all.

But family vacations at this age can still be the best of times together, especially if you share the pre-trip planning with your school-ager. Here are some tips from much-traveled parents:

Show your child how to read a map and let him plot your course before you start. If he follows your route en route, he'll be less likely to ask, "Aren't we almost there?" so often and he'll also learn more about his native land.

Round up travel guides your child can read about your itinerary ahead of time. Let him suggest places of interest to visit and brief you about them when you stop. Most youngsters enjoy being the family authority on historic forts, old battle-grounds and what's famous in the town we're coming to.

Take along at least one book to read aloud to your family as you travel. It's a great way to stop back-seat arguments, lower the noise level in your car and introduce your offspring to books you think are worthwhile. Encourage your child to pack along books to read to himself. Most libraries have vacation loan programs that cover the length of your trip, and reading during the summer is important to keep your child's school skills at pre-vacation level.

Even at this age, it helps to plan a few diversions to surprise your offspring en route. Magnetic Scrabble (if you can manage a fairly steady surface for the playing board), magnetic cards, Mad Libs and board games without too many separate pieces work well for some families. One mother had great success teaching her seven-year-old daughter magic tricks ahead of time with which to mystify and entertain the rest of the family while waiting for the food order at mealtime stops.

Another good travel ploy is to give your school-ager his own responsibilities during the trip: to record expenditures, figure out mileage, inspect your overnight motel each morning for forgotten items, make sure car doors are locked and seat belts secured before okaying the driver to start his engine.

To prevent squabbling in the back seat, you might try a stratagem suggested by the late Dr. Willis J. Potts, famed pediatric heart surgeon. He gave each member of his family twenty nickels or dimes before starting a trip, ruling that any one who began an argument or made a critical remark—parents included—had to forfeit a coin for each member of the family.

If possible, let each child in your family plan a family activity of his own choosing some time during the trip—and veto only on grounds of excessive expense, danger or definite unsuitability.

With careful planning geared to the ages and personalities of your offspring, chances are you'll find that the times you spend traveling with them are among the happiest parts of your lives together.

15. How to Help Your Child

Learn to Talk

When do babies learn to talk? What can you do to help your youngster in the complicated job of acquiring language? What signs mean you should begin to be concerned about your child's speech?

Normal speech development follows a fairly predictable pattern up to the age of about six years, speech experts explain. The average baby should be able to cry, whimper, sigh, grunt and sound some vowels and the consonants k, g, and h by the time he's about one month old. At two months, an infant does more vocalizing that isn't really crying. He has different cries for pain and hunger that you should be able to recognize. And he usually adds the m and ng sounds to his vocabulary at this time. If you talk to him softly, he may coo or sigh back in response.

From birth on, your baby is also learning to listen, to differentiate among the sounds he hears and, gradually, to realize that these sounds have meanings for him. He won't understand the words you are saying at first, of course. But he will come to recognize very soon that the sound of your voice means comfort and relief from hunger, irritation or boredom.

Babbling and vocal play with sounds begin at about four months of age, usually when your baby is by himself, according to speech experts. His vocabulary now includes p, b, t and most vowel sounds. Babbling increases in the fifth and sixth months, with more rhythm, more variety in tone and more repetition. Some speech experts note that a baby enjoys the muscular activity of babbling as much as the sounds he produces. They advise that when your baby babbles, you should babble back at him. Your response to his beginning speech activity encourages him to keep on trying. A deaf infant will begin babbling normally, but stops because he gets no feedback in sound and it becomes exceedingly difficult to help him learn normal speech.

Linguists say that a baby makes all the basic units of sound in every language on earth during the first year of his life. But eventually, he will discard those which are not a part of the language he hears in his home. As an adult, he'll never again be able to make some of these sounds, even if he studies a language in which they are used. This constant interplay between a young child's random babbling and early attempts at producing words and the responses he gets from the people around him accounts for the fact that some youngsters grow up speaking Chinese, while others learn French, Swahili, Russian, black English or standard English.

You can help your baby learn to understand the function and purpose of language if you talk to him from the very first days of his life. You should vary the tone of your voice as you greet him in the morning, change him, feed him, put him to bed. You should listen interestedly when your baby babbles at you. When he stops, you should talk back to him. This will help him get the idea of what language is all about.

You should also be helping your baby learn individual words during these early months of his life by saying them clearly—and individually—at appropriate times so he can begin to associate the words with objects or people or activities. You should say "rattle" or "bottle" or "cereal" when you give him any of these. You can say "blanket" when you tuck him in or "banana" as you give him a slice.

It will be months yet before your baby will begin to say these words back to you. But it's important that you feed these words into his brain during the first year of his life so that he will come to understand them; they are the necessary input for the verbal output to come later on.

By six to eight months of age, a baby is usually having great fun with his babbling, and he enjoys listening to himself and making a rather wide repertoire of babbling combinations, according to speech experts. He begins to make changes in pitch and inflection and to add gestures to his babbling. And he starts using the tip of his tongue in producing sounds.

Sometime between six and ten months of age, a baby usually begins to repeat syllables like "mama" or "dada." At first, the sounds "mama" or "dada" are accidental, produced at random because they are easy to say. But then your baby's environment begins to shape and channel his innate language-learning capabilities. For you react with great joy and excitement to his "mama" and "dada." You smile. You hug him. You repeat "mama" or "dada." You make him feel he has done something wonderful.

The first time this happens, your baby probably doesn't connect his random babbling of the sounds "mama" or "dada" with your response. He still may not, the second or third time the same sequence of events happens. He probably cannot remember what he did with his throat, mouth and lips that produces the sound to which you reacted so happily. But eventually his mind does make the connections. Now he can say "mama" deliberately to mean you—and he uses it when he wants you to come to him or pay attention to him.

This sequence of events and learning is an excellent example of the process psychologists call "behavior modification." By responding joyfully and individually to your child's actions, you encourage him and motivate him to repeat them and to go on learning.

Very slowly, one by one, your baby learns more words. Largely by accident, by chancing to babble syllables that have meaning to the people who are around him and who encourage him to repeat them, he adds more words to the list he knows. It's this response that determines what sounds a child keeps in his vocabulary and what language he will speak as his native tongue.

Even when your baby has learned to associate words you say with objects he can recognize—ball, bottle, teddy bear, spoon—it's a long time before he can say these words himself. Speaking a word is an enormously complicated activity. The throat, the vocal chords, the cheeks, lips, tongue and breathing mechanisms all must work precisely together. And, unlike the hand, these parts of the body are not within range of your baby's sight and the muscles that control them are exceedingly small. So it's no wonder your baby seems to make very little progress at learning to talk during the first year and a half of his life, even though you are carefully laying the foundation for speech.

By ten to twelve months of age your baby should be able to understand such words as "no no" and to respond to "patty-cake," "bye-bye" and other phrases he hears often. He enjoys hearing you name familiar objects. And he may like to imitate the sounds made by a dog, a clock or a cow, or an adult exclamation.

By now you should also be helping your baby learn to recognize words which have to do with feelings as well as objects and people. For example, when he's fussing with hunger and you begin to feed him, you might say, "You'll feel better when you aren't so hungry." Or, when you change his wet diaper, you can tell him, "The dry diaper will make you feel more comfortable." Or, "You're so tired, let me rock you while you rest." The sooner your child can learn to put his feelings into words, the less whining, crying and fussing he will have to do to get the help he wants, and the happier your home life will be.

Even during the first months after your baby's first birthday, he usually makes little obvious progress in learning to speak words. He enjoys babbling, especially if you play with sounds with him. And he adds about a dozen words to his vocabulary. But most of his interest and energy go into learning to walk.

At about eighteen months, when he can walk easily without having to concentrate a major part of his attention on managing his feet, a toddler seems to switch a major part of his interest to learning to talk. He begins putting together sounds he hears and can reproduce in a torrent of combinations, talk that speech experts label as jargon. Most of it is totally unintelligible, even to the toddler's mother. Sometimes this jargon seems so bizarre that parents worry about it. But a child this age often has a good inflection and rate of speech, and if you don't mind not understanding him, the two of you can have delightful "conversations."

Gradually, out of this jargon, your toddler begins to pull intelligible words. By his second birthday he should be connecting one to three words in a phrase with a purpose: "Want cookie," or "Daddy bye-bye." When he is age two, you should be able to understand 50 to 60 percent of your toddler's words, speech experts estimate—if you know generally what he is talking about.

Asking a toddler to carry out a very simple direction can turn into a learning game in which he takes great delight, especially if you praise him and hug him when he's successful. He'll also enjoy games that involve his pointing to various parts of his body—nose, eyes, toes, knees, ears—or having you wash at his direction while he's in the bathtub.

You should be reading to your toddler every day from the age of ten or twelve months on—the same book again and again when he wants it, and new books often, from the library, the bookstore or the supermarket. He'll enjoy looking through magazines with you as you point out the babies, the toys, an apple, a horse, a kitten, other children, familiar products.

Throughout his life—and especially during these first two years—your child will comprehend far more words than he will be able to produce himself. During his second year, language experts estimate, a toddler should recognize 120 to 175 words, be able to connect these verbal symbols with objects, respond to directions and understand simple questions.

It helps during this period to use your toddler's words for objects and actions instead of insisting on adult speech only, some language experts say. This gives your child feedback for his efforts to talk and helps him understand the purpose of words. You should, however, do most of your talking to your toddler in correct word forms, using simple sentence structure that he can understand. He needs correct models of speech from you to imitate as he grows, and you can gradually switch your talk and his away from baby talk.

The year between two and three is the most exciting in your child's speech development. It is also the year in which some speech defects may be created, experts point out.

You will have to expect imperfections in your child's speech during this entire year. It's common for him to mix up his consonants, to say "tat" for "cat" and "dank oo" for "thank you." He'll probably have difficulty pronouncing a double consonant, will say "poon" for "spoon" and "tain" for "train." He'll mix up the syllables in longer words and some of his mistakes will seem delightful to adults.

Gradually a child learns about plurals and tenses and other elements of grammar. And here his mistakes will give strong evidence of just how much he's really learning about good speech. For example, a youngster figures out for himself that adding an "s" sound to nouns indicates more than one, even though no parent has explained the grammatical principle to him. But he adds the "s" to some words which form plurals in other ways, such as "mouses," "womans" and "foots." Rather than being simple childish errors, such incorrect words are actually proof that a child has formulated for himself basic grammatical rules but has simply used a rule in instances in which the English language makes an exception.

Similarly, a youngster figures out for himself which words are verbs, and that verbs can be made to indicate action that took place in time past with the addition of an "ed." So he applies this principle to all verbs and says such things as "eated," "sitted" and "standed." Such words are evidence of the very great intelligence a child applies to the learning of language—and how complex the task really is.

Between two and three, a child usually has great difficulty manipulating his limited vocabulary and incomplete grasp of complicated language structure to express his ideas and feelings, speech experts emphasize. This is the period when a youngster starts to say something, can't find the words, stops, hesitates, repeats initial sounds and acts as if he were stuttering. His ability to think seems to be growing faster than his vocabulary.

These "disfluencies" average about 50 out of every 1,000 words in speech which is considered to be perfectly normal for two-, three- and four-year-olds, according to experts. Many of them persist through the early years of a child's life, gradually decreasing as his control over language increases. But even by age five or six, a few may be noticeable in normal talking.

It's important not to call attention to these disfluencies or to consider that your child is stuttering, most speech experts emphasize. Many experts on stuttering feel that the habit is made worse—or even actually started—by parents who mistake the normal hesitancies and mispronunciations of small children for stuttering.

According to the most widely accepted theories, the problem called "stuttering" usually begins when an adult—father, mother, teacher, neighbor, grandparent—becomes uncomfortably aware that a youngster is repeating or hesitating over words or syllables. Concerned and worried, the adult diagnoses the problem as "stuttering" and, with all love and good intentions, tries to help.

It's what the adult does after he has pinned the label "stutterer" on a child that actually increases the problem, researchers say. Usually the grownup tells the child, lovingly and gently, to talk more slowly. Or to stop and start again with what he is saying. Or to take a deep breath before he speaks. Or to practice saying sounds or syllables. He may even order him to "stop stuttering."

But all of these well-intended home remedies make the child so conscious of his speech that he hesitates and repeats even more. The adult becomes more concerned and pays even more attention to the youngster's talking. The child's hesitancies and disfluencies increase and soon turn into habit.

Once an adult has come to think of a child as a stutterer, it becomes almost inevitable that he will react toward the child in ways that will reinforce his difficulties in talking. What the grownup should do instead, experts suggest, is describe to himself precisely what the child is doing. Usually he's simply hesitating and repeating, especially when he's attempting to express a new thought or enormously excited or is trying to catch the attention of a preoccupied, busy adult.

Dozens of careful, scientific studies have shown that emotional problems, illnesses and shocks do not trigger stuttering. When speech experts interviewed hundreds of parents at the University of Iowa speech clinic, for example, very few could remember any upsetting events occurring at the time or just before their child was considered to have started stuttering.

The best course for a parent to take is to remind himself firmly that disfluencies are normal in children's speech, and to avoid showing—or even feeling—concern about them. It helps, too, to be a good listener when your youngster is talking, to try to give him respect and attention, so he won't feel he has to hurry before he loses contact with you.

Between the ages of two and three, a child's speaking vocabulary increases to 300 to 500 words, and his comprehension vocabulary to about twice that size. By his third birthday you should be able to understand about 70 to 80 percent of what he is saying. His responses average about three words each.

A great many parents do a superb job of helping their youngster acquire the mechanics of language, simply by filling the child's environment with good language models, by matter-of-factly providing him with correct speech forms when he makes mistakes in word usage, and by responding to and praising his efforts. The child delights in his increasing competence with words and in the power that words give him to function in his world.

You shouldn't put words into your child's mouth before he has a chance to say them, of course. And you shouldn't be obvious or strict in correcting his mistakes. But there are tactful ways in which you can supply him with the words he needs but doesn't know. For example, if your youngster comes running to you to complain, "Tommy taked my ball," you can reply, "Oh, Tommy took your ball? Let's go talk to him about it." Your child will soon pick up the proper form of the past tense of "take" without conscious effort on his part and without the discouragement and frustration of being told by you that he has made a mistake.

It also helps to include your child in family conversations. To make talking and listening pleasant and companionable. To ask him interested questions. To comment on what he tells you. To read to him. To play easy word games with him. Too many parents talk to their children only to give them orders. Your child will also be learning many new words from watching television, but TV can never substitute for loving and interested conversation with parents.

By your child's third birthday he'll probably be making mistakes in only about 10 percent of his speech. His vocabulary will be increasing enormously. His sentence structure will be more complicated. In many ways, he will be talking almost like an adult.

Three is the age of questions (between 7 and 14 percent of a three-year-old's speech consists of questions, according to one language expert). His questions now will not be so much a search for the names of things as a quest for information, explanations, understanding. Your job is to answer him simply and honestly and to treat his questioning as a source of mutual companionship rather than an irritation or interruption.

In the year before his fourth birthday, a child usually learns to use 600 to 1,000 words, including personal pronouns, adjectives, adverbs and prepositions. He can now understand complex and compound sentences and even use a few himself, although at age four his responses average only about four words. By the time he is four, you should be able to understand almost everything he says. Increasingly, during his fourth year, a child becomes very conscious of the importance of language and the power it gives him.

By the time your child is six years old, he should have accomplished a major part of the job of learning to speak a language. He should have outgrown the stutterings and hesitancies of two and a half and three and a half. He should be using all of the common consonant and vowel sounds easily and correctly with the possible exception of s and z. And he should have a working command of sentence structure.

But if your child's speech isn't progressing normally so that he'll reach this six-year-old stage in time for first grade, you should be alerted by definite signs much earlier in his life. These signs, suggested by speech experts, are listed here. You'll probably find this list reassures you that your youngster's speech is developing as it should. But it may warn you that he'll need expert help—and the younger the age at which he receives it, the more effective it will be. A typical checklist goes like this:

—Is your child two years old and not talking at all?
—Is he three and not forming sentences? Is most of his

speech unintelligible at this age? Does he omit many initial consonants from the words he does use?

—In comparison with other children of his age, is your youngster more than one year late in learning how to make vowel and consonant sounds?

—After the age of five, does he still often substitute easy sounds for more difficult ones?

—At five, is his sentence structure still incorrect much of the time? Does his speech seem to have abnormal pitch, rhythm or inflection? Is his rate of speaking noticeably different from that of other children his age? Does he have trouble carrying on a conversation with you?

—After age seven, does your child distort, omit or substitute any sounds?

—Is your youngster himself embarrassed or bothered about his speech, regardless of his age?

—Is his voice a monotone, unusually loud all of the time or so soft it's hard to hear him?

—Is the pitch of his voice abnormal for his age and sex?

—Does his speech have too much of a nasal quality to it, or no nasal resonance at all?

If you answer "yes" to any of these questions, you should discuss your child's speech development with your doctor. Serious difficulties in speech and language can often be prevented or minimized if expert help is given to a youngster early enough in the preschool years.

If a child is having difficulty in talking, usually the last place to look for the problem is in his mouth. "Language develops in the brain and not in the mouth," explained one speech pathologist. "Tongue-tie, large tonsils and high palate as valid causes of speech disorders are not much more common than diphtheria."

Social and emotional factors as major causes of speech and language problems in children are also discounted by most speech experts. Parents are often told that a child "doesn't talk because his parents are divorced," or "a baby sister was born just when he started to talk," or "brothers and sisters talk for him," or "he isn't the kind to ask for things," or "his parents spoil him." Declared one expert, "If these were common causes of language disorders, half the country's children would be speechless."

What does cause language disorders and delays? Mental retardation is one of the most common reasons why a child is markedly late in learning to talk or why he speaks poorly. In fact, slowness to learn to talk is usually the key symptom that leads to the diagnosis of mental retardation and other disturbances of the central nervous system. Minimal brain dysfunction, or what is more commonly called "specific learning disabilities," may also account for difficulties in learning to talk within a normal time range.

Another major cause of language delay and speech disorders is defective hearing. Unless a child hears well or has intensive, specialized teaching, he simply cannot learn to talk. Hearing loss doesn't have to be complete to prevent the development of normal speech. Partial hearing loss or loss that affects only certain types of sounds can also result in defective speech in small children. With hearing, as with other causes of speech disorders, the earlier in a child's life the problem is discovered, the better the chances that he can be helped to develop his full potential.

16. KEY WORDS FOR PARENTS

Just as it's reassuring to a tourist to have a few well-practiced phrases like *"J'ai soif"* and *"J'ai faim"* and *"Voulez-vous bien m'indiquer où se trouvent les lavabos?"* ready when he needs them, it's also useful for a parent to keep in stock some handy phrases for coping with common childhood situations. Here's a lexicon of phrases helpful when dealing with children:

"There, there, there" (pronounced softly, almost as a murmur) is an all-purpose, nonspecific, all-occasion comforting sound to be used when a parent wants to convey sympathy and awareness. It is particularly helpful when a child is crying too hard to listen to anything else and in situations in which there isn't much a parent can do to help except to let his offspring know he understands and cares. It is effective from the first few weeks of life for several years and can even be resurrected during the teen years if offered with a slight touch of humor. A patting gesture helps emphasize your meaning.

"It will be better in a minute" is the best response a parent can give to a youngster's physical hurts of the scrape, cut, sting, bump or tumble variety. It offers immediate sympathy (unlike "That didn't hurt, did it?") so a youngster doesn't feel he has

to keep on crying to convince you he hurts. It's honest (unlike "Did that nasty floor hit my darling again?"). And it doesn't encourage malingering or overreacting.

Honest variations of the phrase can also be useful in more serious injuries or illnesses. For example, "You will have a sore throat when you wake up, but it will soon get better" works about as well as can be expected for tonsillectomies. "You'll need to be brave for just a second" helps with inoculations.

"Let's talk about it" gets good results only if followed by a considerable period of attentive, listening silence. Its effectiveness tends to be cumulative, building up with repetition in happy, nonthreatening situations and in routine matters so that its meaning is well understood before it's needed in a crisis.

"Tell me your side of it" is a plural variation of "Let's talk about it," usually used when two children are involved in a dispute or in cases in which a single youngster is being confronted with evidence or testimony of an accusatory nature. The correct way to accent the phrase is to come on like a lawyer for the defense rather than as prosecuting attorney.

"Please" can be incorporated into every request, instruction or order you issue to a child and the sentence structure altered accordingly. Used in the proper context, it won't weaken parental authority, but will lessen the child's feelings of rebellion— and teach him to use similar grammatical construction himself.

"A strong boy doesn't use all his strength with girls or smaller boys" gets better results than "Don't do that" or "Let the baby alone" in the usual boy-hits-baby situations, probably because the older child appreciates the tacit acknowledgment of his physical superiority. It helps to follow the phrase with examples of how Daddy doesn't use all his strength, either, when dealing with anyone smaller.

"This will be a new experience for you" can often entice a youngster into trying a new food, starting off to a new school or attempting to learn a new skill. Used judiciously and usually

in situations you think your offspring will enjoy, it can gradually persuade him to see life as an interesting adventure.

Caution: with many youngsters it's well to taper off with this phrase and to discontinue it well before age sixteen.

"You're just the kind of boy (girl) who likes to do hard things" is a tactful, yet encouraging, acknowledgment of the difficulties a child may be facing when learning to ride a two-wheeler, mastering fractions or learning to jump rope. It's most effective when accompanied by concrete and appropriate recollections about how hard the child worked even as a tiny baby to learn to roll over or to pull himself up or to get the oatmeal into his mouth with the spoon.

"You make me so proud of you" should be applied privately, as quickly as possible after your offspring has done something of which you approve. By reinforcing his good behavior, you make him more likely to repeat it. This is a more effective and happier way to teach children how you want them to act than by spanking, scolding or concentrating on negative activity. If started early in life, you'll usually find you almost never have to punish your child.

"I love you" is the single best, most effective phrase you can ever say to any child of any age, and the words should be spoken, with meaning, at least once or twice every day. When added to any of the phrases above, it immediately increases their effectiveness. These three words can accomplish more with children than anything else—and it should never be taken for granted that your children know you love them without your saying so.

17. Toilet Training Without Fuss

More mothers worry longer and harder about toilet training than anything that happens to a child between colic and college. The worry stems from Freudian-based theories linking a wide variety of emotional problems in older children and adults—everything from lawbreaking to littering—with toilet training.

Yet careful new studies by child psychiatrists and pediatricians show no reason at all for assuming any such links. One long-term study conducted by psychiatrists Dr. Stella Chess and Dr. Alexander Thomas and pediatrician Dr. Herbert Birch indicates that fewer than 5 percent of children have emotional difficulties centering around toilet training. And these youngsters have difficulties in many other areas, too.

Quite the contrary, this study reveals that many youngsters seem to welcome toilet training and enjoy succeeding at this impressive step toward becoming grown up.

Actually, helping a child outgrow his need for diapers isn't much different from helping him learn about other toddler-age skills. The formula is about the same.

You wait until the child shows signs that his body is mature enough to succeed. You provide time and opportunity. You

130

are full of praise and enthusiasm for his achievements. You are matter-of-fact, uncritical and unshaming when he slips. You don't expect too much too soon. And even after he has been quite successful, you expect and tolerate occasional lapses.

You remember that the age at which your child acquires a skill that depends to a considerable extent on physical maturation reflects his own inner growth pattern, just like walking or talking—not your talent as a parent or his "goodness" or "badness" as a child.

Clues that your child is ready to outgrow diapers usually show up when he's between eighteen and twenty-four months old. But ages vary, and girls usually outpace boys. Good indications: Is he dry when he first wakes up from his nap? Can he stay dry an hour or two during the day? Does he tell you by any kind of baby word when he is about to wet or soil? Is he aware of, or uncomfortable about, wet diapers?

It does help, long before your toddler is old enough to control this function himself, to change his diapers whenever he wets and keep him dry as much as possible. This takes extra time and makes extra laundry. But your child will be used to being dry, will be uncomfortable when he is wet, and will be more eager to keep himself dry when he's old enough.

The easiest kind of youngster to toilet-train is the easygoing, placid child who doesn't mind sitting still and whose bowel habits are regular and predictable. This type of baby can often be bowel-trained at the age of about one year, if a mother wants to get herself into the habit of putting him on the toilet regularly, without fail, at the time he usually has a bowel movement.

Bladder training usually follows bowel training for this kind of child at about eighteen months or a little later, without much fuss or trouble.

The hardest type of youngster to train is the active, restless runabout with irregular bowel habits. Any kind of sitting still seems like punishment to him, and when he's put on a toilet seat, he's apt to rebel more about the sitting still than the idea of toilet training itself.

Another difficult type of child to train is the kind who resents and fights against changes in routine. The youngster who fought giving up a bottle or staying with a sitter or switching to junior or solid foods or using a spoon will probably resist toilet training more than an easygoing type.

When you decide your child may be physiologically ready to learn to use the toilet—when he shows some awareness that he has soiled his diaper or when he tells you by facial expression or sounds or a word that he knows when he is about to have a bowel movement or has just had one—get a potty chair or a toddler's toilet seat that fits on a regular toilet. Explain to him that you are going to help him learn to use it, like older children and grownups do. Let him play with it if he wants to. And if possible, give him an opportunity to see an older child using the toilet, so he'll have a good idea what the process is all about.

Then, when you think your toddler is about ready to have a bowel movement, or if he wakes up dry from a nap, put him on the toilet seat for a few minutes and see what happens. If he succeeds, praise him enthusiastically. If he begins to get restless, or resists, let him go off to play with an encouraging comment about trying again later. Then give him another chance in two or three hours, or at a time when success seems likely. If you don't have any results within a week or so, or if you meet with great resistance or feel yourself getting impatient, drop the whole project for several weeks without comment. If you get into a battle with your child over toilet training, you'll just retard his progress and accomplish nothing.

When your child does begin to have some success, you should promote him to training pants and point out how much more comfortable they are and how much easier to manage than diapers and waterproof coverings. Little girls enjoy having frilly panties to wear, and these can often be a happy incentive to outgrow diapers.

As your youngster becomes more independent during the third year of life, he'll begin to rely less on you to get him to the toilet in time and more on himself. When he begins to tell you ahead of time he needs to go to the bathroom, when he starts to manage his underwear himself, whenever he's stayed accident-free for a longer period than usual, you should praise him happily for his progress. He will have some slipups during this learning process, but he will learn much faster and your relationship will be happier if you are casual and accepting about them.

Two psychologists, Nathan H. Azrin and Richard M. Foxx, have demonstrated that it is possible to speed up the toilet-training process and accomplish most of it in a single day, or even a few hours. Their method calls for waiting until a toddler is clearly ready to be toilet-trained—until he is about twenty-four months old, can understand simple directions and seems ready to get along without diapers. Then the mother simply applies behavior-modification strategies in a day of concentrated attention to toilet training. First, the toddler is given training pants and shown how to put them on and lower them. A potty chair—an on-the-floor model with a pot which can be removed from the top—is placed on the kitchen floor, or in whatever area of the house the mother plans to spend most of the day. She also arranges to have supplies of the youngster's favorite treats, salty snacks like pretzels and potato chips to encourage drinking lots of liquids, and his favorite drinks such as fruit juices, colas or milk.

Now, the mother uses a doll that wets its pants to show the child what he is expected to do. The doll is given water to drink. The child takes the doll to the potty, lowers its pants, sees that the doll uses the potty, pretends to give the doll candy or a potato chip as a reward, takes the pot from the potty seat and empties it into the toilet and shows his approval of the doll's behavior with praise and hugging.

Then the youngster acts out the same procedure himself. He is given something to drink. Then he lowers his own training pants, uses the potty, pulls up his own pants, empties the pot into the toilet, flushes it and is rewarded with a treat, a happy hug and lots of praise. His mother talks delightedly about how proud his father, his grandmothers, his friends, the neighbors will be of his great achievement and how happy he is making her. The child reacts with feelings that he is no longer a baby, but a person of accomplishment, and is motivated to keep on trying to repeat his proud achievement.

To accomplish toilet training in a single day, a mother needs to be at home alone with her toddler, according to Azrin and Foxx. There should be no interrupting phone calls, callers, television programs or other distractions. And the prevailing mood should be one of friendliness, happiness and pride. There should be no criticism or scolding about accidents or failures.

All-night control is the last stage of toilet training to be mastered. Azrin and Foxx report that about one third of the children trained by their method also became dry at night at about the same time they achieved day-time control. But many normal youngsters trained in traditional ways do not succeed until they are four or even five years old. A long-term study reported in *Pediatrics* magazine shows that by the age of four, only 56 percent of children stay dry at night without relapsing; 85 percent are dry during the day without further slip-backs. Ten percent of all children relapse on daytime toilet training for a median period of 1.2 years, according to the study. One fourth of all youngsters have relapses on nighttime training, lasting a median duration of 2.5 years.

During this last stage of toilet training, many parents have found it convenient and helpful to wake a child up just before their own bedtime and take him to the bathroom. If he is still dry at 11 or 11:30 P.M., the youngster can then usually stay dry until morning. Some pediatricians advise against this procedure on the grounds that the child should learn to take the responsibility for getting himself to the bathroom. But most parents feel this bit of tactful help just makes the process easier for their children, who seldom need it after about age six.

Children who have the most difficulty with nighttime toilet training are usually those with an especially small bladder and the habit of sleeping particularly soundly. Such youngsters just don't wake up in response to the feelings that send other boys and girls to the bathroom. Children usually produce from five to twelve ounces of urine at night; a bed wetter may have a bladder capacity as small as four ounces.

A bed wetter may also be the kind of child who needs to go to the toilet more often than usual during the day because he can't wait as long as other youngsters. An increasing number of researchers now consider this problem to be genetic—a difficulty inherited from one parent or the other in many cases. Family studies cited by Dr. Harry Bakwin of New York University School of Medicine in the *American Journal of Diseases of Children* show that when one parent recalls (or admits) bed wetting as a child, more than 40 percent of the children also have enuresis (bed wetting) in comparison to 15 percent without a parental history.

Even if bed wetting has a biological basis, it is subject to training and sometimes to emotional factors, according to Dr. Bakwin. Nervous tension may make a predisposed child need to urinate more urgently—just as it sometimes does a non-enuretic individual.

A child genetically predisposed to enuresis is less likely to keep on bed wetting, says Dr. Bakwin, in homes where (1) the parents prize cleanliness; (2) the toilet is convenient; (3) the mother does a helpful, thoughtful job of toilet training; (4) the youngster's intake of liquids is limited before bedtime; and (5) parents take him to the toilet during the night.

A youngster is more likely to be a bed wetter, according to Dr. Bakwin, in a home where (1) cleanliness is not a habit; (2) the toilet is not easily accessible; (3) the child sleeps with another bed wetter; (4) the house is cold at night; or (5) he is afraid of the dark.

If your child is still wetting the bed after age five, you should check out the problem with your doctor. He can rule out such unusual possibilities as urinary tract abnormalities, diabetes and infections. Then the child should be told that he is wetting the bed simply because his bladder hasn't grown big enough to hold all the urine his body makes during the night. He can hurry the growing process along and stretch his bladder by waiting just as long as he can to use the toilet during the day.

Most children accept the challenge to "wait just a little longer if you can" before using the toilet during the day and are delighted to have a positive step they can take in solving an upsetting problem. Some doctors even suggest that a child urinate into a measuring jar and try to beat his own volume record. A youngster can also be urged to practice starting and stopping the urinary stream, to help him feel that he has more conscious control over the process of elimination.

Drugs can also help a majority of bed wetters. These medications aim either to tighten the sphincter muscle so it won't let go so easily in sleep or to prevent the youngster from sleeping too soundly to recognize the need to use the bathroom. The medications must be prescribed by a physician.

18. The Most Difficult Six Months in Your Child's Childhood

If you're staggering with fatigue, lurching from one minor crisis to another, hoarse and hating yourself for constant no-ing and thwarted 99 times a day by an individual one fourth your size and less than one tenth your age, you're a typical parent of a typical two-and-a-half-year-old. You can expect to find yourself out of breath, out of patience, out of sorts and almost out of your mind much of the time.

What helps a parent survive the most difficult six months of his child's childhood—the stage that comes sometime between a youngster's second and third birthday, when he's stubborn, energetic, intransigent, negative and often unhappy even with himself? Here are some tips culled from mothers of ex-two-and-a-half-year-olds:

· It helps to make sure your toddler has a wide variety of things to play with, to handle, look at and listen to. Much of the rebellious misbehavior during the two-and-a-half-year-old stage is due to boredom and can be prevented or diluted by providing your youngster with socially acceptable things that help to satisfy his restless curiosity and drive to learn.

· You can help your child find words to express his feelings. Often the immediate cause of a tantrum or outright rebellion is the frustration a toddler feels because he can't make you understand his problem or his feelings or his needs. By helping him learn to talk and by trying to understand his attempts at language, you're showing him a better grievance procedure than just crying or screaming.

· You can help your youngster learn to work off his tremendous energy and drive in ways you can live with. He has real need to run, jump, throw, hit, bang, yell, pound, push, pull, poke, wrestle, gallop and make messes. There will be far fewer abrasions on your furniture and your temper if you can show him acceptable times and places to do all of these things. Some parents find punching toys, punching bags, cushion-type trampolines and pounding toys useful here.

· During the second and third year of his life, your offspring needs much less sleep and much less food than he did earlier. Many of the frustrations of being a toddler's parent stem from endless battles trying to get a child to sleep when he isn't sleepy and to eat when he isn't hungry. If your child is rebelling constantly against naptime or bedtime, you should reevaluate his need for sleep. He may now require only one nap (some youngsters take none after their third birthday) or a later bedtime. The transition period is fraught with fussiness and there'll be days when your youngster skips a nap only to collapse in sleep while you're mashing the dinner potatoes and then is bright-eyed through the late, late show.

Some days when your child is taut and overtired, you can avoid the gathering storm by rocking him and reading to him.

During the third year of his life, a youngster gains only about four pounds. His appetite is normally small. If your child refuses to eat, you should casually excuse him from the table and not let him eat between meals except for a small, nutritious snack at midmorning and afternoon. Mealtime battles too easily turn into years-long war.

· It helps to remember that your youngster isn't any happier about the way he feels than you are. If you can understand why he's turned into a one-toddler revolution you can usually redirect most of his rebellious energy and maneuver to avoid most of the conflicts. But you can't—and shouldn't—quench his spirit of independence.

Your child says "No" because it makes him feel like a person in his own right—and probably because he's heard it so much from his parents. It helps to give him as few orders as possible and to cut down the opportunities he has to refuse. If you can help him see you as a friendly teacher who aids him in learning what he wants so badly to do, rather than as a master trying to obedience-train a puppy, he'll be much less apt to fight you.

· Often you can find loving ways to lure your child into wanting to behave as you wish, rather than making it a contest of wills. For example, if he balks at bath time, you can try making the tub enticing by adding bubble bath, plastic-sponge cutouts, soap in a different shape or strung on a cord like a necklace, boats, watering can, spray hose, water pistol (with rules on the firing range), washable doll, doll clothes to launder, bubble pipe. If he won't get out of the water once he's in, you can use the lure of a powder mitt, a bedtime story or milk and cookie. (And you can try to increase your own time-tolerance by using his soaking span for a tubside job such as folding laundry or quickie mending, or for a bathroom cleanup.)

· Sometimes orders are easier for a young rebel to take if they don't come directly from a parent. For example, you can set an alarm clock to signal bedtime, or a kitchen timer to announce it's time to leave the bathtub.

· It helps, too, if you show your child you understand his need to be his own person and give him as many choices as possible in running his own life. If you let him decide whether to wear the red shirt or the yellow, he may forget to say "No" to putting on a shirt at all.

· When you can't give your moppet a choice, you should try to set up the situation so you don't give him a chance to refuse or suggest by your attitude or tone of voice that there are any options. You'll get better results if you just take him by the hand, lovingly but firmly, and get on with what needs to be done.

· If your child insists on trying to dress or undress himself, you should try to allow plenty of time for it and cheer him on. But you should be ready with unobtrusive help and a quick suggestion for a change of activity if he's ready to weep with frustration. If he's determined to learn to button and zip and buckle all by himself, you can help him learn by getting him the Montessori-designed learning frames and showing him the step-by-step procedures taught in Montessori schools.

· When your toddler is constantly demanding your attention, you should see that you give him extra loving. His need for your love, shown obviously and lavishly, is as actual as his need for food—especially if you have a younger baby. At two and a half, your youngster has not outgrown cuddling, hugging, kissing, rocking and loving listening, and if you give these freely, he won't try demanding your attention so often with temper tantrums, excessive crying, misbehaving, whining and other unhappy ways.

· All of these suggestions won't work all of the time. There will be days when the kindest thing you can do for both yourself and your offspring is to SOS for a grandmother or a baby sitter and take an afternoon or evening off. And repeat to yourself twenty times, "It will be better when he's three."

19. How to Prevent Sib-al War

Is sib-al war inevitable? Do brothers and sisters always fight? What can parents do to help prevent a child from resenting a new baby?

New, long-term research by psychiatrists and pediatricians now suggests that the Freudian fears about "sibling rivalry" have been exaggerated. It is true that some children do feel neglected and left out when a new baby is born and that brothers and sisters are often competitive and jealous. But if parents use tact and wisdom, the birth of a new baby can be a positive, happy experience for an older child, new research shows. (Upsets and strong negative reactions occurred in fewer than one fifth of the youngsters in one major study.) If they are brought up with understanding of their individual needs, brothers and sisters can live together with no more squabbling and jealousy than takes place in a good marriage.

What can parents do to help?

Your strategy should begin well before your second baby is born. (If your firstborn is younger than eighteen months, this part of your job will be easier, even if the physical work is harder. Research shows toddlers are affected much less, for better or worse, by a new baby than are preschoolers.) Your aim is to make the new baby's birth seem like a natural part of family development and a promotion, not a "dethroning," for your first born.

You needn't worry about that old How-would-you-like-it-if-your-husband-brought-home-another-wife cliché. It is not a valid comparison. You can simply point out to your firstborn that many of his friends have at least one brother or sister and it's time your family grew, too.

You can stress that having a new baby will make him a Big Brother (or her a Big Sister). This is a mighty special kind of status, you can help him understand. It carries several appropriate and cherished privileges—like being permitted to stay up half an hour later, or owning a tricycle or having an extra cookie with his juice. Perhaps it also means passing out lollipops to his friends when your husband hands out cigars.

If you plan to make any changes in your firstborn's life, you should do it well before the new baby's birth, or delay it for a few months afterward. You must make sure he understands he is giving up his crib because *he* will enjoy having a big bed now, not because the baby needs it; that he is going to nursery school because *he* will have so much fun there, not because his mother wants more time with the baby.

Before and after the new baby's birth, you can comment on the contrast between the infant's abilities and those of your firstborn. How lucky your big boy is to be able to use the toilet instead of having to wear uncomfortable diapers. How much more fun it is to walk where he wants to go himself than to cry for someone to carry him. How much more successful it is to be able to tell your parents in words what you want than only to fuss and hope someone will understand.

According to the usual child-care theory, a firstborn may react to these contrasts by becoming more babyish, by fussing for a bottle, or by wetting his training pants. This may indeed happen a few times. But it's more likely that, with encouragement, your firstborn will enjoy noting his superiority and try to act even more grown up, new studies show.

Your firstborn will probably pick up the attitude toward the new baby that you suggest to him, no matter how subtly. If you, or his grandparents, expect him to act displaced or jealous or angry, chances are he'll subconsciously decide this is what he is supposed to do and act accordingly.

Number One child will still need plenty of time with you alone, especially at first (when you're tiredest and your baby most demanding). You will have to let the housework go, rely on your husband as much as possible and try to give your firstborn this attention. If you do, his demands will slack off rather quickly.

One mother made it a practice to find times when the baby did not need her and then say firmly in her firstborn's hearing, "Baby, you'll just have to wait. Billy needs me now." This made it easier for Billy to be patient when the infant's demands couldn't be postponed.

The best way to prevent jealousy is to convince your firstborn that the baby loves and admires him enormously and is trying to grow up to be like him. It's difficult to be jealous and mean to someone who openly admires and imitates you.

You can explain to the older child that babies can't talk, but that they show their love by curling a tiny fist around your finger and holding on tightly. Show him how to slip a forefinger gently into your baby's hand when you bring her home from the hospital. (This is a reflex action that also works with a pencil, but nevertheless, it can be an impressive lesson in love for a preschooler.)

In a few weeks, you can point out how the baby always smiles when Billy comes near. Later on, when your baby starts babbling syllables, perhaps you can make the first sound she says consistently—no matter what it is—sound like your older child's name, or like a special nickname the baby has invented for him. When one baby began murmuring "Ba-ba" frequently, her mother told the three-year-old that the infant was trying to say "Brother." Her firstborn puffed with pride and love at the honor and asked his parents to call him "Ba-ba" too, until the baby learned to say "Chris."

Perhaps you can arrange it so your baby takes her first steps toward her older brother. Perhaps you can help her be the one to find his lost toy. Perhaps he can overhear you telling your friends how he can make her laugh best or stop crying quickest.

You do need to show your firstborn how to pat the baby gently, pointing out that because he is so strong, he can't use all of his strength with her, just as his father can't use all of his might, either. This open acknowledgment that your firstborn is big, strong and capable of self-control makes it easier for him to act just that way.

If you teach your firstborn—chiefly by praise, encouragement and example—to be kind, gentle and loving toward your baby, he and any other children you have will accept this attitude as standard behavior. They will fight and argue sometimes. But the squabbles will be superficial and fleeting.

There are several other good stratagems that parents can use to help their children grow up together in peace, love and mutual respect, without corroding jealousies and wounding competitiveness. Among them:

The don't-try-to-treat-children-equally expedient. Trying to provide equal everything to two or more children is a common booby-trap for parents, because it's impossible, even if you have identical twins. Youngsters don't want to be equal, anyway; each one wants to be unique and special.

What you can do is tell your offspring that you love each one with all your heart, but you show your love for them in different ways, because each one has different needs and wants. You can't assume that because you love both your children equally, they understand that you do.

You can point out that you show your love for your small, cuddly baby by lots of hugging and rocking. You love your older child just as much, you can explain, but because he's outgrown rocking, you show your love in ways he appreciates more, such as inviting his friends to lunch or helping him paint a baseball diamond in the grass in the back yard. This is obvious to you—but not necessarily to him.

The private-property ploy. Learning to share comes easier to a child who has some private possessions that are his alone. You can help each of your youngsters select and identify these favorite belongings, find him an inviolate place to keep them and see that his ownership is respected. Then label other playthings, like blocks and art materials, as jointly owned and to be shared or used on a first-come basis.

The freedom-of-association finesse. It helps if you don't try to turn your older child into a substitute parent, no matter how convenient this may be at times. Nothing breeds resentment between children so much as making a younger child take orders from the older, or forcing the older to let the younger tag along. If your Number Two offspring shows some tag-along tendencies, you can teach your Number One child not to scream, "Get lost, baby," but to come to you privately and explain the difficulty. Then you can tactfully find a same-age friend for Number Two, or an alternative occupation. It takes your time, of course, but less than refereeing constant bickering.

When you can, give a child a choice about helping the other, so he experiences the good feeling of giving, rather than just taking orders.

"Would you like to stay and help make Nancy's birthday party a happy one, or would you rather play at Dickie's house this afternoon?" you might ask him. If he helps by choice, not by order, he'll do it with love, not resentment, in his heart. Afterward you can reinforce the happy, giving, inter-child relationship by pointing out his contributions to the party in Nancy's presence.

The Happy Un-birthday gambit. Someone else's good fortune can be hard to take, even for an adult. If one of your children is receiving a deluge of birthday presents, or a spate of honors, try to find some compensations for your other offspring. Birthdays usually go more smoothly in families with young children if each one gets a small gift. A coveted invitation for one youngster might be countered with a special mother-child outing for the left-out moppet. The need for extra gifts and special plans usually tapers off at about age ten.

The underdog precaution. A parent's first inclination is to jump into a sib-al dispute on the side of the younger child. But often he is not the real underdog. Instead, an older child may be victimized by a teasing smaller sister or brother who knows Number One child won't stand up for his rights. You'll need to observe carefully to determine what usually sets off the squabbles at your house before you begin assessing blame. If possible, it's good strategy to show children how to settle their own disputes. Then you can usually function as a court of appeals, rather than as the cop on the beat.

The walk-in-his-moccasins maneuver. You can often deliberately teach each of your children to understand and deal sympathetically with the other. For example, you can tell your five-year-old, "Bobby's had a hard day at school today. The teacher scolded him. And he struck out three times playing baseball. He feels sad. Can you think of a way to cheer him up?"

Or, you can say to your older son, "Jenny is trying so hard to learn how you put those blocks together. If you move your hands slowly, she will see how you do it. She wishes she could be as capable as you are and she gets cross and upset when she can't do the difficult things you can do."

Stratagems like these won't always work. But they will build a reservoir of understanding and love that will cut down on the length and severity of the disputes that do occur. And they will help your youngsters grow into the habit of loving each other and treating each other considerately.

20. Is Your Child Spoiled?

The question of spoiling a child worries most parents—from a new mother who can't decide whether to pick up her baby every time he cries to an exasperated father who doesn't know what to do about a seventeen-year-old who's goofing off in high school. These guidelines may help:

1. It's spoiling a child to try to buy his love and immediate approval with material things or extra privileges, or to substitute toys for your time and care because it's quicker and easier. Once you start doing so, your child becomes more demanding because his real needs aren't being met, and the relationship can slip into an unhappy battle.

But you don't spoil a youngster by giving him a variety of playthings and seeing that he has all the sensory stimulation he needs for physical and mental growth. And you don't spoil him by bringing him an occasional surprise or gift just for the joy of it.

2. It's spoiling a youngster to let him change your mind by sulking, having a temper tantrum, threatening to run away, whining, crying or demanding. But you don't spoil him by listening to his opinions, considering his preferences and letting him make choices that affect him whenever it's possible.

147

3. It's spoiling a child to let him do whatever he wants for fear you will lose his love, even temporarily, or that he'll be angry with you. You don't spoil him by encouraging him to be self-reliant and by trying to limit your "no's" as much as possible.

4. It's spoiling a child to encourage him to use minor injuries or illnesses to win concessions from you that you wouldn't otherwise grant. You don't spoil him by giving him comfort and extra attention when he really needs it because he is hurt, sick, tired, discouraged or trying something too difficult.

5. It's spoiling a child to let him interfere unnecessarily with your privacy, rest, meals and the entertainment of your friends. You don't spoil him by recognizing that sometimes his needs must take priority over your plans or giving him similar rights of privacy, freedom from unnecessary interruption and hospitality for his friends.

6. It's spoiling a child to give him your time and attention only when he misbehaves, whines, cries, fusses, sulks or acts inappropriately babyish. You don't spoil him by understanding that he does have great need for loving attention and for your interested sharing of your time with him.

7. It's spoiling a child to hand him increasing privileges without increasing responsibilities. But you don't spoil him by recognizing his growing abilities and granting him new privileges without forcing him to whine or fight for them.

8. It's spoiling a child to wait on him constantly and do things for him he can do for himself, on the grounds you can do them faster or better. You don't spoil him by taking the time to teach him, step by small step, the skills he wants to learn because they will make him more independent of you.

9. It's spoiling a child to let him wheedle or dawdle or complain his way out of jobs that are his responsibility. You don't spoil him by helping him out occasionally when he's overloaded with homework or isn't feeling well or is involved in a special activity at school.

10. It's spoiling a child to do his homework for him and to assume the responsibility of seeing that it's done. You don't spoil him by helping him learn points that he's confused about in school, suggesting sources for class projects or showing an interest in what he's learning.

If your child is usually happy, undemanding, relatively independent and self-regulating in reasonable relation to his age, you can feel quite sure you're not spoiling him. But if he's usually whining, demanding, unhappy and behaving in undesirable ways, it might help to take another look at his real needs and your ways of responding to them.

21. Alternatives to Nagging and Spanking

He is six years old, and he was just severely spanked for fighting with his five-year-old brother.

Tearfully, defiantly, he turned to his father and shouted, "You tell me not to hit David. How come you hit me so much?"

Striving for patience, his father replied, "But I'm trying to teach you something."

"I was trying to teach David not to mess up my stuff," sobbed the boy. "So what was wrong with hitting him?"

Deciding when and how to punish a child is one of parenthood's most difficult problems. Some parents are still so influenced by overly liberal interpretations of permissive philosophies that they let their youngsters run wild and become pests to everyone. A few parents punish so brutally that medical associations and government agencies alike are concerned with the serious physical injuries they inflict on their offspring.

But other parents manage to maintain a friendly type of discipline over their children and can't honestly remember when they last punished a youngster.

In deciding how you will handle the situation in your family, it helps to think out your long-range goals. Often you'll discover you can eliminate almost all need to punish your children while still giving them necessary guidance and teaching.

Before you punish a youngster, you should be quite clear in your own mind what constitutes a punishable offense and why. Some parents interpret as punishable misbehavior actions such as interrupting a conversation, spilling milk, messing up the house or losing a possession. Other families consider these to be normal. They would help a child try to overcome such undesirable behavior and to improve. But they would not punish him in these situations any more than they would spank a five-year-old for not being able to do long division.

You should also consider whether any punishments you are using help your child in learning the lessons you intend. Or does spanking, for example, merely teach him that his parents are mean or to stay away from Daddy when he's tired, or that big people can hit little people and get away with it, or simply not to get caught?

It's important, of course, that a child not gain from his misbehavior. But his apparent misdeeds may actually be a symptom of a situation that needs your correcting. David, for example, may be deliberately provoking his older brother's anger and what the six-year-old needs may well not be punishment but some protected privacy for his belongings.

It's also necessary to recognize your own limits of tolerance and to try to keep your children from exceeding them.

Nagging is related to spanking in that it is an unpleasant way of interacting with children—and generally ineffective, especially with continual use. There are other strategies which usually get better results than both spanking and nagging with much less grating, intrafamily friction. (Like everything else involving children, however, all of these techniques need to be adapted to the age level and learning style of each individual boy or girl and none of the methods works with all small fry all of the time.)

The Natural Consequence: The bumps and tumbles that

penalize a toddler until he learns to walk skillfully illustrate the Natural Consequence in one of its purest forms, and no amount of parental nagging or punishment can equal its effectiveness as a teaching technique. It's not always possible for a parent to set up situations in which a harmless natural consequence inevitably reinforces desirable behavior. (A mother can't let a child get hit by a truck to remind him not to run into the street.)

But often a parent can provide, as unemotionally as the floor beneath a toddler, consequences which are so logical and so consistent that they seem natural to the youngster. An eight-year-old who doesn't come to dinner when he's called simply misses the meal (and isn't provided with a snack later on). A seven-year-old who spills milk must wipe it up. A thirteen-year-old who hasn't cleaned her room by Friday can't have an overnight guest.

The Behavior Modifier: This is the deliberate and immediate use of a response from a parent or other individual to reinforce desirable behavior. Usually, this reinforcement is positive—praise or a small reward. To be effective, the reinforcement must come as quickly as possible after the behavior which the parent wants to make a habit.

The key to behavior modification is to catch a child when he's being good—and praise him or otherwise reward him for it. This strategy encourages a parent to pay attention to his child when he is behaving in a desirable way and not just when he's misbehaving or trying to get attention by being disruptive or whining. It's much more effective for an adult to pay attention by means of praise to the good behavior he wants his youngsters to continue than to punish the misbehavior he wants to eliminate.

The use of praise immediately to reinforce desirable behavior should be an everyday part of parenting. Used consistently and happily, it is an extremely powerful influence on behavior and should eliminate the need for punishments and for much nagging. But in some cases, according to psychologists, the praise needs to be backed up with more concrete reinforcements, such as gold stars, bits of candy, cookies, small amounts of money or tokens that can be exchanged for little prizes or valued activities. (This comes close to what many parents consider outright bribery, although the psychologists who use this technique claim it isn't.) But these tangible reward systems must be planned carefully and are usually employed when there is an urgent need to change a youngster's behavior and when less artificial techniques have failed.

The Image Maker: More powerfully than any press agent, a parent can do much to shape a youngster's behavior by the image he creates for him: "You're the kind of boy I can trust with this job." "You behave so well when we go to a restaurant you make the whole family proud."

But the approach must be honest, not exaggerated, and the role must be positive. Negative images such as "You're a bad boy," and "You're just no good" are at least equally powerful in shaping behavior.

The Stage Setter: Often it's better to remove the possibilities for trouble than to nag a child about preventing it, or punish him after it's happened. For example, rather than a constant barrage of "No, don't touch," or "Watch out, be careful," it's easier to put away breakables until a youngster is capable of learning how to handle them carefully.

Sometimes good behavior can be taught, to the delight of a child, by playacting out a situation which is new to him, such as taking a plane trip, going to the hospital or starting nursery school. This strategy gives the youngster helpful information about how he is expected to act, so he doesn't misbehave through sheer ignorance.

The Interesting Challenge: Instead of nagging a child to finish dressing, to put his toys away or to be less messy—or punishing him when he dawdles or clutters—you can turn the matter into a contest. For example, you might challenge him with "Can you get dressed before the sand in the egg timer runs out?" "Can you push the peanut butter all the way into the corners of the bread without getting any on the table?" "Let's have a race to see whether you can put away your toys before I can fold all the laundry."

Strategies like these avoid the resentments and guilts associated with punishments and nagging and they help both parent and child feel happy and loving about their relationships.

22. THE MOTHER BEAR SYNDROME

One hazard parents seldom are cautioned about sufficiently is the Mother Bear Syndrome—the fierce, instinctive drive to come out fighting to protect the cubs against anything or anyone that seems to pose a danger.

Of course, the Mother Bear Syndrome mechanism is an essential part of maternal makeup, revving up the muscles and disconnecting the thought processes in case you have to rescue an offspring from a burning building or snatch him from the jaws of a man-eating tiger.

But few dangers to children these days are in the tiger and burning-building category. And the tendency to come on growling and clawing like a mother bear can have unhappy consequences when threats to your progeny are chiefly mental or emotional rather than physical. It sometimes takes a long time to learn that you can protect your children against contemporary threats far better with a light hand in a velvet glove than by showing your claws.

First symptoms of the Mother Bear Syndrome sometimes develop even before you've left the hospital with your firstborn. You may be quite surprised to hear your usual sweet, shy voice chewing out the nursery nurse for letting your three-day-old cry unsoothed. Or asking her sternly if she washed her hands before picking up *your* baby.

Symptoms increase once you're home. You may have waited until your own appendix almost burst before calling the doctor after office hours. But you're on the phone at 3 A.M., demanding that your pediatrician make a house call when your two-week-old infant sneezes three times—and you turn snarly when he refuses.

You rear up and roar at your mother-in-law when she comes to call with a cold. You question the milkman sharply about the sanitation procedures at his dairy.

But it isn't until you start trying to defend your cub on the playground from the rough-and-tumble fun of his friends that the Mother Bear Syndrome begins to be a problem to your child. After you've come charging out into the back yard a few times to give the neighbor's children a verbal cuffing, your youngster learns not to tell you that Teddy won't play fair or that Nick punched him, and decides to fight his own battles whether he's equipped to do so or not.

You do even more damage if you roar into the phone at Teddy's or Nick's parents. For they usually won't recognize that you are suffering from Mother Bear Syndrome and will write you and yours off as unneighborly or old-witchy. Their offspring usually find dastardly ways to retaliate against yours, too ("I'm not going to invite you to my birthday party next July!").

The worst place of all to mother-bear is at school. All of your maternal protective instincts urge you to go charging over and shake some sense into the teacher who gave Patty a D-minus or the coach who made Scotty a substitute instead of first string. But chances are, you'll discover Patty hasn't handed in her homework for six weeks or that there really are 29 players better than Scotty.

There are times, of course, when children need their parents' help in enforcing fair play on the playground, or coping with a big bully, or straightening out school problems. But you can't do any of these things when your claws are showing.

23. SUCCESSFUL BIRTHDAY PARTIES FOR CHILDREN

Of all the pleasures you plan for your child, none has as many boobytraps as a birthday party. What do you do when three of the guests refuse to play even one of the party games because it's "dumb stuff"? Or when two eight-year olds begin squirting each other with catsup while you are frying the hamburgers? Or when the birthday girl has a temper tantrum when you insist she let her guests play with her toys?

Giving a successful birthday party is an acquired skill, based on fast footwork, the ability to improvise without panicking, superhuman stamina, infinite patience and a tested plan of action. Here are some birthday-party stratagems other parents have found useful—first, general tips and then, suggestions for specific age groups.

· Schedule the party when the guests—and especially the birthday child—are least likely to be tired. When a preschooler's feverish pitch of excitement is combined with the need for a nap, you have an explosive mix that can be ignited by even a small incident or disappointment.

· Do manage some preliminary rest yourself. The guests

157

won't notice if your kitchen floor needs buffing. They will be well aware of any fatigue-triggered irritability.

· Keep the guest list as short as possible, especially if your youngster is younger than age seven. Some child-care books blithely rule: "One guest for each year of the birthday child's age." But practicing mothers know how difficult it is to avoid inviting your child's best friends, same-age offspring of your own friends, school friends, youngsters whose parties your moppet has attended and the small fry next door who aren't close chums but whose disappointed faces will inevitably be seen through the bushes if they are not included.

Remind yourself that some of the most disastrous parties have been those at which a well-meaning mother has tried to include everyone, with guests totaling an unmanageable twenty or more. It's easiest to eliminate the opposite sex completely, especially when the youngsters are between six and thirteen, and those not the same age as your child (which simplifies the games). Hopefully your friends will understand. And you can invite the others for a special treat later on.

· Don't let your child deliver the invitations at school. This hurts feelings. And you can't be sure all the invitations will make it home to every guest's mother.

· Involve your child as much as possible in the party's planning. At least half of the fun is anticipation. Even three- or four-year-olds can decorate invitations and place cards, set the party table, choose the favors and decide on the games and refreshments.

· Let your youngster decide whether his party is to be a dress-up or a play-clothes affair. For some five-year-old girls, a party dress may be the best part of the party. But anything other than blue jeans can spoil everything for most seven-year-old males.

· Run through the party schedule with your child before B-day. For a preschooler, actually acting out events helps enormously in showing him how to greet his guests, what to do with gifts, how to say Thank you.

· Remember that your birthday child is the guest of honor as well as the host. He'll probably be too excited to remember all of his host's obligations until he's at least seven or eight. And the party itself is no time to make an issue of manners.

· Keep the party food simple and familiar. The formula of peanut-butter sandwich, cake, ice cream and milk is still the most foolproof, although you can safely substitute hot dogs or hamburgers. (Add carrot sticks if you worry about nutrition; no one will eat them, but your conscience will be clear.) You can serve familiar food in party form, however. Sandwiches can go into a box lunch or individual picnic basket, for example. Hamburgers can be cocktail size for small girls or the hot dogs "foot-longs" for bigger boys.

· Don't ever turn your back on eating children. This provides an almost irresistible temptation to play catch or darts or dodge ball with the food. The hazards persist, at least for boys, until age twelve.

· Unlike adult parties, you can expect at least some of the children to arrive before party time. You'll have to have a few toys available to keep them occupied until festivities begin.

· Don't try to manage a birthday party by yourself if you have more than four guests. A father with steady nerves is a blessing at a party, especially if he can referee a seven-year-olds' baseball game or grill the hamburgers or read a story to restless four-year-olds. Some mothers have success hiring a teen-ager to help; occasionally a high-school student earns spending money supervising children's parties with happy flair.

· Plan at least two or three more games and activities than you estimate you'll need. It's par for a party to find some small guests refusing to participate in a game or for their interest to lag sooner than you'd expect.

· Every child younger than age ten should have one or more party favors to take home. Preschoolers, especially, are apt to measure the success of a party in terms of take-home loot, and the prospect of a favor sometimes makes it easier for a small child to give up his gift to the birthday youngster.

· Competitive games with prizes usually cause more unhappiness than joy for moppets younger than age eight, unless you can tactfully arrange for everyone to win legitimately at something without much delay. It's better strategy at younger ages to confine the competition to treasure hunts.

· Near the beginning of the party, give each small child a paper bag marked with his name in which he can stow his take-home loot. Otherwise you'll be spending an hour after party's end trying to locate Jimmy's plastic car or the candle Debbie salvaged from her piece of birthday cake. Having duplicates for such emergencies helps prevent these minor tragedies.

· Set a firm end to the party and include the time on your invitations. For preschoolers, a "going home present" of crayons, small truck or doll or magic slate, ball, magnet, magnifying glass, paddle ball, ring or marbles makes the parting pleasanter.

PARTIES FOR PRESCHOOLERS

For a preschooler, a birthday party is Christmas, Fourth of July, Halloween and Valentine's Day all wrapped up together, tied with a red ribbon and tagged "All mine."

By the age of four, most preschoolers are using birthday parties as social currency. ("If you don't let me play with your doll, I won't invite you to my birthday party.") And such an impact does a party have on a preschooler that one child-care book seriously suggests using questions about a child's most recent party as a determinant of his ability to enter kindergarten successfully.

Here are some guidelines, culled from the experiences of dozens of mothers, to help you give parties that will come close to living up to your child's great expectations:

Two-year-olds—Keep the birthday celebration small and in

the family. It's too soon to get involved with a formal party for small-fry at this age, even if this is your firstborn child and you can't wait to get started on the birthday-party circuit. But if sentiment overrules common sense, limit guests to two or three children—and their mothers. Choose an hour least likely to conflict with anyone's nap. Suggest that each mother bring one or two of her youngster's favorite toys and put out a few of your child's playthings you think he might be willing to share briefly.

Don't try to organize games or insist on sharing. Expect tears, wet pants, mess. Limit refreshments to milk, cupcakes, ice cream—and the length of the party to one hour.

Three-year-olds—Depending on the maturity and sociability of your offspring, a birthday party at this age can be a delight or a disaster. The most successful usually include three to six guests (with or without their mothers, as their mothers deem prudent) and often span the lunch hour from 11 to 12:30.

After the gifts have been opened, plan a substantial period of free play. It can be outdoors with swings, sandbox, balls, glider. If you must be indoors, set up your family room or living room like a small nursery school, with toys your birthday child is able to share temporarily. Many of the guests will be content to play by themselves, as they watch the others. You might eventually suggest a circle game of the ring-around-the-rosy level. But don't insist if there isn't any interest.

Refreshments can follow the sandwich-milk-cake-ice cream pattern. Table decorations can be marshmallows and gum-drops the guests can eat and balloons they can take home. Party-insurance policy: Buy small, identical favors (boxes of crayons, toy cars or dolls, bead-stringing sets) you can distribute to ward off tears or trouble, or use as going-home presents if all runs smoothly.

Four- and five-year-olds—These are the golden years for birthday parties, when excitement and anticipation can reach an almost unbearable pitch (and explode suddenly into tears, tantrums or stomach upsets) and when youngsters are most delighted with adult party-giving efforts.

Four- and five-year-olds typically expect and want the traditional birthday party with all the classic trappings: invitations in the mail, paper streamers, party hats, cake with candles, "Happy Birthday" singing, nut cups full of candy, balloons, favors. No additional party theme is necessary.

Many four- and five-year-olds enjoy free play with the host's toys and gifts at birthday parties. But with other groups, especially boys, guests may begin to get overexcited and out of hand. Party insurance: a list of several simple games you can use as needed, complete with equipment and prizes for all. Competition for prizes at this age can spoil the party for many youngsters.

Group treasure hunts, running games outdoors, quiet play with crayons or colored pipe cleaners, a magician keyed to a preschooler's level, a cartoon shown on a screen with a projector, or a father who can read a fascinating story to the group all work well with this age group. Two hours is as long as preschoolers—and their parents—can take of even the happiest party.

PARTIES FOR SIX- TO TEN-YEAR-OLDS

By age six or seven, most youngsters are beginning to outgrow the classic children's birthday party. For six- to ten-year-olds, the most successful parties are those which (1) have an exciting theme; (2) often involve having part of the party away from home; and (3) keep every minute planned.

This is the age span when it's most fun to plan a party with your child, for he will delight in making invitations, corraling equipment for games and shopping for favors and prizes. He will be your best guide in determining which activities are too young or too dull for his friends. (Party guests at these ages will be quick to tell you if you err in this direction—either outright or by withdrawing from the group in boredom or bedlam.)

A good party theme at these ages is one that can be carried out in invitations, guests' clothing, food, games, decorations, prizes and favors and can be adapted to the precise age and interests of your guests and your party budget. Possibilities include the most popular cops-and-quarry program on television (invitations in secret code, games like target practice outdoors with water pistols and a treasure hunt following clues to the stolen loot), circus, shipwreck, monster, Indian, outer space or a recent children's movie. Party themes can also center around a holiday. Or a book all the guests have read in school (*Tom Sawyer, Robin Hood, Robinson Crusoe*). Or a special interest you can be sure the guests share (stamp collecting, cookie baking, dolls, dogs, kite flying, model-making, rockets, baseball).

One unusual party for nine- or ten-year-olds is a millionaires' party, for which invitations are mailed out in the form of a check for one million dollars, which is cashed at the party for large-denomination play money. Guests must pay for everything at the party, like $50,000 hot dogs and $100,000 pieces of birthday cake. They pay to participate in games (guessing and ring-toss types of activity set up so two or three guests can take part simultaneously) and win large sums of money if successful. Guests with the most money at the party's end get first choices from the prize table, which holds enough loot for everyone.

You can adapt and vary most basic types of games to fit your party theme. For example, a treasure hunt can be based on a pirate's map, clues to a murder, pieces of a Valentine heart puzzle, baseball trading cards or canceled stamps. Relay races can challenge guests to walk a "tightrope" at a circus party or follow Friday's footsteps at a Robinson Crusoe affair or take off a shoe to "telephone" a secret agent.

Be cautioned, however, that youngsters in this age range are active and energetic and will run through your program of games faster than you probably estimate. You'll need to have ideas and equipment on hand for three or four more activities than you anticipate using.

This excessive energy is one good reason for planning a party that includes a trip away from home, particularly for six-, seven- and eight-year-olds. Possibilities: a suitable movie, children's theater, miniature golf, museum, zoo. An activity like swimming, baseball game on the beach, bowling or ice skating (a special treat in midsummer if you live near an indoor rink) usually uses up enough energy so that the rest of the party is easy to manage.

PRE-TEEN PARTIES

When your offspring reaches the age of ten or eleven, the whole question of birthday parties needs to be reconsidered. Often the happiest solution is to skip a party completely and substitute some other kind of treat.

Most eleven-year-olds and some tens feel they have outgrown traditional parties. ("We have hosted bowling parties, swim parties, miniature golf parties, baseball parties—you name it, we've given it," commented a mother of three sons in search of a birthday idea for a boy turning eleven.)

Even by age twelve or thirteen, most boys and girls are not ready for teen-age dancing-type affairs. Parents who attempt to give such a party often find themselves trying to cope with reluctant boys who throw food, refuse to dance, start wrestling or wander away and with girls who are hurt by the boys' indifference.

Among pre-teen girls, fast-shifting cliques sometimes make it difficult for a girl to choose guests. ("Debbie said she wouldn't come if I invite Amy; Sally hasn't talked to me since

Monday; and I should ask Janie because she lives next door, but she'll just make fun of everything," said one eleven-year-old, explaining to her mother why she preferred to do without a party.)

Pre-teens are far less interested in collecting birthday-party loot than younger children, especially since they have outgrown toy stores. This is another reason why they often would rather forgo a party in favor of a carefully chosen alternative.

For most pre-teens, a happy substitute for a party is a special excursion involving one to three friends who share a strong common interest. Possibilities for girls include a summer theater performance, a concert by a favorite rock group or folk singer, a grown-up dinner in an unusual restaurant, a folk fair, a day-long picnic or trip.

In one community, "shopping-trip parties" are favorites with eleven-year-olds. The hostess notifies one to three friends well in advance and the girls save or earn a dollar or two of their own to bring with them. A parent drives them to an interesting shopping center, fair or foreign-flavor settlement, where they are permitted to browse and buy on their own, with only discreet parental supervision. A snack or dinner in the area completes the party.

Special trips for pre-teen boys include these possibilities: Jazz concert, trip to a hobby center, rock-collecting expedition, overnight camping trip, sports event.

Boy-girl parties for seventh and eight graders can be successful usually only under certain circumstances: (1) Both boys and girls should have had some experience dancing and enjoy it. ("All you have to do is stand there and act uncoordinated," explained a seventh-grade boy. "You don't have to touch the girl.") (2) You have another couple to help chaperone. (3) You can tolerate the music. (4) You can keep your cool.

Under these conditions, a successful party formula calls for a young rock type combo, heavy on guitars, drums and amplifiers (most junior and senior high schools abound with them), or records chosen by the pre-teens; great amounts of food (soft drinks, potato chips, cookies); supervision; firm rules about staying in the party area, leaving at a specific time, keeping the music at tolerable volume and excluding party crashers.

24. How Playacting Can Set Up a Good Scene

Is your three-year-old afraid to go to the doctor? Your four-year-old leery of starting nursery school? Your six-year-old due for a tonsillectomy? Do you know how to teach a four-year-old to behave at her own birthday party? Or on a cross-country plane trip? Or how to prepare a three-year-old for a night in a motel or a checkup at the dentist's?

There's a good, all-purpose stratagem to teach small children how to behave in new situations and to feel more secure with the unfamiliar: playacting.

Too often, parents just expect a youngster to know how to act in a strange situation, without a script or any previous experience. They consider him naughty or obstreperous or immature if he doesn't perform on cue, when the problem is that he doesn't know the part.

An advance verbal briefing isn't enough to explain a new role to a small child. Your explanation will have to include too many words he doesn't understand. His vocabulary is too limited for him to put his worries into words. And much of his learning is still done through physical movement and co-ordinated activity of hands and eyes.

But if you act out with your child—and any supporting players you can recruit—what's going to happen when he makes a new scene, you can usually be confident he'll perform as you've directed.

For example, you can line up the dining-room chairs to make an airplane aisle, then play stewardess to your child's starring role as passenger. You can welcome him aboard, fasten his seat belt, call the takeoff, give him gum to ward off pressure in his ears, even serve him a snack from a tray.

But you should also talk about how fidgety he may feel after he's been sitting quietly for a long time and that he may get a funny feeling in his stomach if the air is bumpy.

Playacting preparation is particularly important when a new experience is apt to be unpleasant or frightening to a child, or if you will not be with him all of the time.

If your youngster has rehearsed a routine medical checkup and knows why the physician will shine a light into his eyes and ears and thump his chest, and if he has practiced giving shots to you or to a doll, he isn't apt to start screaming the minute he sees the doctor. The playacting not only gives him information but also an opportunity to examine and master his own apprehensions.

Acting out a new experience also gives you opportunity to stress the happy ending. Your child can come to understand that, just as in a television program or storybook, the hero may have adventures which are not always pleasant and which call for courage—but that everything will turn out right.

With a preschooler, it's a good idea to ad lib a bit of action about how his bathroom needs will be met in the new situation. Children who still feel a bit insecure about their control need information about the facilities on trains or planes and in hospitals and nursery schools.

Usually your preschooler will want repeat performances of your amateur theatricals. Then suggest switching roles, with you as patient or passenger and your child as pilot or teacher or physician. Or you can substitute dollhouse people or hand puppets for living actors.

Just as a psychiatrist sometimes uses play with dolls to spot emotional problems in small children, playacting can help you identify your youngster's apprehensions and worries. Then you can put into words, or into dramatic action, the reassurances he needs.

25. Your Child and Nursery School

New research about the importance of early learning has given great impetus to the nursery-school movement in the last few years. Increasingly, four-year-olds, three-year-olds—and even a few two-year-olds, in experimental groups—are spending two to five mornings or afternoons a week in a nursery school of some kind.

The term "nursery school" implies a two- to three-hour program intended to provide social, developmental, or in some instances cognitive, experiences for three- and four-year-olds. The purpose of the nursery school is primarily to prepare pre-schoolers for kindergarten and to give them some experiences in group activities with other youngsters their age. Any free time that results for mothers is distinctly a secondary benefit.

By contrast, "day care" implies day-long baby-sitting services for babies, toddlers and preschoolers, and is intended primarily to help mothers. Usually, in the past, day care has been limited to the offspring of mothers who could not care for their children themselves for a variety of reasons. As more women who are mothers of young children hold jobs, there is increasing demand for a variety of new types of day-care services that will combine physical care with a challenging and appropriate mix of social, mental and physical activities designed to help each youngster grow in an optimal way.

It can be difficult to find a good day-care program in many city and suburban areas today. But most communities have at least one nursery school, and often several, to provide parents with considerable choice.

Most universities, for example, sponsor a nursery school where teachers are trained and where many new ideas about what young children can and should be learning are tried out. Many high schools have a nursery school for community preschoolers in connection with a child-development course for students. There are now hundreds of Montessori schools in the United States, built around a carefully designed series of learning materials which gently lead to writing, reading and mathematical concepts. Churches, parents' groups and other community organizations often set up nursery schools. Many are run by individual teachers. There are sports-type nursery schools, usually limited to males only, with an emphasis on outdoor play and active games. A few corporations and unions have established nursery schools for employees or union members. And there are even some commercial (for profit) preschools, sometimes organized on a franchise basis.

If you have a choice of nursery schools, what kind should you choose for your child? The answer depends on your youngster's individual needs and the kind of home environment you can provide for him. He'll benefit most from the preschool experience if the one you select can offer him activities that complement his life at home.

Preschoolers have several major developmental needs: They should have a great deal of experience playing with other children, learning to share, to take turns, to make friends, to cope with the rights and feelings of others, to play cooperatively. They need the experience of being away from home and parents for a few hours a day to help them begin to feel independent and to prepare them for the separation of formal schooling.

Between the ages of three and five, youngsters need a great deal of active physical play. They benefit from the opportunity to use a variety of outdoor and indoor play equipment, to swing, run, teeter-totter, jump, bounce and exercise all of their fast-growing large muscles. They also enjoy using a larger se-lection of toys and creative materials—sandbox, clay, stand-up easel, books, blocks, dolls, riding toys, trucks, puzzles and games—than the average household can provide.

Three- to five-year-olds are avid learners, eager for new ex-periences and fresh sensory stimulation. All preschools offer considerable learning opportunities in that they give the youngsters a new environment to explore. And as research about the great, innate learning abilities of young children accumulates, an increasing number of nursery schools are developing programs geared to match their language-learning skills and their number readiness.

Lisa is an only child who lives in a big-city apartment build-ing. Her mother has plenty of time to spend with Lisa and enjoys reading to her, talking with her and taking her to inter-esting places in the downtown area. Lisa has a large vocabu-lary, can read a few words, knows numbers and can carry on a poised conversation with an adult. But the only time she can play with another four-year-old is when her mother makes complicated chauffeuring arrangements for the daughter of a friend who lives ten blocks away. For Lisa, the morning play group in a nearby church offers a chance to find same-age friends, to be part of a group, to learn how to play with others.

Marcia has a sister one year older and a baby brother and lives in a neighborhood of small ranch houses where there are several other preschoolers who share each other's backyards and play equipment. Marcia's busy mother seldom has time to sit down and play a learning game with Marcia or read a story to her without interruption. So she chose a Montessori school for her daughter, where Marcia can work on her own choice of independent learning activities in freedom and un-disturbed concentration.

Timmy lives in a high-rise apartment building several blocks from the nearest park. Opportunities for him to play outdoors depend on careful scheduling by his mother, who must also take along a toddler brother. Because Timmy's mother understands how much he needs to run, jump, shout, climb and use his large muscles, and how little chance he has to do so in the apartment, she's enrolled him in an outdoor sports-club preschool. A station wagon picks up Timmy and several other four-year-olds five mornings a week and takes them to a park or beach or farm or playground for two hours of vigorous games and sports activities with three more carloads of youngsters. Timmy comes home at 11:45 A.M. tired and relaxed, ready for lunch and quiet indoor play in the afternoon, and he's gaining a healthy physical self-confidence as he learns to hold his own in the rough-and-tumble play.

These guidelines may be useful in evaluating whether or not to send your child to nursery school in the near future. If you answer "Yes" to most of the questions below, nursery school will probably delight your youngster, stimulate his development and give you a needed breather a few hours a week. More than two or three "No" responses are a warning flag cautioning you to look for a better preschool or to postpone your child's attendance for six months or a year:

Is your youngster at least three years old? Most children younger than three take a long, tearful time to adjust to being away from Mother, and you may find yourself spending as much time in nursery school as he does. A few programs, like an occasional Montessori preschool for two-year-olds, are successful and beneficial, but in these situations special efforts are made to introduce the youngsters slowly to the program, with much support from parents.

Is he self-sufficient and self-confident about using the bathroom?

Is he eager to go to nursery school? Has he visited the preschool you are considering? Does he know at least one child from his neighborhood who will also be there?

Has he learned to share playthings—at least sometimes?

Is he in good health, with enough energy to get through mornings without tired tears or tantrums? A child who comes home from nursery school too often utterly exhausted, too tired to eat lunch, or irritable and weepy probably needs another six months or a year of growth before he's ready for preschool—or perhaps he needs a different type of program.

Does your child have a reasonable resistance to respiratory infections? Some pediatricians discourage nursery school for such youngsters. Preschools not only expose youngsters to new experiences but also to new bacteria and viruses. Childhood diseases that used to be common at elementary-school age are becoming more frequent among three- and four-year-olds, who may not cope with them so easily.

Is your child mature enough to enjoy being on his own in the outside world without you for a few hours a morning? Can you leave him with a baby-sitter without his fussing? Does he react to new experiences with enthusiasm rather than with clinging withdrawal?

Does he understand how he will get to nursery school and is he looking forward to having his own car pool or riding on the big school bus?

Does the school you are considering meet the standards recommended by the National Association of Nursery Education? (See below.)

Are the teachers well trained and understanding of three- and four-year-olds? Are you confident they will work with you if problems develop rather than blame you for causing your child's emotional difficulties?

Does the nursery school make an effort to satisfy some of the youngsters' intellectual hungers, rather than giving them nothing more stimulating than play? Does it offer mind-stretching experiences rather than just group baby-sitting?

Does the program duplicate kindergarten in your area? An outdoor sports group or a Montessori school avoids this common hazard.

Can you afford it? Unless you are lucky enough to find a good, community-sponsored nursery school, you'll probably find tuition rather high. "It costs me more to have my three-year-old go to nursery school for five mornings a week than I paid for tuition at a large private university," one mother commented. She did consider the money well spent. Sometimes parents organize a cooperative preschool, using some of their own labor to keep costs low. And occasionally a mother earns her offspring's tuition by driving the school bus or helping the teacher two or three mornings a week.

Regardless of which type of preschool you select for your child, it should meet certain minimum standards (some of which may be enforced through a licensing program if your state has one). To help you evaluate the schools you are considering, here's a checklist based on recommendations from the National Association for Nursery Education:

Are parents welcome—to visit, to make suggestions, to talk about their child, to ask questions?

Is there ample space, indoors and out, for vigorous activities and quiet play? (The Association suggests at least 35 square feet of free space per child, inside and out.) Is there room to isolate temporarily a youngster who becomes ill?

Do the boys and girls seem happy and spontaneous in their activities? Do they chatter freely with one another? Have they opportunities to tell the teacher about their experiences?

Are the teachers qualified by special education and training in nursery-school work? Are they friendly, warm, understanding, firm and yet gentle with the children? Do they encourage youngsters to learn, to share, to consider the feelings of others? Do they welcome, respect and take time to talk with parents?

Are there at least two teachers for every group of twenty children or less? Can one teacher devote a few minutes to an individual youngster while the other teacher takes over the group on occasion?

Is there plenty of large equipment for rigorous play, such as balls, packing boxes, shovels, carts, climbing apparatus and balancing boards? Is it sturdy and easily accessible to the youngsters?

Does the school have adequate materials to stimulate creativity, such as blocks, clay, paints, large crayons and simple musical instruments? Are there picture books and storybooks?

Do the teachers let children experiment with creative and dramatic materials without constant and detailed directions? Do the youngsters have opportunity to question, to investigate, to experiment?

Is the daily program planned so the children feel the security of a routine? Yet is it flexible enough for new experiences, short trips, special events?

Are the rooms clean and well ventilated, heated and lighted? Are toilets and wash basins clean? Are safety standards high and protection against fire, falls and other accidents as good as possible?

Is a medical checkup required for admission? Are first-aid supplies quickly available? Does at least one teacher have first-aid training?

Are precautions taken to prevent the spread of communicable diseases among the children?

If the school provides transportation for the youngsters, does the bus or station wagon meet safety standards? Does the driver insist that the children stay seated safely en route?

If you decide your child will benefit from nursery school and you can enroll him in a good one, how can you help him take the giant step into the outside world in happy stride? Here are strategies many mothers have found useful:

The It's-Outasight-Man Overture—If you want your offspring to go happily off to nursery school without you, you need to do an effective preliminary selling job. Your child knows he doesn't have to go, as he does to first grade, and he knows that you know it. A parent who says, "Just wait until the teacher gets ahold of you; she'll make you behave," can expect strong resistance to the idea of going to preschool. So can the mother whose youngster overhears a comment like "It will be great to get Larry out of my hair mornings."

You can, however, individualize a positive sell for your small-fry. One approach many mothers find successful, with variations, is "When the big kids go back to school this fall you won't have anyone to play with except the baby, so we've found a wonderful place for children your age, where you will find lots of new friends and interesting things to do." Or, "This is what guys your age do, and we don't want you to be left out of the fun."

You can also talk with anticipation about the big swings, stand-up easels, blocks, story times, new friends to bring home for lunch—whatever features of the program you think most appealing to your child.

The Familiarity-Breeds-Content Caper—The more familiar an under-five-year-old feels with a nursery-school situation, the easier it is to start him off on his first mornings. It helps to tell him in advance what his new school looks like, how he will get there, who the other children will be, what he will do there.

Your offspring may be worrying about how his bathroom needs will be met, when and how he will get back home, who will help him if he feels thirsty or lost or sick or scared. He may not be skillful enough with words to voice all these concerns, so it's a good idea to take the initiative and casually work the answers into reassuring comments.

Because a small child has no way of telling time, your youngster may appreciate some concrete way of knowing when he will come home. It helps to tell him, for example, "Right after you have juice and crackers, you'll play with blocks or paint a picture, then you'll have a story and after that the bus will bring you home, where I'll be waiting for you."

It's a good idea to take your child for a visit before he's due to start school. It's even better if you can do so on a day when a playmate he knows will be there and can show him around. Playacting out the whole session, from your casual goodbye at the school or bus door to your happy hug at his homecoming, can also be reassuring.

Some nursery schools urge you to stay two or three mornings with your youngster, until he's so busy playing with new friends he scarcely notices you. Others recommend a clean break, right from the start. Whatever the policy, your child should have a clear understanding of it in advance. And unless there's strong reason not to, it's a good idea to conform to the rules of the school about separating from your child. You don't want him to have the idea that he's the only three- or four-year-old who still needs his mommy to come with him— or the only preschooler whose mother doesn't care enough to come along with the other parents on the first day.

The Preschool-Speak Strategy—You should make sure your child understands words and phrases he'll be hearing from his new teacher and new friends. Three- and four-year-olds have only a hazy understanding of many words adults around them use, and some youngsters have been confused and upset by such expressions as "car pool" and "juice break." You should also be positive that the bathroom words your child uses are understood by the teacher and won't expose him to teasing by the other youngsters.

The "I Won't Sit Under the Apple Tree with Anyone Else but You" Assurance—Some preschoolers are reluctant to spend a morning at nursery school for fear of missing something exciting at home, especially if there's a younger child still there with Mother.

Often you can alleviate such unspoken concern by saying something like this: "Today while you're playing with your new friends, I'll do the housecleaning and give the baby her bath. Then I'll fix your lunch, and when you come home, you can tell me all about your fun, and we'll have time for a story while the baby is having her nap."

One three-year-old was greatly comforted about separating from her mother when her mother told her, "I'm not allowed to ride on the nursery-school bus. No mother is. But my love will go right along with you wherever you go. When you're playing this morning, I'll send you a special loving thought. You'll know I'm thinking about you."

The Security Is a Stuffed Animal Move—Most nursery-school teachers don't mind if small-fry tote along a furry, fuzzy friend. In fact, they prefer a stuffed animal to a thumb as an emotional crutch for difficult moments.

The Reserve Clause—Some three-year-olds, and more four-year-olds, go happily to nursery school without a tear, sometimes without even a backward look or a wave. Others adjust contentedly in a day or two days or a week. If your child is still crying or balking or having tantrums or saying he's sick or insisting on going to the bathroom for a long stay just when it's time to leave for nursery school, or if he comes home teary, tense or tired, reserve the right to reconsider nursery school for him at this age. Chances are, in another six months or a year he'll welcome the experience he's rejecting now—if you don't force it on him now, when he's not ready.

26. How to Cope with a Sick-in

All the trials, troubles and tediums of child care are doubled in spades when a youngster gets sick. He usually acts half his age, is twice as difficult to keep contented and demands ten times as much of your time as he normally does.

Once you've done the nursing your doctor ordered, the problem is basically how to keep your child as happy as possible while he recuperates. With some thought on your part, his convalescence can be a gentle hiatus in your family's hectic life, a time of mutual warmth and closeness, instead of fussing, demanding, bickering boredom.

"When I was sick as a child, my mother used to spend hours reading to me, playing games with me and showing me fascinating things to do," recalled a young lawyer. "That's the mental picture I get when I hear the word 'mothering.'"

When the sick-in is at your house, these suggestions can make the Florence Nightingaling a little easier:

· Unless your doctor has specifically ordered your child to stay in bed, both of you will save fussing and friction if you don't try to keep him down. If he's sick enough to need bed rest, he won't want to be up, most pediatricians now tell parents. (Hospitalized children who are ordered to stay in bed actually are more active than youngsters with similar illnesses who are permitted to be up whenever they wish, as most mothers have long suspected, and one study has shown.)

· Your feelings and attitude about your child's illnesses will influence him far into his future. So you'll want to be loving, sympathetic and supporting. But you should also try to be casual and confident that he'll be better soon. If you are calm and matter-of-fact, your youngster probably will be, too.

· Give your youngster as much reassuring information about his illness as you honestly can. Being sick can worry a young child into being sicker simply because it's a relatively new experience for him, or because he considers it a punishment for misbehavior or even for thinking bad thoughts about others. A simple explanation about the disease, stressing that it will soon be over, can usually prevent this kind of misery. He may also be relieved to know that other children get sick—and recover, too.

· A sick child often reverts to younger, outgrown behavior and demands more active mothering than usual from you. He may decide he can't feed himself or dress himself or put away his toys. If you accept these temporary changes casually— perhaps rocking your four-year-old or helping your five-year-old with his buttons and shoes—the regressions will be short-lived. He will act his own age when he's well if you matter-of-factly assume he will.

· Because he is sick, your child is probably low on energy. He's cut off from his normal sources of sensory stimulation, from active play, friends, exploring, physical exercise. Yet, sick or not, he has real need for things to listen to, look at, handle and learn about—and for distractions to keep his mind off his aches and on something pleasant.

· Television, used with discretion, can be a major help when your child is sick. But you shouldn't let him watch indiscriminately, no matter how much you need time to cook dinner or do the laundry. Even cartoon programs, which often contain violence, can be upsetting and cause bad dreams in preschool children, medical studies show. Older youngsters sometimes worry excessively about domestic comedy programs which depict family situations they don't understand and which seem threatening. Doctors have reported several instances in which sick children left to watch TV for hours grew so listless and disturbed that they couldn't sleep and drifted into chronic illness.

Since it's rare for a family with young children to get through a winter without being virus-ed in or bacteria-bound, mothers find it helpful to develop a repertoire of home-nursing skills. For example:

· To make your youngster happier when bedbound, you can improvise a back support, using a beach backrest, or a tilted, firm-sided suitcase covered with a blanket, or a sturdy cardboard carton sliced in half diagonally and placed, open side down, under a pillow, or, simply, lots of pillows.

· For a firm surface on which a youngster can play, you can set up your ironing board at a height to angle over his knees. Or use a breadboard or a dining-room-table pad if it's the kind with a stiff backing. Or you can make a bed table by cutting out a half circle from two opposite sides of a large, lidless cardboard box, so it fits over your youngster's legs.

· It helps make a sick child more comfortable if you can arrange handy storage spaces for his belongings, to avoid clutter. A shoe bag can be fastened to his bed to hold small miscellany. Or you can roll down the tops of half a dozen paper bags and stand them in a shallow carton for close-at-hand supplies.

· If your physician prescribes medicine for your persnickety preschooler, your best strategy for getting him to take it is to avoid open confrontation and begin with the calm assumption that he will. Matter-of-factly feed it to him while talking about some other subject, if you can get away with it. When a child rebels against swallowing a pill, you can crush it and mix it in a teaspoon of pureed fruit, honey, jam or pudding. Liquid medication can be masked with honey or maple syrup. But be wary of combining bitter-tasting medicine with fruit juices your child routinely enjoys. Instead of making the medicine more palatable, your strategy may backfire and trigger long-term dislike of the juice.

Scientifically minded six-year-olds sometimes can be persuaded to test the theory that sucking on a piece of ice will numb the taste buds long enough to take medicine. Others will cooperate if you let them choose their own chasers.

· If your physician orders extra liquids, novelty works better than nagging as a way to lead your child to drink. You can find dozens of interesting ways to serve up milk, fruit juices and special concoctions. A mason jar with a straw inserted through a hole in the lid makes a spill-proof container for a bedbound child. Or try peppermint sticks to stir cocoa, or pineapple sticks in punch. Or freeze fruit juice into suckers or marshmallows with food-coloring faces perched on plastic straws. Mugs, tall iced-tea glasses, pop bottles, paper milk cartons and paper picnic cups also add fun to drinks.

· When your pint-sized patient doesn't feel like eating, prodding him to do so can sometimes produce long-term problems. But as gentle persuasion for a convalescent, you can try serving him a meal on doll dishes or hobo-style on a pie plate, or paperbagged for a bedroom picnic. Or you can deliver his lunch skewered or toothpicked in ready-cut bite-sized pieces as hors d'oeuvres.

· Sometimes you can nudge a recovering appetite back to normal by playing restaurant. Chalk a menu with three or four easy-to-fix entrees, take your child's order waitress style and let him pay the check you present with play money. Another good technique is to write out happy fortunes and tape them to the bottom of your youngster's glass and plate. He has to finish the servings to read the messages.

You yourself will probably be your sick small-fry's favorite diversion. If you can find time to read to your offspring, to play easy games with him, to have relaxed visits with him or just to work in the same room where he is, you can often turn at least part of an illness or convalescence into a long-remembered time of special closeness, warmth and love. Here is a compilation of suggestions for quiet activities for a child who is abed and bored—collected from mothers, doctors and sick children themselves:

· Reading aloud—mysteries, fairy tales, poems, jokes, riddles, newspaper articles, biographies, adventures—is excellent diversion for any sick youngster, even those old enough to read by themselves. It sometimes helps to explain to your patient that reading won't take away the earache or the nausea, but will fill up a big part of his brain so he won't pay so much attention to the hurt.

· Good talk is another effective antidote to illness and usually comes easiest if you can find some simple activity to share, like rearranging things in a dresser drawer, stringing beads or sewing on buttons.

· Round-robin stories can be a mutual delight, as parent and child take turns improvising on a story theme for a few sentences, then tossing the plot back to the other to continue.

· Word games can be helpful, too. "I'm thinking of something in this room that's red" usually works well for three- or four-year-olds. Variations on "Categories" ("What color is seven? What kind of weather is Donald Duck?") are fun for older invalids.

· Set up your phonograph or tape recorder by your patient's bed and let him use it to play disk jockey with a pile of records or a stack of tapes. Or help him make a tape recording of his own. Or record special messages to him on tape that he can play back by himself.

· Artwork, in a hundred variations, is good therapy because it takes more mental than manual energy and can be distracting for long periods.

· If your walls can take it, tape a large sheet of wrapping paper by your patient's bed for crayoning a mural or just for doodling. Or suggest that he make a few new drawings to decorate his bedroom.

· Many bedridden children enjoy making their own personalized bedspread, using an old sheet or large piece of unbleached muslin. A child can decorate it himself with crayons (you can press the color in later with a warm iron) or with marking pens, or he can ask visitors to autograph the material.

· Your small invalid can try making collages from scraps of paper, cloth and bright miscellany. He can create lacy snowflakes from paper doilies. He can experiment, using crayons on paper plates, ballpoint pens on tiny scratch pads, chalk on construction paper or washable marking pens on stationery.

· Depending on the season, you can encourage your moppet to start making Christmas cards or valentines by providing him with an assortment of appropriate stickers, bright construction paper, crayons, marking pens and odd bits of rhinestone jewelry, sequins and glitter.

· Starting a scrapbook on a favorite subject or filling one with old Christmas cards or valentines can take several convalescent hours. (You can make an inexpensive scrapbook by folding separate sheets of newspaper in half and stitching through the middle with yarn.)

· Some small children enjoy creating new dust jackets for favorite books, or making their own illustrations to tip into a book of poetry or stories, or drawing to the inspiration of a favorite phonograph record. Betsy, six, delights in pretending she's a dress designer. Her mother gives her assignments such as "a warm outfit for playing in the snow" or "something special for a party" and she crayons her own creations.

· You can suggest that your small patient sort through your collection of old photographs and help you bring your albums up to date as you share some warm, "remember when" talk.

· Introduce your offspring to a quiet new hobby, such as

stamp collecting, coin collecting, model making, weaving, jewelry designing or knitting. But be sure it's not too challenging for the amount of energy and patience he has. One mother we know bought her fenced-in cowboy, age eight, two penny-collecting folders and ten rolls of pennies from the bank. The boy spent two contented days sorting through the coins, keeping about forty for his collection. Then, with help, he rerolled the rest to return to the bank.

· Books of jokes, riddles and magic tricks are good morale boosters for a sick child, especially if his father is willing to play straight man when he comes home.

· Help your youngster write a letter (or picture-letter) to a friend, to Daddy, to his classmates, or to a grandmother who'll write back.

· For a child who is particularly lacking in energy, a small pet can be fascinating to watch from bed. Among the easy-care possibilities are gerbils, parakeets, ants in a glass-sided farm, hamster, goldfish or turtle. Building a bird feeder for a child who is going to be abed for some time can also be a happy distraction.

· Puppets are good therapy for a sick youngster, too. You can make simple ones by painting faces on peanut shells and working them on your fingertips, or stitch or glue hand puppets of felt, or mark faces on spools and mount them on pencils. You can put on a puppet show for your child, if he is very young. Or you can encourage him to plot, plan and produce a show for you.

· Paper dolls are fun for homebound kids, especially if you can find the kind of dolls that punch out and wear clothes that can be laced on. A shoe box lined with wallpaper scraps makes a good house or theater for paper dolls or small puppets. Or you can cover a shoe box with corrugated paper to make a log cabin as a setting for cowboy and Indian puppet action.

· Start a jigsaw puzzle for your child to work on by himself or with you when you have free time. Or make, or help him make, jigsaw puzzles by pasting a photograph or picture on cardboard and cutting it into puzzle-shaped pieces.

· A few dime-store or other surprises can be valuable distractions for a child toward the end of a long, sick day, or for times when you really need to work elsewhere. Possibilities include: snowstorm ball, kaleidoscope, magnet with a collection of bottle caps and nails, prism, harmonica, magic slate, magnifying glass, puzzles, paper punch, collection of bolts with nuts to match, stamp with ink pad and paper, old alarm clock to take apart, packet of colored pads, paper punch (use the circles to make paper mosaic designs) and pipe cleaners for making "people." For extra fun, wrap these little items as gifts and let your child have one at special times—after his nap, when he's had his medicine or when you most need time away from him.

27. Your Child and the Hospital

If your child has to go to the hospital, how can you make it easier for him?

Hospitalization, even under the best of conditions, may be a frightening ordeal for a small child. The likelihood that he will bring home psychic scars as a result of the experience is greater, the younger he is, the longer he stays in the hospital and the less time you are permitted to stay with him. Many children who are hospitalized for as little as 24 to 48 hours have subsequent emotional disturbances. Some youngsters have been emotionally upset for weeks as a result of their experiences as outpatients in hospital emergency rooms, even when their own injuries were minor.

Long after he's home again, a youngster may be unusually withdrawn. He may be overattached to his mother, or reject her angrily. He may revert to babyish habits, have nightmares or be reluctant to try new experiences.

The problem is particularly acute for toddlers and preschoolers. A very young baby can usually be comforted in a hospital by a motherly nurse who has time to cuddle him and hold him for feedings. Children over six have had some experience being away from home and from their parents and can understand why they are in the hospital and that "Mommy will come right after lunch."

But a toddler who fights separation from his mother even for an hour's Sunday school can be hysterically frightened by the combination of illness, separation from parents and home, and the strangeness of the hospital. He may be withdrawn or apathetic instead of screaming, but this indicates even greater emotional upset.

Yet these emotional aftermaths can be drastically cut or even eliminated by (1) parents who know how to guide a child intelligently and lovingly through a hospital experience, and (2) hospitals and doctors who adapt their healing services to the special needs of sick children rather than forcing small patients into convenient hospital routines.

Here are suggestions you may find useful if your child has to go to the hospital:

· Cut the hospitalization as short as possible, especially if your child is younger than age six. If he needs a tonsillectomy, for example, perhaps you can bring him in for the necessary lab work the afternoon before, then return with him early the next morning, so he won't have to spend a night away from you in the frightening surroundings of a hospital.

· Make a calm, matter-of-fact effort to prepare your child for the hospital experience. Try not to let your own anxiety and worry show, but don't be so cheerful about it that you mislead your youngster into thinking it will be some sort of picnic. In talking with your child, you may find that seeing programs about doctors and hospitals on television may have scared him—or perhaps reassured him.

· Never deceive your child about the purpose of a trip to the hospital, or what will happen there. To do so may make it easier for you to get him there, but you'll forfeit his trust and make the experience more difficult for him to handle.

· Don't promise your youngster that nothing will hurt him in the hospital, when you know this is not true. The pain and fright involved in any surgery are hard enough for a child to bear without feeling that his parents have betrayed him.

· You can, however, be careful of your choice of words. "Fix your throat" sounds better to a tonsillectomy patient than "cut your tonsils out." And do explain why any operation is necessary, perhaps along these lines: "It's better to have your throat fixed, even if it hurts some, than to be sick as much as you have been lately, when you've missed out on so much fun."

The late Dr. Willis J. Potts, pediatric surgeon, said, "Never, but never, let your child, if he is old enough to understand, be taken to an operating room before someone, preferably the doctor who is going to operate, has explained in simple words what is going to happen. He will not like the idea of an operation, but will not harbor resentment if told what he may expect. The explanation needn't be elaborate, but honest and suited to the child's age."

· It is possible to help a child see hospitalization as an adventure—one which includes hardship and suffering, but ends in triumph for the hero, just as on TV. Sometimes an explanation along these lines is useful for a child of five or older: "This will be a new experience for you. As you know, some people become frightened about anything new. Others see a new experience as an adventure. Part of being in the hospital isn't going to be pleasant. But much of what you'll see going on around you will be interesting, if you look at it this way."

· If you aren't sure of what will happen to your child in the hospital, check with your doctor and hospital authorities. If your child is to have surgery, he needs a simple explanation about anesthetic, why he will be dressed in a hospital gown, why the doctor will be wearing green (or white), and most of all, when he will see you again.

· Do *not* tell your child you will be with him when he wakes up from the anesthetic, unless you are sure your hospital will permit it. Many hospitals now insist that patients stay in the recovery room until they are fully conscious and do not permit parents to see a youngster until he has returned to his own room. Unless your child knows this ahead of time, he's apt to be terribly frightened as he struggles to consciousness through the anesthetic fog without finding you by his bedside.

· A preschooler facing surgery is usually helped by play-acting out the procedure at home first—from packing his suit-case, to riding the cart to the operating room to eating ice cream before he comes home.

· It helps, doctors suggest, to emphasize the coming-home part of the experience, for most children are aware that occasionally people die in hospitals.

· If your child is very young and apt to scream in terror at separation from you in strange surroundings, ask your doctor if he can be given enough sedation to put him to sleep in his own hospital bed, with you at his side, before he's taken to the operating room. One of the most miserable experiences of parenthood is to hear your youngster being carted screaming down a hospital corridor for surgery while you sit helplessly behind in his empty room listening.

· If possible, you should room in with your child at the hos-pital if he's younger than age six, and take over as much of his care as possible. Your presence can be particularly important in a short-term hospital stay involving surgery. Good, modern hospitals increasingly welcome mothers for overnight stays, realizing that they can relieve nurses' aides of considerable child care and can comfort a small patient far more effectively than anyone else.

If you're up against an emergency with your child and your hospital has sticky rules excluding parents, there isn't much you can do at that point. It's a good idea to find out when you first choose a pediatrician or family doctor how the hos-pital where he takes his patients feels about parents—and keep looking until you find one that understands these emotional problems.

· If you can't room in with your child, stay with him as

much as possible. When you do have to leave your child alone in the hospital, tell him as specifically as you can when you will be back. If he can't tell time, tell him you'll come right after lunch, or whatever association he will understand.

· Let your youngster take a favorite toy or two with him, or his baby blanket, if he is used to sleeping with it. Said Dr. Potts, "No matter how worn or dilapidated it may be, let him take it along and don't allow a germ-proof observer of rules to take it away from him."

· Don't worry about overindulging and overattention when your child is in the hospital. He needs all of your emotional support and reassurance while he's ill. Once this special need has passed after he recovers, so will the necessity for extra attention from you.

· Hospitalization limits the amount of essential sensory stimuli a child normally receives from his environment—partly because he's usually in bed and partly because his intake abilities are curtailed by fear and tension. So efforts should be made to replace the stimuli—by reading to your child, talking to him, telling him stories, rubbing his back, bringing him small surprises and suitable gifts. The longer a child is hospitalized, the more he needs you to provide extra stimuli.

With this kind of careful thought and preparation on your part, chances are good that your child will come through his experience in the hospital without any emotional aftereffects at all.

28. How Do You Handle the
God Question?

"My wife and I have a three-year-old daughter," one father wrote in a letter. "We are becoming concerned about how to handle her religious training.

"Neither my wife nor I believes in organized religion. My wife believes in the existence of God. I do not. One of us grew up in a Jewish home, the other as a Protestant.

"We both want to be honest with our child. We don't attend religious services now and we don't think that going for the child's sake is fair to her or to us. Yet we want her to make the decision for herself and she can do this only if she knows what religion is all about. Also, we do not want her to feel left out when her friends go to religious school.

"As to the existence of God, I can't—_won't_—pretend to believe, just to set a good example. So what do I do if our daughter comes to me and asks if there is a God? Do I say 'No,' and have my wife say 'Yes'?

"When I got out of school I went to services to please my parents and felt like a hypocrite reciting the prayers and singing the songs. Doing the same thing with my daughter seems wrong, although I suppose it's the 'right' thing for a parent to do. What *is* best?"

Many parents have problems with their children's religious upbringing in these days when there is a crisis of belief in many denominations, when moral values are changing and old orders stand in doubt. Even parents who agree about a centuries-old religious faith with extensive dogma and parochial schools for children are faced today with unprecedented ideological schisms and controversies.

There are no pat or "best" answers to the questions this father raises. There is no persuasive research on the subject that applies to all families. There is no consensus among child psychologists, psychiatrists, religious leaders or educators. What helps one family won't necessarily work for another.

What is sure is that parents cannot escape making certain religion-oriented decisions for their children. It is true that every adult can decide for himself what he will or won't believe. But his faith, or lack of it, will inevitably be shaped by the religious experiences he has or hasn't had as a child, and whether he accepts or rebels against his teachings, teachers and parents.

Practically, parents in this particular father's position seem to have three alternatives, each of which carries its own difficulties and disadvantages.

First, as a father, you can simply try to ignore the whole idea of religion in your family's life. On one level, this is increasingly easy and common. Weekly church attendance in the United States has slipped considerably from its high of 49 percent of the total population in 1958. Sunday-school attendance is down in many areas. Secular activities, including shopping, are increasingly available on Sundays. Religious exercises and symbols have been systematically removed from public schools and public places.

If you spend Sunday mornings sleeping or grumping around the house, your child may fuss occasionally about why you don't go to church like some of her friends and their families. But if you fill your Sundays with loving, happy family activities, your child will rarely give Sunday school another thought.

You will have some trouble answering the kinds of questions four- to six-year-olds bring home after inevitable theological arguments with friends of the same age: "Who is God's Daddy?" "Is God down inside my stomach? Mark said He is everywhere." "Cathy's mother said my kitty that got runned over is up in heaven; why can't you get her back for me?"

But then, even parents with a firm, well-defined faith often stumble over questions like these.

Like the questions young children have about sex, you can subtly turn off your youngster's queries about religion by the time she's six or seven by showing embarrassment, discomfort, anger or reluctance in answering. But just as they often do about sex, children may stop asking parents for information and continue to piece together their own crazy-quilt of answers from comments made by friends, from overheard conversations and later on from references in reading.

It will be impossible for your daughter to miss the significance religion has in the lives of many other people, if only in the obvious trappings of weddings, funerals, invocations, references to God in the Pledge of Allegiance, in holidays and in friends' first communions, confirmations and bar mitzvahs. She will encounter religious references and influences in art, music, literature and history—and in common words in her vocabulary.

Some parents try to counter religious influences by acquainting somewhat older children with the concept of the Bible and other religious stories as myth, invented by primitive, non-scientific people to help them understand the uncontrollable forces in nature—but not needed by contemporary, rational people.

However, you may encounter more problems than you solve by trying to keep religion out of your daughter's life. Will your wife, for example, be content to demote God to mere myth? Will she give the same kind of answers to your child's questions as you do? What about her parents and yours? Will they be tempted to teach their beloved granddaughter just one little prayer or read her a few religious stories?

What will you do about celebrating the great holidays children enjoy so much and which provide such loving mortar for a family's foundations? A few of the traditional religious festivals, like Christmas and St. Patrick's Day, have secular equivalents. But it is almost impossible to keep Passover or Yom Kippur nonreligiously.

Even if you can avoid all of these problems, you must still consider what beliefs you can offer your daughter. Four- and five-year-olds often seem to feel a need to believe quite urgently, especially as they become aware of the ecclesiastical labels of their playmates and even if they are vague about what the identifications mean.

When Laura was about four, her mother, who is a Protestant, spent considerable time explaining to her about a religious observance being marked by Jewish neighbors. Laura became increasingly upset and finally burst into tears, sobbing, "I don't care what Linda and her family believe. What do I believe?"

Early adolescence, when confirmations and bar mitzvahs traditionally take place, seems to be a stage in life when commitment to a religious faith or a higher belief or ideal satisfies a great innate need. Simply not believing may not be enough to fill this void for your daughter. Substitute philosophies of life—humanism or existentialism, for example—may be intellectually sufficient for an adult, but are usually not specific or satisfying enough for a young person.

Recently a newspaper reporter was interviewing a family who had adopted several children of mixed and different races. As he talked to the parents, a three-year-old began teasing one of the other youngsters, finally hitting him to get attention.

"Don't do that, Jeff; it isn't Christian," corrected the father.

Few parents put their religious convictions into words as matter-of-factly as this father. But for most parents, religiously based moral convictions and codes of right and wrong still form the basis for the decisions they make and the values and standards they try to teach their children.

You and your wife may have an adequate value system in operation. But what standards, what rationale for existence, what moral code will you encourage your daughter to use when she must make decisions for herself?

You must be ready to do more than expect your child to adopt your moral values just because you are her father. You must supply some rationale. Relying solely on contemporary mores may leave your daughter dangerously dependent upon peer-group pressures, fads, fashions and pragmatic considerations and make you defenseless against the argument "But Daddy, everyone else is doing it."

Still another function of religion you will have to try to replace in your daughter's life as she grows up is that of consolation and comfort. This is a major reason why a large part of present-day congregations go to church, sociologists point out. You must have something to say to comfort your child when a grandparent or a playmate or a pet dies, or an injustice seems to go uncorrected, or she wonders about the meaning of existence. Most non-God views of the world in which man is just a biological accident adrift in an empty void seem cold and futile in contrast to the warmth, the love, the hope and the eternity offered by religions.

You can raise a child without religion, of course. Millions of parents do. But there are other options.

You can send your daughter to religious school when she is old enough without attending services yourself, but it isn't likely to accomplish much. If your primary purpose is to help her gain a knowledge of religion in a historical sense, you should not expect her to acquire it in a religious school set up to instruct youngsters in a particular faith. And it seems hypocritical to expose her to indoctrination in a religion you have rejected for yourself, or to send her to religious school just for social reasons.

Another alternative is for you and your wife to try to work out a searching, open-ended kind of attitude about religion which you can honestly and lovingly share with your child as she grows up. If you examine the basis of your own current opinions, you may find you have more common ground of positive agreement and belief than you realize.

For example, what is the definition of the God in which you do not believe? Is He the kind of anthropomorphic Santa Claus on a golden throne that young children sometimes picture? Or a spy-in-the-sky bogeyman? Or a celestial CPA keeping account of your needs and misdeeds in a heavenly ledger? Or the God the Russian cosmonaut announced couldn't exist because he didn't see Him when he orbited the earth at 125 miles out? Or the God who didn't give you a new bike or keep your goldfish from dying when you were seven years old?

But how many of the concepts of God suggested by contemporary theologians have you heard or read? Could you, perhaps, accept as a beginning Paul Tillich's definition of God as "the Ground of Being"? Or the idea of God as life force or creative energy or first cause?

With some searching, you may find there is a form of God you can accept. You may find that what you have been rejecting is someone else's idea of God, and not the concept of God. Then you can explain more easily to your daughter in a way that won't turn her off, as you have been turned off.

When she starts asking questions about God, you can give her simple answers, suggesting at the same time that God is a very big idea which is hard to understand all at once and that she will want to learn more about it and talk about it many times. Gradually, you can help her see how difficult it is for man, the finite, to comprehend God, the infinite. And you can explain that mankind, wherever he has existed, has felt a great innate need to know and worship God, but because there are so many different ideas of what God is like, the ways of talking about Him and worshipping Him are often quite different. This is why there are so many different kinds of churches and places to learn about God and worship Him.

You can also tell your child that her grandparents have different ideas about God than her parents do, and that even you and your wife don't completely agree. But all respect each other's right to learn and think about God for himself.

You can also, in honesty and wonder, talk about ideas of God, past and present, which might be appropriate for your child as she grows. The youngster who asked if God were in her stomach because He is everywhere could have been told something like this: "One of the big ideas about God is that God is love. You know I love you, but you can't see my love as you can see my nose or hair. My love for you isn't in the living room or in the kitchen sink or even under your pillow at night. My love for you is really everywhere and yet nowhere you can see or touch. Yet you know my love for you is real and that it is good."

An Indian legend appropriate for children suggests that God may be like the life force in a seed. You cannot see it if you cut the seed open, yet it is there and its power is tremendous.

Another way to help your child think about God is to suggest that you can sense God's presence and importance by what many men have done in His name. Because of God, people have composed great music, created famous paintings, built cathedrals, freed slaves, fed the hungry, written psalms. (This also leaves an opening to talk about how the concept of God has been misunderstood, distorted or deliberately invoked in perverted ways—without diminishing the concept of God Himself.)

You can explain that because the idea of God is hard to

understand, people sometimes make symbols or develop rituals to help them, and that some begin to think the symbols themselves are what is important and forget the real ideas behind them. You can then say that even though the symbols or rituals of a religion don't make sense to you, it's helpful to understand why people have them.

This kind of open-ended, exploring attitude, developed gradually as your child grows up, will help her to be tolerant and appreciative of other religions without feeling threatened. It should make it possible for all of you to participate in the religious observations of grandparents without feeling hypocritical. And it should give your child an appreciation of the great force—usually for good—that religion has been throughout human history.

If you decide on this approach, you may want to look for a church congregation in which your whole family can participate. Many churches are increasingly concerned with social action rather than worship and are experimenting with new forms of services, drawing upon contemporary kinds of music, art and writing, in an effort to keep traditional symbolism from getting in the way of understanding.

A search for a relevant faith today can be intellectually demanding and difficult. New theologians can be just as obtuse as old ones, and there is considerable faddiness involved in some of the new theologies. Unless you are willing to give the search for a meaningful faith your best mental efforts, you will simply be shopping around for a more comfortable pew.

29. Gender Roles in the World of Women's Liberation

How should you raise a small daughter in this era of women's liberation? If you encourage her to be free from traditional female roles and stereotyped feminine attitudes, will she be likely to be happy as an adult?

Women, argue many feminist groups, should no longer have to choose between career and marriage with children. Like men, they should be able to have them both—free not only from socially imposed menial work but also from cultural pressures and attitudes that impose supposedly "female" traits like passivity and lack of dominance and drive on girls almost from birth.

But it isn't easy to free female children from the limitations of cultural attitudes and expectations about sex roles, even if parents try. And it isn't as simple as the anatomy-is-destiny-is-baloney theories make it sound.

No one is precisely sure, for example, just how much of what psychologists call "gender role" is learned behavior and how much of what is considered "femininity" is actually determined by genes and hormones.

Another difficulty is that there's no consensus on what women's "gender role" should be in the liberated future. Yet all societies in history have imposed such roles on both sexes from birth, and psychologists stress the importance of helping a child become comfortable in his gender role early in life.

There is increasing awareness, of course, that much of the "gender role" imposed on females by society has been unnecessarily limiting. Too many women who might have been physicians are shunted into nursing; too many women who could have been successful as executives are turned into secretaries instead of management trainees; too many women who should have become scientists are discouraged from taking the prerequisite math courses in high school.

Yet the role of the working woman may not fit all, or even most, of the girls growing up now by the time they are ready to make their own decisions. Certainly a considerable percentage of young women will become full-time wives and mothers, even a generation into the future. And most women will probably spend many years of their lives at least as part-time homemakers and mothers. So the gender roles parents teach their daughters now must be broad enough to make them comfortable with a wide variety of lifestyle choices in the future.

"I am telling my daughter that she can succeed at any career she wants," explains a professional woman in her forties. "But I also point out she will be missing one of the central joys of human existence if she doesn't have children. And I suggest she consider a life plan that would include a top-notch education, a year or two of full-time work, then part-time or volunteer work or study in that field while her children are young, with full-time career concentration afterward. That's the best lifestyle I can find that fits cultural realities today, doesn't shortchange the children too much, and gives a woman the best of two worlds."

What else can the parents of a daughter do to prepare her for life in a fast-changing society?

From toddler and preschool ages on, parents can make sure they are choosing for a daughter toys and activities that are geared to her interests as a person and not to a sex-imposed stereotype. A little girl should have just as much opportunity to play with a dump truck as a doll, to use a pretend doctor's kit as a nurse's outfit.

A girl should have books and stories—even at an age when parents are still reading to her—which don't always portray women in traditional roles of keeping house and tending babies. Most books for children are still sexist, showing men as doers, rescuers, wage-earners and decision makers and women in subordinate, traditionally female, passive activities. But a few publishers are now making an effort to put out books for children in which girls and women share active, heroic roles and which avoid sexist stereotyping and vocabulary.

Most television programs—and commercials in particular—are sexist, showing women almost exclusively as homemakers, wives, mothers and subordinates, and interested in nothing more than housekeeping and making themselves physically attractive to men. This inaccuracy needs to be pointed out to a girl, and she can be helped to see why this image of girls and women is inaccurate and unfair.

Parents of a daughter can see that she isn't shut off early from areas of interest and expertise because it's "man's work." This happens still in myriad subtle and obvious ways, from showing boys, but not girls, how to change fuses and run a power mower to trying to talk girls out of pre-med or engineering in college.

Parents of a daughter who shows an early interest and talent in math and science should be wary lest cultural and school pressures dampen these sparks. Studies on creativity show that girls produce as many imaginative ideas in these areas as boys do until about fourth grade. After that, most girls tend not to try very hard, assuming society's attitude that "Girls don't know much about those things."

Generalities that begin "Girls don't . . ." and end with

a lowered expectation or a limiting assumption should be avoided. And they can be contradicted or fought when they are heard.

A girl, especially one with superior abilities, should be encouraged not to turn off her talents deliberately and lower her academic sights during the preteen and teen-age years in hopes of being more popular with boys. She should be encouraged to take a full sequence of math courses in high school; many women lose out on possible careers in science because they enter unprepared to begin calculus and to take the math program required for most science majors.

As changing laws and public attitudes open up more opportunities in sports for girls and women, a daughter should be encouraged to take advantage of expanding possibilities for classes, teams, training and competition. Developing skill in sports during childhood and adolescence can lead to lifelong recreational interests, promote physical development, and help girls, as well as boys, to become more self-confident and poised. In communities where opportunities for girls in sports still lag markedly behind those for boys, parents can take the lead in pressuring public schools and community facilities to provide more equality.

Feminist activities, women's-movement progress, and gender roles in general should be discussed openly and frankly with a daughter and she should be encouraged to keep her options open and not be frozen by early choices into limited, traditional attitudes and work. At the same time, the emphasis should be on freedom of choice, so that a girl can feel comfortable if she eventually decides she wants to fill a traditional role as wife and mother without trying to hold a paying job outside the home as well.

A mother can help point the way to a freer future for her daughter by being active and involved herself in the world beyond supermarket and PTA. A father's cooperation and interest in a woman's widening role can help a girl understand that masculine approval need not be contingent on passivity and dependence.

Parents can also make sure that they don't usually show approval or otherwise reward a girl in subtle as well as in obvious ways when she is acting "feminine" in the traditional sense rather than when she is behaving more independently. A father whose most frequent compliments to his daughter are along the lines of how pretty she is and a mother who seems more interested in her daughter's dates than in her grades in school are leading her into old sexist patterns, whether they intend to do so or not.

However, a girl still needs to be helped to see the values in being female, to become comfortable in a feminine "gender role" in its newest and broadest meaning. It's not doing a daughter a service—and may do considerable psychological harm—to raise her merely to be more like a man.

How do you raise a male child in this era of women's liberation? If the traditional sex roles aren't going to work for the coming generation, what will?

Avoiding instilling sexist attitudes in children is considerably harder than eliminating racism. For the lifestyles of most fathers and mothers are still dominated by prevailing man-woman stereotypes; the Daddy-works, Mommy-changes-diapers role models are what most children still see from birth on.

Male chauvinism begins early, even in homes where mothers hold full or part-time jobs and fathers freely and naturally help with household chores and child care. Parents sometimes see that male-superiority attitudes can be caught like chicken pox, usually from other small boys who have older brothers.

"I hate girls" is as much a part of the vocabulary of four- to six-year-old males as impolite bathroom words—and almost as hard to stop.

The prevailing myths about what's inherently masculine and what's feminine—and which is better—are reinforced by almost every aspect of contemporary life that touches children. In school, the teachers are usually women, the principal a man. In the pediatrician's office, the doctor is male, the assistant female. Daddy drives the car, mother sits passively by.

On television, men read the news, fight the gun battles, sit in judgment on women's efforts to please them with offerings of coffee or breakfast food. Women blither about the delights of detergents, watch the action from the sidelines and try to justify their existence by producing the right cup of coffee or the perfect shade of blond hair or the shiniest waxed floor.

It's no wonder that small males get the idea early on that they are a superior breed.

But male chauvinists aren't going to be any more welcome in the world of the future than racists are today. So parents of boys do need to find ways to help their sons develop a healthy masculine identification and appreciation of their gender role without the sexist assumptions that maleness has traditionally implied.

Parents, for example, can make an effort to avoid the sexist stereotypes that put down women or limit their roles. Sexual generalities shouldn't be used, either, to prevent young males from expressing and developing tender, nurturing aspects of their personality. A man who tells his preschool son, "Boys don't play with dolls," may be making it more difficult for the son to become a father himself some day.

It's particularly important to avoid turning boys away from early artistic or creative interests because they seem "sissy" to some fathers. Studies show that the creative talents of many boys are stunted by about fourth grade because they seem too feminine to adults who influence them in other directions.

Household tasks children are required—or hired—to do can be divided up on a nonsex basis. Boys shouldn't be excused from making beds or doing dishes merely on the ground that it's girls' work. And they should be taught to cook and sew enough so they won't be dependent upon women to wait on them.

Parents can try to avoid sexist books for children—which are astonishingly prevalent. And they can talk about contemporary changes in sex roles and sex stereotypes, just as they do about racism and what alterations in society must be made to give not only racial minorities but also the female majority equal opportunities to develop and use their abilities.

But the best way to prevent limiting sexist attitudes in boys is by example. A loving, involved, active mother and a sharing, caring, nonthreatened father who are at ease and happy in an egalitarian marriage provide the best role models for young sons and daughters today.

30. Sex Education: How Much,

When and by Whom?

Children's need for sex education has grown enormously in recent years. Our society has greatly increased its exposure of the young to pornography and to commercial erotica in best-selling books, plays, magazines, movies and even on television. Teen-age pregnancies are increasing. Abortion is on the rise. Venereal disease is epidemic among the young.

Yet at the same time, we have removed many of the traditional safeguards against premature sexual experience by giving young people easy access to cars and open college dormitories and by limiting chaperones, supervision, rules and many traditional moral and religious sanctions. It is essential that young people be helped to reach a better understanding of sex and sexuality. But even in the midst of what may be a revolution in sexual mores, many parents are still too uptight about the subject to talk straight to their offspring.

Sex education in school seems to many concerned adults the best way to reach almost all young people. But the problem is that because there is no consensus among adults today about sexual standards, there is no basic agreement about what children should be taught. And as of now, there is little reliable evidence about what kind of sex education in school is most useful, when it should be given, by whom, to whom and how.

Parents are rightly concerned about questions like these: How can sex education be taught in school without a framework of attitudes and morality? But whose attitudes? What morality? How can you avoid group sex education coming too soon for some children and too late for others? What can be done about the teacher whose sexual views are far more liberal than parents believe to be appropriate for their children—or about the teacher who foists his own sexual hang-ups on his students?

So what should parents do about sex education? Just what they always should have done in the past and must continue to do, no matter what kind of program their local school district has now or decides to adopt in the future. Parents must teach their own children what they need to know to handle sex intelligently. By being responsible for sex education yourself, you can be sure your children are exposed to sex as an aspect of love, a mortar of marriage and an instrument of creation—rather than just a gimmick to sell movie tickets or books or deodorants or as the subject of dirty jokes.

But is sex education really necessary for young children? Can't it wait? Take a thirty-second look at the newspaper ads for movies. Or at some of the films and commercials on prime-time television. Or the magazine advertisements with nudes or near-nudes and suggestive copy. Or listen to the talk about the latest unmarried pregnant celebrity.

There's no way you can prevent your children from being bombarded with "sex education" of this kind both inside and outside your home. All you can do is to make sure they get enough facts and philosophy from you to put it in its proper perspective.

If you don't answer a child's questions (spoken or unspoken) early in his life, you can be quite sure some five- or six-year-old friend will. Or your youngster will piece together for himself a funny-scary-right-wrong-mixed-up montage of assumptions and impressions that will continue to color his feelings even when he is exposed to facts.

Dodging these first questions (which a mother or father can do quite adroitly) conveys to the youngster the impression that this is an off-limits area. The child soon stops considering his parents as a source of information about sex and no longer voices his questions. Without the queries, it's easy for the parents to postpone giving the child sex education "until he's ready and asks." The older the youngster gets, the harder it becomes for parents to initiate conversation about sex and they begin thinking, He-probably-knows-it-all-already, and We'll-just-buy-him-a-book-he-can-read-himself when he gets ready. This laissez-faire attitude can produce a teen-ager with disturbing, even dangerous, gaps in his knowledge.

Are there any guidelines parents can follow in teaching a child about sex in today's world?

· First, remember that what parents do and are, as individuals and as a couple, influences a child's ideas about sex and sexuality far more than little talks about the facts of life. Sex education consists of much, much more than a description of the reproductive processes and the moral values surrounding these processes. It also involves the whole concept of marriage, family, babies, the roles of man and woman, respect, responsibility, love and life goals.

· Use correct anatomical terms when you discuss sex with your child. If you don't, he will be forced to use baby words or gutter terms and may be embarrassed later on by his lack of ease with correct vocabulary.

· Do answer your child's questions when he asks them. If you can't right at the moment because you're on a crowded bus or have guests or the baby needs quick attention, take the initiative in bringing the subject up when it is convenient.

· Help your youngster to feel secure enough psychologically to ask you more questions on the subject—or any other— when they occur to him. You might say something like "You'll probably want to know more about how babies grow some day and I'll be happy to tell you." Or, "I'm glad you asked me about that word. I want you to know what it means so you won't use it in the wrong way."

· Always tell your child the truth, but in a way that is suitable for his age. Once a child realizes he's been told a fairy tale, he'll turn to his friends and classmates or some other source of information the next time he feels curious.

· Be wary of using words your child will misunderstand. Many a preschooler, told that a baby is growing "inside Mommy" or "in Mommy's tummy," reacts by wondering if it's "down there with all the hamburger and mashed potatoes." It's not uncommon for a girl—or a boy—who has been informed that babies grow from seeds Daddy plants inside Mommy to try swallowing some orange or watermelon seeds or even prune or plum pits with the intention of creating a great surprise for everyone. One five-year-old accidentally overheard her mother telling a neighbor that she had once "lost a baby." Later, the five-year-old was found tearfully reassuring the three-year-old, "Don't worry. I'll take care of you if Mommy ever loses us."

· Most parents find books useful in providing sex education for children. Reading aloud from volumes with drawings and pictures make the subject easier for preschoolers to understand. Older boys and girls appreciate having their own books about sex information to which they can refer in private. But books about sex for youngsters in all age groups vary markedly in their approach and quality, and you should carefully scan any book you want to share with your child before you make a final selection.

At what age should you begin teaching a child about sex?

Indirectly, your first lessons begin in the first weeks of your baby's life, as he learns the differences between his father and his mother—that his father's voice is deeper, his shoulders broader, his hands bigger than his mother's. A baby comes, quite quickly, to associate his mother with being fed and tended most of the time and to expect his father to go away and return at intervals and to play with him in a somewhat different way than his mother cuddles him.

Long before he's able to ask a single question about sex—or anything else—a baby has already absorbed considerable information about male and female, about roles in marriage and about family relationships. His feelings about his body are already being shaped by how his parents handle him, bathe him, change him, toilet him and love him.

Questions about sex begin sometime after age two or two and a half, usually along with questions about everything else. All of them should be answered with equal casualness and simplicity. They have no emotional loading until an adult hesitates or an older child snickers.

What does a two- or three-year-old need to know about sex? Primarily, he should be helped to understand that people are divided into two sexes—boys and fathers are males, and girls and mothers are females—and that their bodies are different in some ways.

Parents who don't have a new baby of the opposite sex for a preschooler to observe closely should wangle an invitation from a neighbor who does. Watching a mother bathe, diaper and dress the baby—and talking casually about his tiny body—can be an excellent early lesson in sex differences.

Most nursery schools have a casual, open-door arrangement for toileting, which makes the acquiring of information about sex differences matter-of-fact and unemotional.

Not all little girls react like the three-year-old who lamented about a neighbor's toddler, "He's so fancy and I'm so plain!" But psychologists say it is important that parents make it quite clear to girls that they are not just boys with a missing part, but that, instead, they have a special place inside their body where it will be possible some day for a baby to grow. A boy, too, may assume that girls are mutilated males and worry lest he, too, be injured, unless parents provide an adequate explanation.

It's also a good idea to point out at this time—and later, in other contexts—that biological differences between males and females involve only sexual roles, not mental abilities or aptitudes, and that the presence or absence of a penis is not a factor in the ability to handle any job except fatherhood.

When do children begin asking about where babies come from? Usually between the ages of three and four, depending upon whether there is a new baby in the family or in the neighborhood or whether the youngster's interest has been triggered by something he's heard or seen on television. If your child has not asked a question of this kind by four and a half or five, it's a good idea to answer it anyway, using a friend's new baby, a picture in a magazine or a baby animal to lead into the conversation.

What's the best answer? Most three-year-olds are satisfied with an answer along this line: "A baby grows in a special, warm, soft place inside the mother." With somewhat older preschoolers, you can add that this special place is called the uterus, that it is quite like an upside-down balloon that is all folded up, and is little until the baby starts to get bigger; then the uterus stretches and expands just like the baby.

Youngsters are usually four years old, or a little older, before it occurs to them to ask how the baby gets out. The balloon analogy makes it simple. You can just say that as the baby grows, it gets so big that the balloon-shaped uterus can't stretch any more. So it gently pushes the baby out through the end of the balloon, which is really a special, extra opening between the mother's legs which stretches to let the baby out.

Not until age five or older do many children ask how the

baby got into the uterus, or what makes it start growing. Parents should then describe the father's part in creating a baby in the same simple terms.

All of these conversations should be loving and gentle. You should talk about the beginnings of life with the sense of miraculous wonder you might use in showing your four-year-old a daffodil bud or a new baby kitten. If you wish, you can add that the way babies grow is a part of God's wonderful plan for living beings and also a reflection of the love that a father and a mother have for each other.

What should you do if a child starts using words you consider obscene? Calmly explain to him what the words really mean and point out that when he is using the words he doesn't intend to convey that meaning. Tell your offspring that the process of starting a baby to grow, of waiting for it to be born and of cherishing it afterward is important and beautiful, and that the words that describe these wonderful parts of life should be used privately for these purposes. Sometimes it helps to suggest other words a child can use when he is angry or upset. (None of this will be effective if the adults around him set contrary examples.)

What else should children be taught about sex before the teen-age years? Usually, during the years between six and ten, children's questions about sex and reproduction seem to reflect more of a scientific interest than a personal curiosity. In fact, some psychologists refer to these years as the "latency period," although there is considerable controversy about how "latent" sexuality really is during this period.

If you've kept the channels open, your youngster will probably ask you many times about how babies grow and how they are started. Sometimes he's asking for information he's forgotten, sometimes he's checking a classmate's version of the facts, sometimes he's just thought of more details he wants explained.

With a six- or seven-year-old, you can add more information

about the ovum and sperm to your account of reproduction. Eight-, nine- and ten-year-olds may be interested in genes, chromosomes and heredity. How animals and plants reproduce and how these processes compare with those in humans fascinate six- to ten-year-olds.

Toward the end of this period you should begin to prepare your child for the changes of adolescence. Both boys and girls need to know how their bodies will alter during puberty, that these changes come at different ages—all within the range of normal—for different individuals, and that it is common, almost universal, that young people feel awkward and unattractive at times during this transition.

This is also the time to point out to them how much a baby needs both a father and a mother who are mature, stable individuals prepared to take on the responsibility of a baby, and to explain about contraceptives, in general.

If you have always talked freely to your child about sex and if he feels secure in coming to you with his questions, you won't find this stage so difficult. If love and responsible morality have been at least an implied part of all you've said to your offspring about sex and sexuality—and if you've provided him with a loving, moral example—you'll have greatly increased the chances that he will find sexuality to be wondrous and joyous, despite the cheapening influence of our society.

31. Is Television Harming Your Child?

A wise and loving mother recently had to tell her four-year-old that his grandfather had just died.

"Who shot him?" was the boy's first response, for he was a child of the television generation and no stranger to sudden death by violence.

How many murders does the average child see every day? How many fist fights? How many shootings? What does he see of adult behavior, of family relationships? What image is he shown of minority groups, of women, of policemen?

What is television doing to your child?

Today you can find experts and studies to back up almost any answer you want to this question. Sometimes it's easy to trace a nightmare to a TV show, or excessive whining for a new toy to a commercial. But it's often difficult to measure precisely how much television distorts a youngster's concepts of reality or influences his behavior, or whether it sharpens or blunts his concern for others.

There's no doubt, of course, that television—the plain, run-of-the-channel TV without educational pretenses that most small children watch—does teach youngsters innumerable good and desirable things. It enlarges their horizons, introduces them to a world beyond their block, builds their vocabularies and entertains them when they are sick, or their mothers are sick of them. It has even helped some preschoolers to read a few words.

But is TV hurting your child?

The most massive attempt to answer this question can be found in a 2,499-page, six-volume report on children and televised violence prepared for the U.S. Surgeon General at the request of Congress and published in 1972. This great mass of data—some of it researched to order for the Surgeon General's committee—leaves no doubt that there is a definite link between violence on television and violence in some children. But the report's conclusions are stated so softly, with so many marshmallow words, that its message has been largely ignored. Even in the face of much clear evidence from its five volumes of research findings, the report hedges, stumbles, weasels, dilutes.

The report nitpicks about the definition of "violence" on TV and "aggressive behavior" in children. It puzzles about whether a child can be considered to be "viewing TV" if he is also doing homework or talking or eating or just swinging his foot or picking his nose. It frets about the size of its samplings and the fact that human behavior is complex and has many interrelated causes.

Eventually, the report concludes: "Violence depicted on television can immediately or shortly thereafter induce mimicking or copying by children . . . under certain circumstances, television violence can instigate an increase in aggressive acts. The accumulated evidence, however, does not warrant the conclusion that televised violence has a uniformly adverse effect nor the conclusion that it has an adverse effect on the majority of children. It cannot even be said that the majority of children in the various studies reviewed showed an increase in aggressive behavior in response to the violent fare to which they were exposed. The evidence does indicate that televised violence may lead to increased aggressive behavior in certain subgroups of children, who might constitute a small portion or a substantial proportion of the total population of young television viewers."

The same could be said about most viruses: Exposure produces symptoms only in certain children.

Many critics of television found it surprising that the report to the U.S. Surgeon General reached even this mildly critical conclusion. For, they charged, the 12-member committee that produced the massive study was set up in a way that made it prejudiced toward the TV industry.

Despite the controversy, however, the study does contain a mass of research data about children and television. Among the findings:

· Almost every child in the United States has access to TV. At least 98 to 99 percent of the homes where there is a child or a teen-ager have a TV set. One family in three has more than one TV.

· In the average home, the television set is turned on for about six hours, 18 minutes every day, chiefly during late afternoon and evening. Most youngsters watch television at least two hours daily. Many children put in considerably more time in front of the set.

· TV viewing begins very early in a child's life. By age three, he's already a habitual watcher. One study puts preschoolers' average weekly viewing time at almost 35 hours for boys and 32 hours for girls.

· The amount of time spent watching TV continues to be high until about age twelve, when there's a considerable shift toward listening to music on radio and records. From this teen-age low, TV usage begins to increase again in early adulthood, with marriage and the starting of a new family. It remains stable during the middle adult years, then rises again when offspring grow up and leave home.

· Typically, during the first sixteen years of his life, a child in the United States spends at least as much time with television as he does in school.

· The more TV programs children share with their parents, the more violent the shows they tend to watch.

· Bright youngsters watch television more than other children during the preschool years. But this pattern shifts after age six, and their viewing totals drop to less than average. Among junior and senior high-schoolers, A students see considerably less television than their B and C classmates.

· Black children and their parents watch television more than do whites. Blue-collar families put in more time in front of the screen than do white-collar families. The lower the socioeconomic background of families, the more they use their TV sets and the less critical and more accepting they are of television as "realistic."

· Like adults, children don't pay complete attention to what's on the screen, even when they are in the same room with a turned-on set. But when a violent episode comes on, their level of attention increases. This means that some children may often see only the violence and not the context in which it occurs on the program.

· As children grow up, the proportion of their TV time spent on shows containing violence increases.

· Only one family in ten has established rules about what and how much children can see on television—but many more parents worry that they should be making such rules. The poorer the family, the less adult control there is likely to be over TV watching by children.

The results of all this research, as the report to the U.S. Surgeon General shows, are as simple as ABC (or NBC or CBS):

A. Children are exposed to a substantial amount of violent content on television and they can remember and learn from such exposure.

B. There is a definite relationship between watching aggression and violence on TV and behaving aggressively and violently.

C. Violence on television can be a direct cause of aggressive behavior in youngsters. It can not only suggest to children new ways of acting violently, but also teaches the idea that aggression is a powerful technique for getting their own way.

"The greater the level of exposure to television violence, the more the child was willing to use violence, to suggest it as a solution to conflict and to perceive it as effective," the report to the Surgeon General states. "When the home environment also tends to ignore the child's development of aggressive attitudes, this relationship is even more substantial and perhaps more critical."

No evidence came out of the massive studies to back up the frequent claim that watching violence on TV would help children work off their innate aggressiveness and anger, making them less likely to fight, hit or try to hurt others. Just the opposite was found: The more filmed violence children watch, the more likely they are to copy that kind of behavior themselves.

The presence of an adult does cut down on the amount of violence children imitate from TV, experiments cited in the report to the Surgeon General show. But such aggressiveness increases when children are with other youngsters of the same sex and age without a grownup around.

Currently, television also suggests to children that they themselves may easily become the victims of violence. Two out of three leading characters observed on prime-time television during these studies were themselves victims of acts of violence. The "overriding message" of the medium is the risk of being a victim of violence, noted one researcher. And unlike real life, most violence on television is committed against strangers or casual acquaintances—again suggesting the possibility to children that they may become unwilling victims. Typically, violence is pictured as a way to enforce a "personal goal, private gain, power or duty" rather than because of some broad moral or social issue. Female leading characters are much more likely to be the victims of violence than to be violent themselves.

"Exposure to a diet of violent television" as a child can also result in aggressive behavior in the late teen years, according to the research. In one major study, the amount of televised violence seen by a large group of third-graders was observed and recorded. Ten years later, the same individuals were rated as to aggressive behavior. Those who had seen the most on-screen violence as children grew up to become the most aggressive young adults, the research clearly showed.

"An eight-year-old boy cannot very effectively be aggressive in adult fashion, but if that sort of behavior fascinates him, he may well enjoy watching it on television," suggests the report. "Some years later, as he matures physically and acquires various social and combative skills, he should find more situations in which to act out his predisposition to adult forms of aggression." At the same time, this eighteen-year-old may not spend much time seeing TV any more, explains the report. He has already "become more or less habituated to the stock clichés of television aggressiveness."

Does watching violence on television just before bedtime give a youngster bad dreams?

About 40 percent of first-grade boys and girls in one study told researchers they could remember having dreams about incidents they'd seen on TV. Thirty percent of mothers reported their children had trouble getting to sleep at night after seeing exciting television shows; some were convinced that TV triggered nightmares in their youngsters.

But when the researchers screened violent and nonviolent clips for children in their laboratories, and later awakened the sleeping youngsters to question them about their dreams, little evidence of the influence of TV turned up.

Sleep disturbances were traced to violence on TV in a much

clearer fashion in a report given at an annual meeting of the American Academy of Pediatrics by two Air Force physicians. Captain Richard M. Narkewicz and Captain Stanley N. Graven linked excessive fatigue, poor appetite, headaches, sleep problems and abdominal pains with prolonged and excessive watching of TV.

The pediatricians indicted television after studying thirty youngsters, age three to eleven, who were brought to them with a variety of symptoms including chronic fatigue, nervousness, vague stomach pains, vomiting, lack of appetite and disturbances of sleep. No cause could be found in repeated physical exams, lab tests and X-ray studies. And the children's families were all stable, with no unusual stresses or economic problems.

But all the youngsters were avid TV viewers, the doctors finally discovered. They averaged three to six hours before a television set every weekday and six to ten hours daily on weekends. TV filled them with anxiety and tension. This interfered with sleep, leaving them too tired for outside play and less able to face emotional stress the next day. So they spent more time watching television, growing more anxious and sleeping less well because they were too tired to do anything else.

In several cases, a mild illness triggered the cycle of excessive TV. For other youngsters it started with stress at school, such as a new teacher or a new class, or the departure of a close friend.

Even cartoons caused symptoms in small-fry, particularly the three- to five-year-olds, the physicians observed. Youngsters were also troubled by many programs classified as family entertainment, but filled with emotional conflict.

To help these addicted youngsters, the two doctors prescribed stopping all TV. "Limited or selected viewing is in itself a source of conflict because it requires decisions as to what can or what cannot be viewed," they said. Some children also were given sedatives or tranquilizers for a few days. Active play after school was recommended.

Dramatic improvement resulted within three to ten days in all cases. All symptoms were gone within three to six weeks. Checking on the youngsters months later, however, it was found that only nine remained free of symptoms, and all of these were restricted to less than two hours of TV daily. Even with restricted TV, four children had mild symptoms, usually related to what they watched. Of the thirteen youngsters permitted unrestricted TV, eleven had an increase in symptoms.

Concluded the physicians: The children were fine as long as TV was restricted. But it was surprising, in view of this fact, that so few parents were able to control the television, probably because of their own viewing habits.

There is no doubt that television is a highly effective way to sell children almost everything the medium chooses to sell. From the impact of *Sesame Street* to the TV networks' sales pitches to advertisers, evidence is overwhelming that children are enormously affected and their behavior changed—in ways ranging from learning the alphabet at age three to demanding brand-name products—by what they see on television. Most major advertisers bet a big part of their advertising budgets on the effectiveness of TV in altering the behavior of viewers.

Is television hurting your child? These questions will help you answer on an individual basis:

1. Does your child have a fairly good idea of what is fact and what is fantasy on television? Most preschoolers have difficulty separating reality from make-believe in their own lives, let alone appreciating the distinction between the man who dies on the 6 P.M. newscast and the one who dies at 6:30 in a drama and who will live to spy and die again next week on another channel.

2. Are his concepts about the world considerably or undesirably distorted by what he sees on TV? Small children constantly are trying to make sense out of the world around

them by forming tentative concepts which they test against reality and then discard or revise with new evidence. A preschooler who thinks murder is a common kind of social interaction or that mouthwash is the key to happiness will have considerable relearning to do.

3. What does your child's televiewing cost him in time not spent reading or in active outdoor play or creative explorations or with friends or in family conversations?

4. Does your youngster frequently have nightmares that seem to be related to what he has been watching on television?

5. Is he beginning to build an effective sales resistance against commercials on TV?

If you're not satisfied with your answers to these questions, then what?

The report to the Surgeon General had little to offer concerned parents. "We are able to say that, beyond the junior high level, both violence viewing and aggressive behavior are apt to decline in frequency," notes the report. "Time and maturation are on the side of the parent, but this is probably of little comfort to the parent whose child appears in imminent danger of getting into trouble."

It may help for parents to set a good example, to lessen the amount of televised violence they watch, the report indicates. How much TV violence children see and how aggressively they behave are related to how much television their parents, especially their mothers, view, according to the study.

How aggressively a mother acts—by fighting, yelling or using physical punishment, for example—is also linked to aggressive behavior and excessive watching of televised violence, the report shows.

Attempts by parents to control what children see on TV don't seem to be effective, the researchers conclude. "In fact, arbitrary control might serve to increase the child's frustration and make aggressive behavior more likely."

Trying to reduce a youngster's aggressive behavior by cutting down on the violent TV he sees is really too indirect a method of solving the problem, says the report to the Surgeon General. It's much more effective to deal directly with the child's behavior, teaching him not to fight with other children, not to use force or threats to get what he wants, not to imitate the behavior he sees on television.

It also helps not to use physical punishment on children and not to discipline them by taking away privileges or grounding them. The report found that children who are punished in these ways are likely to watch TV excessively and to behave aggressively.

This "should not be mistaken for advocating permissiveness," cautions the report. Youngsters who are treated permissively turn out to be "about average in aggressive behavior and well above average in attitudes approving aggression," according to researchers.

The bulky Government study acknowledges how inadequate its few suggestions are for coping with the vast and pervasive influence of television in the lives of children today.

After two years of research, 2,499 pages of data and large expenditure of Government funds, the report concludes, "The concerned parent at the present time has few alternatives to making his own assumptions about the effects of television and to follow advice based on thin evidence and speculation."

But parents can't give up as easily as the Government report-writers. There are several steps fathers and mothers can take which have been found effective. For example:

· You can make sure your child has plenty of interesting activities, available, challenging playthings, reading materials, art supplies, playmates, a wealth of satisfying things to do so he won't be so likely to turn to television out of boredom for hours every day.

· You can set an example of not watching television for long hours yourself or making an obvious habit of turning on the set whenever you have nothing urgent to do.

· You can teach your child to turn on the television for one particular program of special interest, then to turn it off and do something else when the show is finished, rather than indiscriminately watching program after program. And you can do the same thing yourself.

· You can initiate a rich family life together, full of shared fun and conversation, as another way to make your child's real life more interesting than the shadows he sees on television.

· You can watch TV with your youngster, so you can talk over programs with him and help him understand and evaluate what he sees.

· You can help your child learn how to identify what's real and what's make-believe on the screen. One mother, for example, took time to devise a "TV producer" game with her six-year-old son, in which they wrote and read newscasts about what was happening in their neighborhood and invented Western dramas to stage in front of a box "camera" mounted on old doll-carriage wheels. Both father and mother made it a point to tell the boy at the beginning of every TV show he watched whether it was "real" or "made-up."

· You can use television commercials to help your child develop into a discriminating consumer. Many families make it a rule never to buy anything advertised on television without the most careful scrutiny of the product in person. You can also make a game of helping your offspring detect flaws, omissions, exaggerations and suspicious claims in TV advertising.

Teaching your child to use television wisely is a time-consuming project. But given the amount of time television will undoubtedly take of his life, you really have no choice but to help him use it to the best advantage.

32. How to Make a Good Move with Children

Jim is an organization man's child. Amy is an army brat. Peter's dad has been offered a great new opportunity on the coast. Sally's parents have finally found a house in a suburb they can afford.

Millions of youngsters like Jim, Amy, Peter and Sally—one child in five each year—faces the difficulties of being achingly, anxiously, acutely new in a neighborhood and in a school. For moving has become almost an inevitable part of growing up American. And helping a child adjust to, cope with, learn from and enjoy moving has become almost as essential a part of parental expertise as readying a youngster for kindergarten or nursing him through chicken pox.

Of the youngsters who move cross-county or cross-country annually, about three in ten will enjoy the move, studies show. A similar proportion will have minor difficulties getting settled. About three more in ten will have some problems connected with the move—and one will have serious difficulty in becoming adjusted to his new surroundings.

Yet there is much parents can do to reduce the emotional

227

strains on a child and make him feel less like a pawn in moves dictated by impersonal corporations and military contingencies. Here are suggestions garnered from several conferences held by psychologists and related specialists on the subject— and from parents for whom biennial moving is a way of life.

It's a good idea to begin by telling yourself privately, until you believe it, that the move will be an exciting adventure and a great new experience. (Never mind the new living-room drapes you just finished or the play-reading group you were just asked to join.) Then tell your small-fry enthusiastically about the move and include him, from then on, in the when, why and where of the shift so he'll feel a part of the planning, too. You owe it to your child to make sure he hears about any forthcoming changes in his life directly from you—not from overhearing a phone conversation or unexpectedly seeing a "For Sale" sign in your yard.

When a family move is caused by an unhappy reason, such as divorce or economic difficulties, a child usually has much more trouble adjusting to a new home and school than other young movers do, research shows. In these cases, parents need to recognize that their offspring is more vulnerable and must try particularly hard to be encouraging.

Because a parent's attitude is so contagious, it helps to emphasize all the adventurous, exciting experiences your new community can offer, its geographical blessings and special events, and the advantages to your family in making the transition. You can talk about the nearest big league baseball team or ski area or beaches or weekend fun. You can make plans seem real in every way possible—with maps, brochures, Chamber of Commerce handouts, descriptions from Daddy-who-has-been-there. As soon as you know where you'll be living, you can make paper floor plans and scale cutouts of furniture so your youngster can practice arranging his own room.

You can sympathetically acknowledge the inevitable feelings

of loss, anxiety, tension and complaints your small-fry voices about moving away from his old friends, school and place in society. Then you can gently counter with plans for new fun and new experiences to come.

No matter how busy they are with the logistics of moving, it's important that both father and mother spend as much time with a youngster as possible until he's serenely settled in his new home. Studies show that the length of time a child is separated from one or both of his parents during the move affects how easily and happily he adjusts to the transition.

If your child finds it difficult to leave a particular pal, you can sometimes make a realistic plan to help the youngsters keep in touch, at least for a while—perhaps a summer-vacation visit or matched boxes of stationery for correspondence or the promise of a long-distance call on a special occasion.

One much-moved mother asks some of her youngster's pals to draw pictures for him to display on the walls of his new room, as evidence of continuing friendship. An understanding teacher has each pupil in her class write a letter, a collection of jokes or a paper-pencil game to give the departing classmate, to be read en route to the new home and cherished afterward.

The more of a child's familiar possessions that can make the move, the easier the switch for the youngster. Nothing that belongs to a child should be dismissed lightly even if it means two extra packing crates and a $29.56 freight charge. Familiar objects make it much easier for a youngster to cope with new surroundings, and he needs more bridges to the past than many parents realize.

If you possibly can, keep all the family pets, even if it means traveling cross-country with an ant farm on your lap. If you can't figure out how to manage the white rat or the goldfish in transit, help your youngster to find a suitable home for them. If your child's best friends can't give them shelter, cross your fingers and ask the teacher if they can be donated to the classroom. Use the local animal shelter for pets only if your youngster does not know what happens to unwanted animals and if he can be assured his pets will be given a good home.

On the day you actually move, it helps to spend as much time as possible with your offspring, even if it means letting the movers manage without your constant direction. A baby needs to be kept as closely as possible on his usual feeding-sleeping schedule. A toddler should have constant protection from unexpected hazards. And older children benefit enormously from the reassurance of your interest and attention in all the confusion.

A baby, toddler or preschooler will need toys to play with, even on moving day. And you'll have to pack playthings, security blanket, snacks, changes of clothing and clean-up supplies in your car for use en route to your new home, no matter what it does to your image as incoming neighbors. A child who is three or older should have some choice about the possessions he totes with him in person during a move. You can give him a small suitcase or box and let him decide what to put into it, subject to your veto only if it will break, spill or spoil.

Once the movers have departed and you've all had something to eat and a tour of your new premises, it's good strategy to start a fascinating outdoor project with your progeny: building a fort or snowman, or setting up a tire swing or playing baseball. This quickly attracts neighborhood small-fry of appropriate ages, explains a much-transferred mother, and once your youngsters are involved with other children, you'll have time to start hanging curtains.

The more a family moves, the more parents should emphasize the rituals and family celebrations that give their offspring emotional security. Celebrations to mark special achievement by individual family members, holiday traditions, shared experiences, family vacations, mealtime conversations, seasonal events, family visiting, anniversaries, milestones in children's lives and shared reminiscences all play an important part in giving children inner security they can carry with them, psychologists suggest. These symbols, rituals and memories can provide much-moved children with the same kind of emotional roots and sense of family solidarity that previous generations found in long-time living in the same house in an unchanging neighborhood.

HOW TO HELP A YOUNGSTER MOVE INTO A NEW SCHOOL

"Do you think the boys will all gang up on me and fight?"

"What if they are all studying something I haven't had and I don't know any of the answers?"

"What if everybody teases me and nobody likes me?"

It's a stomach-churning, knee-shaking, panicky feeling to be the "new kid" in school after a move to a new home in a new community. How long it takes to get over it depends on the innate temperament of the youngster, his experiences in meeting new situations and the care with which you prepare for the shift.

Outgoing, easygoing youngsters like Mark usually adjust to a new school without much difficulty—even with a sense of adventure. But shy types like Maggie who always have been slow to warm up to new situations may not feel secure and at ease in a new school for weeks. A few youngsters, particularly those who were having difficulties in school before the move, may encounter prolonged problems.

Girls tend to find moving more difficult in many ways than do boys, psychologists report. They are more preoccupied with being accepted, worry more about being rejected, feel badly treated more often, are more concerned about their personal appearance when they enter a new school, and their grades are more likely to decline in a new classroom. The easy camaraderie of sports makes it somewhat easier for boys to become accepted by new classmates, especially if they are relatively good athletes.

Strategies for helping a child succeed in a new school situation lie basically in strengthening the youngster's feelings of self-confidence and worth. Your role is to encourage and support but to stay firmly in the background.

It helps if you encourage your offspring to voice his fears about starting the new school and talk over ways to handle possible problems. You can ask him to analyze why certain children he knows are well liked (Are they friendly, good at sports, enthusiastic about others' ideas?) and why some youngsters aren't popular (the bullies, braggarts, goody-goodies, cheaters).

Then you can point out his assets. Perhaps he's a good center fielder, was president of his class one month, did a good job of caring for.the class goldfish at the teacher's request, is always invited to parties. You can reassure him that his new teacher and new classmates will see all of these same assets as soon as they have had a chance to know him.

You can also help him, gently, to understand that all newcomers are likely to be teased and that such initiation rites last only a short time if the youngster takes it gracefully and good-naturedly.

Just talking about the feelings your child will probably have the first days at school may help him to cope with them. For example, you can explain that he can expect to feel a bit lost and confused about his academic work for a while until he gets used to a new teacher and new texts. You can add, "These feelings are what everyone experiences in a strange situation. If you make a silly mistake or feel left out on the playground, don't think you're stupid or that no one likes you. Just say to yourself, 'This is what it's like to be new and this feeling will go away very soon.'"

Before you actually enroll your new transferee in his new

school, it pays to do some behind-the-scenes checking to make sure he gets off in the same kind of clothes as his classmates—even if you have to observe unobtrusively from the playground during recess to find out. He shouldn't show up the first day with a Mickey Mouse lunchbox if his new classmates all brown-bag it, or wear neatly pressed slacks if they are all blue-jeaned.

"I take my youngster to a new school for the first time about five minutes after the pupils have left in the afternoon," one mother who is the veteran of three executive transfers explains. "I phone ahead for an appointment with the new teacher and we talk to her.

"Then my daughter and I tour the school building and I help her find the office, the drinking fountain, the girls' room, locker, nurse's office, telephone. The next day she can start off knowing where she is going—without her mother tagging along."

At your first meeting with the teacher, it's a good idea to arrange for a brief conference with her and your child about ten days hence, explaining that your child will probably find there are a few areas in which he needs help to catch up with his new class and that the conference will be a good opportunity to discuss these points. You can say that you'll gladly work with your child to make up lessons if the transfer has put him behind or if he must switch from one reading method to another.

This helps your youngster think objectively and positively about his schoolwork instead of panicking when he discovers that his new classmates put /'s instead of –'s between syllables or that his new third grade is already multiplying by eights when his old one was only up to sixes. This technique also shows your child that problems are something to be talked about and solved actively and objectively, rather than worried about in aching solitude.

Occasionally, a few sessions with a private tutor make it

easier for a confused transfer student to catch up with phonics or new math or French when he's far behind his new class. Surveys show that many teachers consider the newly transferred child to be a burden who will require extra help and time to learn class routines other pupils already know, and will also require extra after-class help to catch up academically. Anything you can do to ease your child into his new class without making his teacher much extra work will make his adjustment much smoother and quicker.

Being left out socially often upsets a new student more than being behind academically. If you can help your offspring gain a respectable skill in whatever play activity is most popular in your new community, social acceptance usually follows quickly. And this will give your child enough self-confidence to recover from the rest of the transfer trauma.

Barbara, for example, had a giggly group of jacks-playing friends in her Phoenix school. But she was spending school recesses moping by the fence when her family moved to a Chicago suburb—until her observant mother gave her a quick crash course in how to jump rope.

Children often develop their own strategies for making friends, and it's a good idea to encourage them—within reason. One ten-year-old told his mother the best way to avoid having to eat alone at his new school was to pack along extra potato chips in his lunch sack for trading. He considered himself socially accepted the day he parlayed them into two cupcakes, a cookie and an extra carton of milk.

With this kind of emotional support, most youngsters won't experience more than temporary tensions and anxieties about being "the new kid in school." As you can point out, learning how to cope with this kind of new situation well may be one of the most valuable lessons of a childhood, for it will give your youngster skill and confidence for all the other times ahead when he will be "new."

33. How to Teach Your Child

About Strangers

Teaching a child to be wary of strangers is an unhappy necessity in this age, regardless of how pleasant the community in which you live or the average income level of your neighborhood. Hopefully you can impress your youngster with your warnings about strangers without making him leery of every new person he meets, or frightening him unduly. These suggestions should help:

Before the age of three or four, a child isn't old enough to understand and heed the usual don't-talk-to-strangers warnings. He needs constant protection and supervision from you or another reliable adult. You should not leave him alone in the car at a shopping center or permit him to go alone outside your yard (where you should keep a watchful eye on his activities when you are not outdoors with him).

But when your child is old enough to be away from home without you—even as far as the next corner—you must make sure you've armed him against danger from the kind of adults who might possibly harm him. Because you can't always be with him as he grows old enough to walk to school by himself, or to go down the block to a playmate's house alone, you must teach him to protect himself, without scaring him into distrusting all adults he doesn't know or confusing him about sex.

You must teach your child that he is not to talk to any stranger. He is not to go anywhere with anyone he does not know for any reason, or even get close enough to a stranger's car to be pulled in. One gentle girl was lured to death by the request that she "come cheer up my sick little daughter who is just your age."

You must warn your youngster never to trust the stranger who says, "Your parents told me to get you" and promise never to send for him in such a way. He is not to take candy or a toy or anything else from a stranger. He must not let a stranger touch him or handle him.

You should make sure your child understands that he is to report to you any adult who tries to join in children's games, who hangs around the park where he plays, who tries to touch him in a movie theater or follows him toward home. If he is old enough to be left at home by himself on occasion, he must be instructed never to let in anyone he doesn't know.

Telling your child about avoiding strangers is less frightening if you make it a part of a long-range safety education program between the ages of four and five. You do need to include a "why" in your warnings. One girl, for example, assumed her mother was just snobbish and decided to speak to every stranger she encountered when she was by herself.

You can explain along these lines: "Once in a great while, a person's brain may get sick or be injured and he may do something that hurts a child. You can't tell this by looking at him. That's why you must make it a rule not to talk with anyone you don't know and especially you must not go with a stranger anywhere or take anything he offers you, like candy or toys."

You have never seen such a person, you can probably assure your child. You doubt that he ever will. But it is part of his safety training to know what to do. You can remind him that his school holds fire drills, although his school has never had a fire and probably never will. And when he's old enough to be a Boy Scout, you can point out that he will learn how to give artificial respiration in the unlikely event he ever sees anyone drowning.

A child who has been taught to speak in a friendly way to adults when you are along and who is outgoing by nature may feel uncomfortable about not replying to an adult who starts a conversation with him when he's alone. He may be further confused if he sees you answer a stranger who makes a casual comment to you in an elevator or store.

The best all-purpose solution is to teach your youngster something positive to say and do, rather than the blanket "Don't talk." Instruct him to reply to any stranger who talks to him or asks him to do anything, "I'll go and get (or ask) my mother (or teacher, if she's closer)." Then he must go quickly and do precisely that. This gives the youngster something reasonably polite to say, but it will also remove him from real danger quickly and get an adult on the scene in a hurry.

You should word your warning so it includes not only men but also women and teen-agers. And tell your youngster that he is to tell you immediately if anyone—even a relative or adult he does know—tries to undress him or play with any part of his body. A surprisingly large percentage of molested children are the prey of adults they know.

If you incorporate these teachings into an overall plan of safety education, your child should not be unduly upset. You may be wise to renew your cautions each time your child is preparing for another big step toward independence—when he begins to walk to school on his own, when he is first permitted to go to a shopping center alone or attend a movie without an adult. You may also want to discuss the subject with him should he read of a case of molestation or kidnapping in the newspaper or hear about such a tragedy on television.

34. Child-Pet Problems

When you give your child a pet, you don't just add a dog or cat or gerbil to your household; you change the emotional dynamics and psychological undercurrents of your family. You may do your youngster great emotional good—but you also must be wary of several possible pitfalls.

So says Dr. Boris Levinson, professor emeritus of psychology at Yeshiva University and an expert on people-pet relationships.

"A pet is too important and plays too great a role in the child's personality development for its choice to be left to mere chance," Dr. Levinson emphasizes. His answers to common parental questions may save you hours of cleaning up after a problem pet or fretting about what to do with an unwanted animal.

What kind of pet is best for a child?

Whatever the youngster has been asking for—provided it doesn't cause more inconvenience than you can tolerate, says Dr. Levinson. Before you get any pet, work through your own feelings about animals, decide how much time you can spare for pet care and discuss the choice thoroughly in a family conference, he advises.

If you can't manage the kind of pet your youngster wants, sit down and reason out with him what kind of animal would fit into your family.

A pet a child can take outdoors and play with around other youngsters has the most value, explains Dr. Levinson. An animal that is soft and cuddly, responds to a youngster's actions and shows its love and loyalty gives its owner more satisfaction than one that doesn't. Dogs are the first choice of both boys and girls, but girls rank cats higher than do boys as second choice.

What should you do if your youngster fails to care for his pet as he promised? Remind him constantly? Get rid of the pet? Do the work yourself?

It's best to sidestep this dilemma completely, according to Dr. Levinson. A parent should realize that caring for an animal is a learned skill acquired gradually by children, with considerable backsliding. If you praise your youngster enthusiastically when he does help care for his pet but don't rush turning over total responsibility to him until you are sure he will do it, you avoid this problem.

What is the best way to handle the death of a pet?

Realize that your youngster will have to go through the work of mourning and learn the agony of losing something he loves.

"If you don't work through a bereavement, you can't love anyone else again," Dr. Levinson points out. Like a vaccination, the loss of a pet can immunize a child against overwhelming emotional shock at the death of a family member.

Permitting a child to hold a burial service for a dead pet helps in the work of mourning. "Let him mourn for a week or two and then replace the pet," Dr. Levinson advises. "If you give him a new pet right away he may get the idea that life has little value and that he could also be replaced just as quickly."

What if a child feels he has contributed to the death of his pet by carelessness?

Discuss it with him, saying, for example, "You didn't know

your dog would run into the street just when the car was coming." Talk about other families in which pets have had accidents. And if your child continues to have guilt feelings, get psychological help, for such emotions can be repressed for years, only to cause depression later in life, Dr. Levinson notes.

Will it be harmful to a child to have an old pet put to sleep?

Parents should avoid this move, cautions Dr. Levinson. Instead, they should use the pet's old age to teach their youngster how valuable life itself really is.

When a youngster brings home a stray animal you can't keep, what should you do?

First, praise the youngster for his goodness in caring about the animal, advises Dr. Levinson. Then discuss with him what kind of plan you can make together to find a home for the animal. "This helps the child learn that his parents aren't arbitrary and that his own innate feelings of caring are good."

35. How Not to Waste a Wait

The mother waiting in a doctor's reception room to have her glasses checked was trying to read a magazine. But her three-year-old daughter was standing beside her, fussing at her, patting her, talking to her, wanting to be read to, spoken to, paid attention to or hugged.

Annoyed, the mother snapped, "Stop bothering me!" The three-year-old was quiet for about twenty seconds. Then she started fussing again.

"Can't you be good and be still?" commanded the mother more sternly. The little girl started to cry.

"If you don't stop that we won't take you with us on vacation next week," threatened the mother. The child continued to cry. The mother spanked her. The little girl cried harder. The mother yanked her up by one arm and slammed her down hard in a chair next to her five-year-old sister, who was intently picking a scab on her knee that was beginning to bleed.

"Keep her quiet," the mother ordered the five-year-old. She kept right on teasing the scab.

The three-year-old cried for about sixty seconds. Then she slid defiantly down to the floor and sucked her thumb, sobbing sporadically. Two minutes later she was fidgeting beside her mother again, pulling at her dress and fussing.

At this point, the receptionist came over to take the mother into the doctor's office. The mother gathered up the three-year-old and curtly ordered the five-year-old to "sit still and be good."

"I don't want to stay here by myself," said the five-year-old defiantly, jumping up and clutching her mother's dress. The mother gave her as hard a spank as she could manage with her free hand, glanced at the waiting receptionist with a poor-martyred-me expression, and struggled into the doctor's office with the five-year-old tagging right behind.

With minor variations, this scene is played a million times a day—in a shoe store waiting for a salesperson, in a restaurant waiting for a waitress, in a barber shop, beauty salon, dentist's office—everywhere a parent and a small child spend enforced time together in public with nothing to do.

Usually, such common scenes are dismissed with the explanation that this is how threes and fives behave. Or with the comment that the mother should have disciplined her children more effectively. Or with the sugary cliché that the mother really should enjoy her children now because some day they'll be grown up and gone.

But recent research on the mental development of children makes clear that the reason why young children are so fidgety, so easily bored, so fussy, in these sit-still-be-quiet-and-wait situations is their innate need for great amounts of appropriate sensory stimulation.

Young children just can't sit still without something to do for more than a few minutes, any more than they can go hungry very long without fussing. They have an inborn drive to touch, to move, to manipulate, to experiment, to listen, to see, to explore, to learn, that psychologists now say is just as basic and urgent as other primary drives.

So a parent's most effective strategy is to use this innate drive to shape a child's behavior—not to try to thwart it or to ignore it.

It's not difficult to do, with a bit of advanced planning. The mother might have anticipated the wait and brought along a small drawing pad and colored pencils. Or a magic slate. Or pipe cleaners to make dolls or sticky-backed paper strips for free-form constructions. Or a suitable pocket puzzle.

The mother could have brought a book to read to her daughters. Or dropped a dozen little familiar toys into a paper bag and let her children put a hand in the bag and try to identify each one sight unseen before pulling it out. The three could have played quiet word games or discussed the sound of letters of the alphabet or talked about how doctors work or what would happen during their vacation.

With a little advanced preparation, a child of five, or even younger, can be encouraged to stay uncomplainingly in a waiting room while a mother sees the doctor. The strategy is to tell the youngster ahead of time what to expect, even to play-acting it out; to acknowledge that she'll feel fidgety and ask her to bring along books or small toys she thinks will keep her busy and quiet; then to praise her lavishly and lovingly for her cooperation.

A mother who thinks of these inevitable waits as tiny oases in time in which to enjoy her children and delight in finding stimuli that match their intense need for mental nourishment earns a fourfold blessing. Her children are easier to manage because they aren't so bored and frustrated. She isn't embarrassed by their behavior (or hers) in public. She creates new bonds of shared pleasures. And she helps enrich their fast-growing minds.

It doesn't work all the time. Nothing does with children. But it's a cinch the mother wouldn't have got any reading done anyway.

36. TEASING

"My daughter is almost four—obedient, affectionate, bright —and timid," worries a mother. "I know children have to learn to get along with each other and they fight and tease in the process. But my daughter is very sensitive and cries over the least thing. If the other youngsters take her toy, don't want to play with her or tease her, she cries. The children know this and pick on her even more.

"I don't know the right thing to do any more. Every day I have a different strategy. I have tried punishing her by taking her in when she cries. I have tried talking to the other children. It doesn't help. What can I do? I want her not to take her little friends so seriously. Not once has any of them cried over her. They don't care if she stays or goes. This hurts me very much. I am so upset over this situation I feel like I'm getting a nervous condition."

Sometimes right from birth a baby seems to be extra sensitive and less outgoing than most others. This tends to make his mother extra protective, which in turn usually makes the youngster feel he is so defenseless and so helpless he isn't safe without a parent to intervene.

Every child gets teased or picked on or left out or rebuffed

244

by others occasionally. The friendly, self-confident youngster takes these slights casually, forgets them quickly, and keeps on expecting the world to be a friendly, accepting place. But the timid, shy youngster almost seems to invite teasing or meanness by his distrustful attitude. He expects to be picked on and he usually is. Like an adult injustice-collector, he broods about these rebuffs and grows more unfriendly and unsure of himself.

Most children tease at one time or another—and four-year-olds are among the worst. Most neighborhoods have at least one bully. Teasers and bullies possess an uncanny knack for feeling out the child most vulnerable to their tactics. You can't change the other children. You'll only make life more difficult for your daughter if you fly to her defense continually by scolding the others.

Your best strategy—and it takes long-term patience—is to strengthen your daughter so she'll be less vulnerable. You can work on building her self-confidence and her image of herself as a likable person. You can arrange her life so she'll meet with many small successes. You can love her warmly and let her know it. You can praise her enthusiastically even for small achievements. You can be casual and easygoing when she is teased. And you can show her by your quiet confidence that her world is friendly and she is competent to handle it.

Children take their cues on how to react to most situations from their parents. If you are worried and upset about what happens to her when she's out playing, your child will know it and feel her position is even worse because an adult is so concerned about it.

You can teach your child at least one skill which is admired by neighborhood children (no matter how trivial it seems to you). You can see that she's dressed like the other youngsters and isn't held to more adult standards of grooming and behavior than her playmates.

You can encourage your daughter to see her relationships with others as normal give-and-take, not in terms of injustices and slights. You can avoid getting upset yourself about what seem like rebuffs; this only makes her feel she is so inadequate and the other children so unfriendly that she'll find it even more difficult to venture into social relationships.

If your daughter's playmates are as young as she is, it's expecting too much for them to play together fairly and happily all the time. If they are older than she, you need to find friends nearer her age who won't consider her a baby.

Instead of turning your girl loose to cope with a blockful of youngsters, you can arrange social experiences where you're sure she will succeed on her own. You can invite just one friendly little girl to your house for lunch or for a small excursion to the playground where you can be inconspicuous, yet present. (Even the least popular child is liked by a few youngsters, a study of popularity among children made at the University of Toronto shows.) Each successful occasion will build up your daughter's confidence in herself.

When your child is with a group that is getting unruly, you can be ready to step in—in a friendly, casual way—to suggest a change of activities (such as cookies and milk all around). But you shouldn't be scolding or defensive of your daughter while you're doing it.

Sometimes a father can help. A dad who starts a fascinating activity in the yard (building a giant snow fort, constructing a tree house, hanging up a tire swing) with your child can often be a magnet to draw playmates. But any such efforts need to be low key and casual.

If possible, it will help to find a nursery school where your daughter can have a happy, social experience and opportunity to be with other children her age in a setting where teasing should be at a minimum and youngsters are encouraged to play together in friendly ways.

Popular children have two chief characteristics, according to the University of Toronto study: They have lots of energy and they use it for purposes approved by their peers. It might help to evaluate the amount of energy your child has available for playing. She might need more rest, or a medical checkup. Or she may simply be using up too much energy worrying. It's one more way you may be able to help her.

37. TUNING PARENTS OUT

It is late afternoon on a sweltering, sticky, late-summer afternoon at the airport. A father and mother, caught in the push of deplaning crowds, stop for a minute to reorganize their grip on luggage and children, a boy about five and a girl, four.

Suddenly the mother's voice shoots cold and sharp at the little girl, "You're the one I'd really like to lose. Your brother, he's all right. But you I can get along without."

In the toy section of a dime store, a mother shrills at a seven-year-old, "I'm buying this game for your sister, and if you ever touch it, you're really going to get it."

In the supermarket, a father promises angrily, "Just wait until we get home. I'm going to spank you so hard you'll never forget it."

Listen to parents talking to small children in public places and it's obvious where the communications gap between the generations begins. What can a youngster say when his mother announces in public she would like to lose him or intends to spank him or knows he's hopelessly stupid? He has two choices: to close his mind to what his mother is saying or to take her literally and gradually turn into a clinging, dependent,

248

insecure individual with a self-image that discourages him from even trying.

Most small-fry are resilient enough to tune their parents out, to convince themselves by indifference that they didn't really hear the cold words, the sharp tone, the threat.

But the more a child tunes out, the louder the parent turns up the volume, and the more adept the youngster becomes at not hearing or believing. The wider this communications gap becomes, the harder it is to bridge afterward.

In public places, at least, parents say "Shut up" to their children far more than they say "I love you." They shake and yank and hiss "You're really going to get it when you get home" far more than they smile and encourage and say, "Thank you for helping me with the shopping; now let's get an ice-cream cone."

Of course children are often annoying, pesty, irritating, demanding, fussy and in the way. Of course parents get exhausted, weary, exasperated, overworked, impatient and harassed. But talk should be used to make matters better, not worse.

There are practical as well as humane reasons why parents should talk to their children with as much courtesy, respect and interest as they show to their adult friends. It simply gets better results.

Parents who liberally sprinkle their talk to children with praise and love are listened to, not ignored. Parents who do not make empty threats are believed and trusted. Parents who don't shout at youngsters are seldom shouted at, and rarely hear their offspring bullying younger children. And parents who don't call their children "stupid" or predict "You'll never amount to anything" or "You'll never get into a good college the way you're going" seldom have to wonder why their children don't try.

38. Teaching a Child to Tell the Truth

"My four-year-old granddaughter lies and makes up the wildest stories," complained a grandmother. "Sometimes she'll tell her mother at least six different stories about the same incident. She is a bright girl and seems eager to learn. Is the fibbing something to be concerned about in one her age?"

Most four-year-olds sometimes have difficulty telling the difference between what's real and what's pretend, between wishful thinking and fact. They often enjoy telling imaginary stories so much they almost begin to believe in their reality themselves. Many four-year-olds have make-believe friends and build up such elaborate and long-lasting fantasies about them that their parents may be halfway convinced, too.

None of this should be considered lying.

Besides the great fun of creating stories, there's another reason four-year-olds seem to fib. Preschoolers are trying to make sense out of the complex world around them by formulating concepts that explain what they observe. They constantly revise these concepts as they discover new evidence, or are given new information, or are able to understand accurate explanations.

Tommy, for example, told his mother that Mr. Jones, next door, was going to have a baby. When his mother questioned his announcement, Tommy said defiantly that he had heard Mr. Jones say he was going to the hospital and when Jill's mother and Ron's mother went to the hospital, they came back with babies. That's what hospitals are for, said Tommy, to give away babies.

This type of concept formation can sometimes explain why a child seems to lie in explaining to his parents why he lost his new sweater or why there are muddy footprints on the floor.

A parent should help a child learn to tell the truth, of course, even before he is four years old—and should help him understand clearly the difference between fact and make-believe. For example, you can make a point of labeling every story you read to your moppet as real or pretend. You can point out which television programs he watches are make-believe and which picture something that actually happened.

You can encourage your child to report accurately to his father or grandmother about experiences you have shared. And, on occasion, you can join him in a deliberate game of making up stories for fun, being careful to label the fantasy as fiction. You can also help him satisfy his boundless curiosity about the world around him by explaining simple, scientific facts.

Sometimes a small child does not tell the truth because he is too severely punished for minor misdeeds and actions other parents would consider normally childish or harmless accidents and merely would correct in a friendly manner. Usually, if your child has disobeyed you, there's no point in asking him, "Did you?" and tempting him to lie. It's better just to take appropriate action and explain to him again what he has done amiss.

Occasionally a child is careless about truth because he has been taught to be—unthinkingly—by his parents. "A small child almost always tells the truth, as he sees it, until he is taught otherwise," says a family counselor. "We sometimes call it being rude."

A father who instructs his four-year-old to tell a persistent salesman he isn't home, or a mother who pays a compliment to a guest and then says just the opposite after she has gone, should not be surprised when their child bends the truth to his convenience, too. Neither should the parent who shows the child by example that it's all right to exceed the speed limit if you don't get caught. Other lessons in lying are taught by parents who give easy, inaccurate answers to a child's searching questions, such as explaining death as "going to sleep." Or by parents who pretend to know more about a topic than they do.

Other ways you can help your child learn to tell the truth include these:

· You can point out to him that you would like to trust him and believe him, but that you can't if you discover he is violating this trust. And you can explain to him the value of mutual trust and confidence.

· You can avoid giving him the opportunity to lie unnecessarily. When you are sure your youngster has done something for which he must be corrected, simply correct him without demanding that he confess.

· You can be sure you understand and make allowances for extenuating circumstances before you punish or scold. You should give your child time to explain his actions fully and be sure you judge fairly, especially if punishment is involved.

· You can avoid severe punishments. Many children lie because of fear. And you can make the consequences of lying more severe than the penalty for the action the lie is intended to avoid.

· You can also gradually teach your youngster appropriate ways to handle his goofs and accidents, so he'll have something better to do when he's in trouble than to lie about it.

39. How to Help a Child Handle His Goofs

The neighbors were out of town when the batter hit a long fly ball into left field—and against the kitchen window. The glass shattered. The baseball team scattered. Not one of the eight boys said a word to his parents. But during the long week until the neighbors returned, they whispered together fearfully about what would befall them when the accident was discovered.

What happened? Nothing much. The neighbors cleaned up the glass and mopped up the rain that had soaked, fortunately, only the tiled kitchen floor. Then they called the team together.

"We don't care about the window," the man said to the boys. "We told you long ago we'd rather have you play here than in the street, that we'd rather take a chance on losing a window than losing a child. But why didn't you tell someone about it, so it could have been boarded up?"

Children need to be taught to handle their mistakes, the damage they cause accidentally to other people and others' property. It's good manners. It's simple justice. And it helps prevent children from developing deep-seated feelings of guilt which, psychologists say, are more common than most parents realize.

Youngsters also need help to overcome a natural tendency to run away from unpleasantness and to deny responsibility for what has happened. (A child's comment, "Somebody spilled something on me," became a traditional joke in one family.)

Adults often fail to realize how hard children try to be good, how devastated they feel when they fall short of their parents' expectations. There is no point in punishing a child for accidental damage. But it is important to teach him to make amends.

Like punishment, the way in which a child makes amends should be a logical consequence of the mistake or accident.

Spilled milk, for example, need be no greater domestic crisis for a child than for an adult. You can simply tell him to clean it up, pour another glass and forget it, unless he is deliberately careless.

What should a child be taught to do when he breaks something that belongs to someone else? To say he is sorry and offer to pay for it, and then to tell his own parents, so that they can back up his offer of restitution.

If a youngster's allowance won't cover the damage—and chances are it won't—he can contribute a reasonable percentage of it while his parents make up the difference.

A child who accidentally hurts another—a swing pushed too hard or a baseball bat flung in the wrong direction—should be taught to come at once to the nearest adult, to see that the injured child is taken home and to report the matter to his own parents.

In most cases an accident isn't serious and requires only a bandage, a drink of juice and a little sympathy. The sympathy can be furnished by the child responsible, via an apology and perhaps an offer to keep the victim company until he feels better or the loan of a prized toy.

40. Should Your Child Start

Kindergarten This Year?

"Kindergarten roundup in our community is held in May, when parents must register their children to start school in September. Please help us decide whether our son should be enrolled for next fall. He will be five years old on September 26. He is large for his age. People who know him say, Of course he is ready. But I worry about him being one of the youngest in the class. From everything I can read on the subject, it is not good for a child to be the youngest in his class unless he excels not only scholastically, but physically and socially as well. I do want him to do well in school."

Spring is open season for concerns like this, usually about children with birthdays from August through December. But such questions can't be solved with a simple yes or no, or by setting an arbitrary cutoff age.

For chronological age is only one factor that helps to determine how well a child will do in kindergarten and first grade, and it's not always reliable. Recent research has demonstrated that at least a dozen other indicators need to be considered, especially in the case of youngsters whose fifth birthday falls close to the legal school deadline.

Only by looking closely at an individual child and the particular school he will attend can parents decide whether or not to hold him back when he is legally eligible to start school. These questions can be useful guidelines:

1. Does the youngster seem immature for his age? "Immaturity" is often listed as a characteristic of children who don't do well in kindergarten and first grade. Sometimes these immature youngsters are simply the youngest in a class where ages cover a full 12-month span. But often the immaturity itself is an indication of a neurologically based learning disability that probably will not be outgrown, even if the child is kept out of school for an extra year.

2. Does the youngster seem overactive, easily distracted, jumpy and unable to concentrate even on something he enjoys —in comparison with friends of the same age? These symptoms also suggest a learning disability that requires active help, not merely postponing school.

3. Is he physically within normal range for his age? Physical and mental maturity don't always go together. But a youngster who is smaller in size than would be expected for his age and his family heritage should be carefully evaluated before he enters school.

Even if small physical size isn't a handicap in the elementary grades, it may be a discouraging disadvantage by the time a child—a boy, especially—reaches junior high level. If his father and grandparents are short or were late in starting their preadolescent growth spurt, this might be one of several factors to tip the decision toward postponing school entrance for a year.

4. Is the child's speech normal for his age? Marked difficulties in learning to talk at the usual age or the persistence of babyish speech may be predictive of reading problems. (Don't count a few mispronunciations; they are normal at this age.)

5. What kind of learning style does the child have? A youngster who approaches a new situation with enthusiasm,

who enjoys challenge, likes learning, is independent and well organized, will usually do well in school, research shows. Children who are more likely to have school problems tend to be either (1) boisterous, hyperactive, uninhibited and unable to concentrate their energy on any plan or activity; or (2) passive, dependent, worried types who are too tense and anxious to focus on what they are supposed to be doing.

6. Is the child a male? Boys with school problems outnumber girls by several times. Reasons range from the theory that girls identify better with the female teachers, who like them better because they sit still, to the fact that girls have superior verbal skills and are more mature biochemically and neurophysiologically than boys at this age. Being male isn't enough reason by itself to keep a child with a borderline birthday out of school an extra year. But it might give a little more weight to some other indicators.

7. Was the child a premature baby? Despite all the theories about prematures catching up physically and mentally, a strikingly large percentage of children who fail in the early grades were born prematurely. The former prematures who do well almost always have a stimulating home and good mothering; premature birth seems to make children particularly vulnerable to damage by an unfavorable environment.

8. How much mental stimulation has the child had at home? Has he been read to, talked to, listened to, taken with his family to many fascinating places? "Maturity" is not just the result of an innate developmental timetable, but an interaction between genetic patterns and a stimulating environment, recent research makes clear.

9. Has he been to nursery school or a Head Start program? Does his teacher think he's ready for kindergarten? If so, there should be little reason to hold him back. But if most of his future classmates have had preschool experiences while he has not, and if he is at the young end of the age range, he might benefit more from a year of nursery school.

10. Is the youngster eager to go to school? Are the children he usually plays with going next fall? If he regularly plays with three- or four-year-olds, even though five-year-olds are easily available, this may suggest he's not quite ready for kindergarten.

11. What is the kindergarten he'll attend like? Some are essentially nursery schools, focusing on social adjustment. Others introduce reading, simple math, elementary science and other learning opportunities. An immature five-year-old might succeed in the first, perhaps not in the second.

12. What happens after kindergarten to the children who aren't ready for first grade? A developmental, diagnostic or transition class to which kindergarteners who aren't quite ready for first grade can be assigned takes most of the risk out of sending an almost-five child to school. More important, it helps find the youngsters with learning disabilities before they fail first grade and gets specific treatment for them.

Unless a parent can find compelling reasons for delaying school entrance, it's probably a good idea to give the child the benefit of the doubt and enroll him. If he's kept out, his parents have, in effect, demoted him a year without giving him a chance to see what he is able to do—and indicating a lack of confidence in him that they might find difficult to explain when he asks about it later.

If there are good reasons for not letting a child start to school with his age-mates, then he needs careful evaluation and help—not just another year at home.

"Julie has an I.Q. of 139; we had her tested privately by a psychologist to verify our own opinions. She can read at third-grade level and she has been reading with enthusiasm since she was three and a half years old," writes another mother. "The psychologist who tested her told us she is socially and academically ready for kindergarten and has what he described as a 'readiness that is almost an urgency' for school experience at this time. But the school won't take her because her birthday comes 19 days after the cutoff date for kindergarten, and no exceptions are ever made, despite our requests and recommendations from the psychologist and an educator on her behalf. Why can't something be done for a child like ours?"

Julie's parents fear that delaying kindergarten until their daughter is almost six years old and first grade until she is almost seven (and her mental age about nine and a half) will blunt her eagerness to learn, that she will be bored and unchallenged in school for years. They, like many other parents, educators and psychologists, are raising the perennial question: Should children be admitted to kindergarten on a basis of readiness, ability and mental age—instead of just by birth date?

Most states and school districts find it expedient and politic to stick to a firm cutoff date based on age for kindergarten (and first grade) entrance. It is usually specified that a child must be five years old before November 1 or December 1 to qualify for kindergarten in September. No exceptions are usually permitted, even for a youngster like Julie.

Such a ruling creates serious problems not only for the immature youngster who isn't quite ready for school, but also for the child who is bright, mature, a veteran of one or two years in nursery school and eager to start formal schooling. Many recent studies by psychologists and educators have probed the problem of the immature kindergartener. Serious attempts are being made to find ways to screen him off before he enters school or to reroute him into a transition class between kindergarten and first grade, to spare him what seems to be inevitable failure by the end of first grade.

But almost no one speaks up for the bright youngster who finds kindergarten a repetitious bore and whose inborn drive to learn is in serious danger of being dulled by reading-readiness exercises and endless "Show and Tell" a year or two too late. Those who do plead the case for the early admission to kindergarten of bright, mature youngsters are almost always their parents, who are typically brushed off quickly as being "pushy" or as pressuring their children because of their own neurotic needs.

Schools which have tried a flexible early-admission plan based on testing are generally enthusiastic about it. It's a better method than double promotion for helping keep a bright youngster challenged in school because it avoids the possibility of educational gaps and makes it unnecessary for the child to form another group of friends when he skips a grade.

Dozens of research studies which have traced early entrants to kindergarten through the elementary grades and in some instances through high school, show that as a group the bright youngsters who start kindergarten before the usual age do academically as well as or better than their older classmates. They get better grades, have fewer failures and trial promotions and score higher on tests. They have fewer emotional, social or personality problems. They have more friends. And they rate higher than other youngsters in teachers' evaluations with regard to health, coordination, achievement, acceptance by others, leadership, attitude toward school and emotional adjustment. In physical size and maturity, the early kindergarten entrants cannot be distinguished from their older classmates after they've reached first grade.

By high-school age, the early kindergarten entrants have increased their margin of superiority over the other boys and girls. A larger percentage of them are graduated with honors, are leaders, take part in extracurricular activities, get elected to office and are admitted to college. They do not differ from their classmates in athletic and social standings. And they can cash in on that year they've saved when they begin graduate study or embark on a career.

"There is one full chronological year's difference among children in any kindergarten normally," pointed out the principal of an elementary school which does admit bright youngsters to kindergarten before their fifth birthday. "Add to this the normal variations in maturity and about a three-year span of mental ability. Admitting the brightest youngsters a year early helps keep kindergarten classes more nearly at the same mental ability level. It won't solve all the problems of the gifted child. But it does help."

But what can a parent do if the school district has no early-entrance plan for bright pupils and if, as in Julie's case, it refuses to make an exception?

Then, the child's parents must continue to take almost total responsibility for giving their child the mental stimulation she needs. The parents must encourage her to read at her ability level at home, and make sure she has a continuing supply of books that interest her and the time and privacy to enjoy them. They'll have to continue helping her find exciting, challenging ways to learn on her own. (Many bright children not only learn at a different rate than average youngsters, but in different ways as well.)

Parents like Julie's can encourage a child to develop hobbies and new interests that are challenging enough to make her want to concentrate and learn. It's easy for a bright youngster to slide through grade school without needing to study; but eventually in high school or college the need for study skills catches up with even the brightest.

Parents can keep the conversation in their home at a stimulating level and share some of their own interests and enthusiasms with their child. Youngsters like Julie can be given private lessons in music, art or another specialty in which she shows interest or talent. Such lessons not only give mental stimulation but provide some chance to work at the youngster's own natural accelerated rate of learning.

It also helps children like Julie to find at least one or two friends whose minds work as fast as hers does. Too often, a bright youngster feels socially out of step and tries to hide his abilities in order to have friends.

41. Countdown for Kindergarten

If your boy or girl is scheduled for an initial launch into kindergarten soon, it's a good idea to make sure well ahead of time that he's been briefed about what he'll encounter, that his preparation has been adequate and that he knows safety routines.

Here's a quick pre-launch list you can use to check him out on his readiness for school during the pre-September countdown:

· Does your child know how to survive in an unfamiliar environment? Have you taught him how to drink from a bubble fountain, how to use a public bathroom, how to smother a sneeze, how to wash his hands effectively?

· Can he manage all of his personal equipment? Does he know how to use a handkerchief and will he, when he needs one? Does he know how to put on rubbers and boots, button his coat, zip a jacket? (You can help by buying only clothing with simple fastenings and big enough boots or rubbers to fit over nonskid shoe soles.) Can he tie his own shoes? (Teachers don't insist on tying skill, but count as blessings the five-year-olds who can.)

· Have you researched the clothing requirements? It helps if you consult with mothers of last year's kindergarteners to ·

make sure you're assembling clothes that conform to the current preferences of the five-year-olds in your school district. Jeans, for example, are a uniform for boys in most schools, but not all. In some kindergartens, girls usually wear pants, especially on cold mornings; in others, skirts are usual, with or without a formal school-dress code.

· Does your child feel comfortable and familiar with the clothes he'll wear to school? It only adds to his sense of strangeness if you send him off the first day of school in still-new shoes and unbending new jeans.

· Is he sure of his identification? Does he know his own name, his parents' names, his address, telephone number? Can he recognize his own name on labels?

· Has your offspring passed a recent physical examination? Are his vision and hearing normal? Are his vaccinations up to date? Has he been to the dentist?

· Does your five-year-old know which natives are friendly? Does he feel free to ask the teacher for help and expect to enjoy learning from her without fear? Does he understand the role of principal, office secretary, custodian, patrol boys?

· Have you taught him not to talk to strangers and why?

· Does your child have at least one friend who will be in his class in the fall? If not, canvass the neighborhood and arrange some playtime for him with at least one other freshman kindergartener. Having a friend to go with—or meet in the classroom —the first morning does much to ease the transition.

· Is your new kindergartener familiar with his destination? Has he visited his new school, walked around the playground? Does he know which door he should enter, where his room will be, where to board his bus if he will ride one?

· If your child is to walk to school, have you practiced going over the route with him? Has he been trained to look both ways before crossing streets and does he—always and automatically? If you live in a suburb without sidewalks, does your youngster know how to walk safely in a street?

· Are there any large, barking dogs on the way to school

about which your child may need reassurance? He should know that he must never pat a strange animal or try to stop a dogfight or tease an animal or bother an animal that is eating.

· If your kindergartener goes to school by bus, has he been briefed on proper passenger behavior? Can he identify his particular bus if his school has several? Does he know what to do should he miss his bus on either end of the line?

· Have you tried a simulated launch? Letting your child pilot you to school carefully, making sure it's safe for you to cross each street and calling all the turns for you is good practice.

· Have you briefed your child on playground hazards? Does he stay clear of the sweep of swings when other children are using them? Can he dismount properly from a teeter-totter? Does he know he shouldn't try to run up a slide or stand too close to a baseball batter?

· Have you worked out procedures for possible emergencies? Does your youngster know what to do if he should feel sick in school or mislay his jacket or get lost himself? If you will be at work during his school day, does he know how to reach you in an emergency—and does he know that his school does?

· Has your preschooler had experience being away from home for short periods of time—in nursery school, summer day camp, at Grandmother's or visiting friends—so that he is beginning to be independent of you?

· Does your child understand reentry procedures? Does he have a general idea about when he'll come home (if he can't yet tell time, at least in terms of what will be happening at school) and how to get there? Have you impressed it upon him that he is always to come straight home from school? If he wants to play with Kenny, he must report home first, unless you have made clear and prior arrangements with Kenny's mother. The same rules hold, too, about his bringing Kenny to your home.

· Have you done what you could to prepare your child's

mind for learning in school, helped him learn how to learn, and encouraged him to appreciate the excitement and pleasure of learning?

· Have you been sharing the joys of reading with your youngster? Do you read to him daily? Give him opportunity to choose his own books from the library and buy him books of his own whenever you can? Do you show him pictures in newspapers and magazines you think will interest him? Do you let him see you reading and enjoying it? Have you shown him how to get information by reading? Do you answer and encourage his questions about written letters and words?

If your child indicates an interest you can begin teaching him to read by himself even before he starts kindergarten, although no kindergarten teacher expects a five-year-old to be able to read at all. Many a preschooler is so fascinated by words that if you tell him the sounds of the consonants and the long and short vowels, plus general rules about which to use when and how to combine sounds into words, he will begin reading without apparent effort and with great joy. Many preschoolers also learn to read a few words by watching TV programs for children and commercials for adults.

· Have you encouraged your child to understand basic mathematical concepts? Ideas about relationships such as "more than," "less than" and "equal to" can easily be taught to preschoolers. You can help him distinguish geometric shapes, such as squares and circles. And you can teach him to count and give him concrete experiences with numbers, such as putting six napkins on the dinner table or cutting out nine cookies from the dough.

· Have you helped your child to learn to listen—to directions, to an adult who is talking, to a story, to his friends, to what music suggests? Have you played listening games with him, or helped him try to isolate and identify particular sounds such as a bird's call or a jet plane's passage?

· Have you given him opportunities to be creative? Has he

had ample supplies of art materials such as fingerpaints, poster paints, colored chalks, paper, clay and other creative media to use freely and often?

· Is your child convinced that even though he may encounter some difficulties, starting school is going to be one of the most exciting experiences of his life and that you are confident he will succeed happily in this big adventure?

You should be careful not to overdo your enthusiasm here. Some parents oversell kindergarten to such a degree that their children are disappointed in school, particularly if they have been led to expect a wealth of exciting learning opportunities and instead encounter a traditional play-oriented situation. "Kindergarten is just like nursery school, except you rest with your head on the table instead of having to lie on a rug," one indignant five-year-old told his mother after the first two weeks of school.

Many new ideas for kindergarten curriculum, based on new research about how much and how five-year-olds can learn, are being developed in several university centers and pioneering school systems. Already it has been demonstrated that kindergarteners can learn to read and that they can absorb some major concepts about history, geography, science and economics—when taught by teachers who understand their special kind of learning abilities.

Most kindergarteners, however, are still likely to get a traditional readiness program. You owe it to your child, in any case, to give him a realistic explanation of what he can expect when he takes that big step into formal schooling.

42. How to Give Your Child a Good Start in Reading

How well a child does in school depends, in large measure, on how well he can read. And how well he can read depends, in larger measure than is usually acknowledged, on how skillfully his family has encouraged him to read.

These are two major conclusions that can be drawn from several new studies about school achievement by youngsters from various home backgrounds. Differences in reading abilities become greater as youngsters progress through school, and the gaps between good and poor students widen instead of narrow, research shows.

What can a parent do, in the irreplaceable years before first grade, to start a child off toward high achievement in reading? Here are several ways you can help:

· You can give your youngster good language models to imitate, for the language he brings to first grade will reflect exactly what he has heard in his home—whether it is English, Spanish, Southern drawl, slum patois, swear words or "Shut up." If you speak grammatically, your child will absorb correct speech patterns without obvious effort.

· You can also help your youngster build his vocabulary in the same general way, by casually introducing new words into your everyday conversation. Usually your offspring will comprehend the meanings from the context of your talk and learn the new words naturally and almost automatically.

· You can make reading to your child a part of your loving, warm relationship with him, starting no later than his first birthday. If you cuddle him beside you or in your lap and read to him almost every day—starting with picture books and simple, factual stories, and growing into the whole range of poetry, imagination and information—he'll subconsciously associate reading with happy times.

· You can keep interesting reading material handy to fill impatient, unhappy moments with your youngster. You can pack a book along to read while you are waiting in the doctor's office or for the shoe salesman. You can read to him in the car when you are not the driver, and in a restaurant while waiting for your order. You can read to him to distract and comfort him when he is sick or lonesome or tired. (It's easier on you, too, to read than to cope with tears, frustrations or fidgets.)

· You can make bedtime reading to your child a habit. It's a good way to help a youngster unwind and relax and it ends the day with a comforting closeness between parent and offspring.

· You can encourage your youngster to watch an educational TV program that helps children learn to recognize letters and numbers and increases their awareness of words and their meanings.

· You can take your child with you to the library, starting at least by age three, and let him select some of his own books. Books make excellent birthday, Christmas and just-because-I-love-you presents. So do gift certificates that permit a youngster to buy books of his own choosing. You can see that your child has his own bookshelf to store his books. And you can even add to his delight in ownership by buying him inexpensive bookplates with his name—or encouraging him to create his own with crayons and contact paper.

· You can provide your child with ample and interesting materials for writing, such as crayons and manila paper, blackboard and chalk, ballpoint and felt-tipped pens, pencils and paper in various textures and sizes. There is evidence that for some children an interest in writing comes before a curiosity about reading, and that encouraging this interest can lead to reading.

· You can call your youngster's attention to printed words, beginning at a very early age. You can show him stop signs, names on mailboxes, his own name on his clothing labels, brand names on products he sees in the supermarket, titles on books and records.

· You can start pointing out to your child, even as a preschooler, in a casual and informal way, the relationship between sounds and the letters that convey these sounds. Even a two- or three-year-old can learn quite easily that the letter "m" makes an "m-m-m" sound and what sounds other consonants indicate. If your youngster is interested in these observations, you should consider teaching him to read yourself. Nonpressuring, easy phonetic reading methods are available for parents and young children. And they have been used by hundreds of thousands of parents—to their children's great advantage and with mutual delight.

· You can play all kinds of simple word games with your child. These help to increase his skill in using words and in recognizing sounds—and to keep him contented while you're driving or doing housework.

· You can help your child learn to identify words that are important to him, even if you don't consider this to be "reading" per se. For example, most four-year-olds can master words like "men" and "women" when they are looking for the proper rest room. Or a word that helps them identify the record they want to play. Or names on cereal boxes. Or "stop" on a sign.

All of this helps a child understand that printed letters are symbols with meaning.

· You can answer your child's questions about reading, letters, and what signs and words in books say. Even a little help of this kind can benefit a preschooler a great deal, research shows. There is no evidence that it will confuse or conflict with first-grade teaching, but many parents have been so intimidated by warnings to keep hands off the learning-to-read process that they hesitate even to answer their children's interested questions.

· You can write down your child's words for him until he is able to do so himself—in a letter to a grandparent, a note for father, a thank-you for a birthday gift, a shopping list. This helps him understand that writing is just spoken words in another form.

· You can avoid limiting your child's reading to books prescribed for his age level. Your own experience with him will be your best guide. If a book matches your youngster's mental development, he'll probably want you to read and reread it to him and he'll listen contentedly while you do. If it's too easy or too difficult, he'll probably wiggle away and do something else.

· You can let your child see you reading frequently, too, for learning and for pleasure. A youngster who grows up seeing his parents get most of their information and entertainment from television is quite likely to do likewise and may never become happily addicted to reading.

When a child comes home from first grade to recite (almost certainly from memory) the words in his reader, it's tempting for parents to trust that the teacher has now taken over responsibility for reading and put the subject out of mind. But there's still much that parents can do all through the elementary grades to encourage a youngster to read—happily, easily, competently, enthusiastically and often. To neglect to do so may make a major difference in a child's progress all through the rest of his schooling.

Here are more ways you can help your child:

· Even though your youngster can read first- or second-grade-level books on his own, you should continue to read aloud to him. It will be a long time before he's able to read by himself at the level of his comprehension. And he's probably become so adept at getting information from other sources—television, radio, conversation, records—that he finds the content of the usual readers incredibly dull. By reading to him at the level of his interest, you can help keep him convinced that books are worth the learning effort. (Sometimes parents stop at a most exciting part of a story because "I'm too busy to read any more right now" and then discover their child has picked up the book himself in his eagerness to know what happens next and has managed to read material considerably more difficult than his supposed grade level.)

· Your youngster should always have a fascinating variety of reading material readily available. Because most books for children are short, you'll probably need to schedule weekly, or at least biweekly, forays to the library with him. You can let him select a book himself to buy to celebrate a small triumph or for a gift occasion—or just because you love him and books are a delight.

· You can subscribe to a suitable magazine for your child. Most new readers are excited about getting mail of their own.

· You can encourage your young reader to write letters to people you know will write back. (A drawing with a few words suffices for first- or second-graders.) You can ask any traveler you know—grandparents, father, neighbors—to send him postcards with easy-to-read messages. And you can let him choose and write out birthday cards, Christmas cards, party invitations.

· You can post messages for your youngster on your family's bulletin board, even if you are at home and could tell him the information. A few can be casual reminders about chores, but most should be happy news, like "Look for two peanut-butter cookies in the big jar."

· As your child begins to make progress in reading, you can help him see practical uses for his new skills, such as reading a recipe for a cake mix or instructions for making models.

· You can provide your child with a TV schedule, show him how it is arranged and suggest he check program times himself. With this kind of motivation, and having seen program names on the screen, most children can read a television guide long before they can handle anything else of comparable difficulty. You can also use TV to lure your offspring into reading more by looking for books on subjects he's seen on television or stories with plots of a type he enjoys on TV.

· You can ask your new reader to read to you for your pleasure when you are busy driving or ironing or doing dishes. Then you can thank him enthusiastically for making your work go more pleasantly. If you have a younger child, you can encourage your beginning reader to read to him and praise him delightedly afterwards. Most youngsters respond warmly to the admiration of a smaller child—and having them both occupied will give you a few extra minutes.

· You can arrange for your child to have a quiet, private place with a good reading light where he can sit or sprawl in comfort. It's surprising how little unscheduled time some school-age children have and how casually some parents will interrupt a reading youngster because "he isn't really doing anything."

· After your youngster has been in first grade for two or three months, you can check up on his knowledge of phonics. If he doesn't know letter sounds or how to decipher a word phonetically or if he guesses wildly or says "We haven't had that word yet" when confronted with a new word, you'd be wise to get some instructional material and teach him yourself. He'll progress much faster and more happily with this essential information. (Although teaching phonics at the beginning of reading instruction is increasing rapidly in this country, there are still many classrooms where children are expected to learn to read by memorizing one word at a time and trying to identify words by their outline. Yet repeatedly, research shows that children learn better and faster when they are taught sound-symbol relationships first of all, so they have a logical, systematic way to go about deciphering new words.) If you haven't seen a good, modern phonetic or linguistic reading method—or if you learned to read by a sight-word method yourself—you'll probably be surprised and delighted at how much it helps.

· You can invent a dozen simple games that help your child practice on troublesome sight words or on sound-letter relationships. For example, you can make bingo-type cards using sight words or phonetic sounds instead of numbers, then write duplicate words or sounds on slips of paper and draw to play the game.

Or you can paste a sight word on the front of each card of an old deck. Then turn them face down and let your child and a friend take turns drawing for a card. Each card they read correctly they can keep. Mistakes go back into the pack. The player with the most cards at game's end wins.

You can also buy bingo, lotto and dice-type games that help a child learn sounds and letters. And board and card games that require some reading to win are excellent motivating forces for primary-age youngsters.

· If your child shows an interest in a typewriter, you can encourage him to use it. With a little preliminary instruction, most youngsters six or older can handle a machine carefully. If you put caps over the keys and paint them with bright colors keyed to colors you have painted on the fingernails of your youngster, he'll almost automatically use correct fingering.

· You can make it a family custom to share interesting reading—perhaps at the dinner table. You can begin by reading short news items, jokes, riddles, science reports or apt quotations and gradually encourage your offspring to contribute, too. This kind of "hey-guess-what!" approach, which children often use with each other, can lure your youngster into wanting to read these sources for himself.

· You can let your child stay up half an hour past his bedtime—provided he spend the time reading. Many parents have found this strategy the most effective motivation of all.

· The summer vacation following first grade is a particularly critical time in the development of reading skills for most youngsters. Some first-graders, particularly if they have been taught by a word-recognition method, forget much of what they've learned during the hot-weather hiatus. A post-first-grader doesn't need formal lessons to keep up his interest and his level of achievement—but he does need opportunity to use his skills in practical ways and in happy games. With this kind of help, he can go back to school in September reading better than he did at the school year's end.

43. How to Evaluate Your Child's School

How good a school is your child attending? And what can you, as a parent, reasonably expect your school system to do for your child? Your answers to these questions will give you a good idea of how your youngster's school stacks up:

1. Is your child learning—in reasonable proportion to the amount of time he invests and to his intelligence? (Good measures: Can the first-graders read competently and independently by the end of the school year and decipher new words intelligently? Do nationally standardized tests show your child and your school functioning at grade level or better?)

2. Does the school provide a wide variety of learning opportunities and recognize that not all children learn in the same way at the same rate? Does it make it possible for every youngster to succeed? If the school groups children by abilities, does it make special effort to use appropriate materials and methods for bright youngsters and for slow learners? Does it have established ways in which children can move up easily when they

275

are ready? If the school does not practice some form of ability grouping, has it a reasonable and workable alternative, such as individualized, programmed learning, to handle the great spread of skills in each classroom?

3. Are adequate provisions made for children with special problems? For children who have specific learning disabilities? For those with other handicaps? Are youngsters who need these special aids encouraged, respected and valued equally with other pupils?

4. Is your school's administration reasonably open to new ideas and innovations in education? Are teachers alert to new research in educational fields and willing to change when better methods and techniques are available?

5. Will your school's administrators and teachers discuss new ideas in education with parents and PTA groups without acting threatened and criticized? Is the parents' association considered to be a working, intelligent partner in the school and not merely a fund-raising appendage?

6. Does your school consider its primary function to be education—rather than the implementation of social or political change or life adjustment?

7. Does the school have a library-learning center with a variety of effective materials? Are children allowed to go to the center freely? Can they move around in the center quietly without being scolded?

8. Does the elementary school introduce children to a foreign language? Teach any science? Have much audiovisual equipment? Make use of films, slides, records, games, newspapers and a variety of up-to-date learning materials?

9. Does your school willingly share with you information it garners about your child? If it uses I.Q. or achievement tests and makes decisions concerning children on the basis of such testing, these results should be shared with you—with sufficient interpretation to make the scores meaningful to you. Does your school refrain from using psychological tests on your child without your permission and without sharing results with you?

Do parents have any difficulties exercising their legal right to see whatever is placed in their child's file at school?

10. Does your school have a satisfactory system of reporting your youngster's progress to you? Whether it uses parent conferences, A-B-C-D-F report cards, percentage grades or descriptive letters, such reporting should be specific enough so that you know how your child stands in relation to his own abilities and in comparison with others in his class and with nationwide grade levels. And such reporting should be frequent enough so you can spot potential problems before they become full-blown.

11. What is the school system doing about integration? There are no rigid right-wrong answers here, because communities vary too much. What's important is that school administrators and teachers be progressing with honest intent and in the best interests of the children toward solving whatever problems exist locally.

12. What methods are used to teach reading in the early grades? Even if your child has progressed past first and second grade, this remains important. A good phonetic or linguistic program begun no later than the start of the first grade means fewer reading problems (and teachers' time spent on problems) and a higher level of achievement, not only in reading but in other subjects dependent on reading.

13. How old is the school building your child attends? How well is it kept up? The second question tells you more about the quality of the school than the first.

14. How large is the annual turnover among teachers? How does the teachers' salary scale compare with state and national averages? What percentage of teachers has a master's degree? A high turnover in teachers indicates dissatisfaction with the school, its administrators and/or community support of the school.

15. Are you welcome in your child's school as a visitor? Are teachers and principal available by appointment to talk with you about your child?

16. Is there an adequate safety program in force—on the playground, in school, on nearby streets? Are younger pupils protected against bullying by older boys and girls?

17. Is learning—at least some of the time—considered an adventure to be shared by teachers and pupils, rather than a chore to be imposed? Does your youngster enjoy going to school—at least some of the time? Does he become excited about the ideas he is learning and absorbed in the projects he is assigned? Are his individual interests encouraged? Is he being helped to develop his own unique talents?

18. Do teachers and school staff like, respect and appreciate all the children—and let them know it? Or do comments from your youngster and complaints you hear from other parents suggest that some of the teachers may play favorites or be prejudiced against some of the children because of their sex, race, socioeconomic background or I.Q.?

19. Does your school treat you as an intelligent working partner in the education of your child—acknowledging that the ultimate responsibility for him is yours?

44. How Would Your Child's School Evaluate You?

How effective are you as a parent—in the eyes of your child's school? What can your school system reasonably expect you to contribute to your youngster's education? Your answers to these questions will give you a good idea of how you stack up as an asset to your school-age child:

1. Do you send your youngster off to school every morning on time, clean, suitably dressed, emotionally secure, well-breakfasted, healthy and open (if not eager) for learning?

2. Are you interested in your child's school activities and do you make sure he knows it—by participating in school functions, by listening and encouraging him to talk about school, by sharing his enthusiasms and his problems, by treating his life at school as of major importance? Are you active in the parents' organization?

3. Are you reasonably well informed about your school system and aware of its current problems? Do you know, for example, whether your school system has problems of integration? Increasing or decreasing enrollment? A salary scale for teachers equal to or better than average? A bond issue under discussion?

4. Are you willing to help your child's school in any way you can—by checking out books in the school library or supervising the lunch hour or chaperoning field trips or campaigning for needed funds?

5. Have you made some reasonable effort to encourage and help your child learn—during the urgently important years before age six and as a matter of course all during his childhood years? (Research shows that children in families lacking such stimulation begin first grade behind other pupils and slip even further back by junior-high-school age.) Are you yourself still interested and involved in learning—and does your child understand your feelings?

6. Are you reasonable in your expectations of what any school can do for children—without holding it completely responsible for solving problems triggered by segregated housing, urban crowding, inadequate families and unequal learning abilities? Do you resist asking the impossible of the school—that, for example, the teacher make Tommy behave properly or break up a friendship you consider undesirable?

7. Are you informed about current issues and innovations in education in general—and do you realize that every new idea in education is not a panacea and every new method is not applicable to your child's class?

8. Do you generally back up your child's teacher and school with regard to safety rules, codes of conduct and homework assignments? If you disagree with a school policy, do you talk the matter over with the teacher or staff rather than make your child a pawn in a school-home argument or broadcast your criticism all over the community?

9. Have you taught your child the rudiments of safety so that he can get to and from school safely and use playground equipment without danger to himself and to others?

10. Have you helped your child learn social skills and attitudes necessary to get along well with others that are appropriate for his age?

11. Do you treat as confidential information given you by the school about your child?

12. Are you judicious about the amount of time you spend at school? You shouldn't hesitate to ask for a conference if you want to talk to Molly's teacher or to visit her classroom. But school is Molly's world, not yours.

13. Do you love your child, respect him, appreciate him, encourage him, so that he will have the self-confidence to keep on trying?

14. Do you work with the school in educating your child— always remembering that the ultimate responsibility for him is not the school's but yours?

45. WHEN YOU'RE THE MOTHER OF THE BRIDE OF FRANKENSTEIN

Small-fry that go spook in the night on Halloween scare safety experts, who each year repeat a haunting refrain: Unless you safety-proof your ghosts and ghouls before you send them freaking out into the night, what started off as trick-or-treat may well turn into trick-and-treatment at the nearest hospital emergency ward.

Car accidents, burns and falls take an unhappy toll of trolls and witches and moppet-sized monsters every Halloween. To make sure your grade-school goblin or size six Superman gets through the night with nothing more serious than too much candy, here are cautions from accident-prevention experts:

Make sure your ghost or ghoul or goblin isn't invisible to mortal motorists. To help him materialize clearly in the October dark, decorate his costume with light-reflecting tape or metallic spangles (most fearless freaks enjoy the psychedelic effects and don't object). Insist that he carry a white trick-or-treat sack, that at least part of his costume be light in color and that he take a large lighted flashlight wherever he ghosts.

Your facsimile Frankenstein needs to see as well as be seen.

But the eye slits in most Halloween masks are so small and so poorly placed in the face that at best they give a child only tunnel vision; if they slip off nose center, they can blind him completely.

The safest solution is to make a mask of makeup. Most toy and dime stores carry inexpensive theatrical makeup sets with putty and grease paint in crayon colors, and most mothers can get a sufficiently macabre effect with mascara, lipstick and eye shadow to satisfy a miniature mummy. If your vampire complains that he doesn't look scary enough, suggest he hold a lighted flashlight under his chin and check the effect in the dark. One look in the mirror will probably convince him that he really has freaked out.

When you begin witch-ful thinking about your child's costume, remember that even a monster must have easy mobility. Vampire, ghost or creature from outer space, he can still get thrown for a painful, down-to-earth bruise by a too long costume. Do make sure that your youngster's costume will stay well anchored through the evening's expeditions, that your pillow-stuffed tramp won't trip over his father's long trousers, that your Raggedy Ann's granny dress is short enough for running, and that your King Arthur's sword won't swashbuckle between his knees when he tries a fast getaway.

Even an ersatz astronaut can crash-land painfully on an unfamiliar step or an obstacle in strange terrain. So, as mission control, insist that your small spaceman light every step of his way with a flashlight before you let him blast off into his trick-or-treating orbit.

Even though most parents now use flashlights instead of candles to light up doorstep jack o'lanterns, you should make sure your child's costume is flame-resistant, especially if it is flimsy or trailing. (You can treat the material by dipping it in a solution of two quarts of warm water mixed with seven ounces of borax and three ounces of boric acid. The protection will outlast ironing, but not washing.)

Don't let your friendly freak fend for himself in the October dark. He'll have much more fun with a pride of pirates, a school of ghouls or a gaggle of goblins than he will on his own —and he'll be safer, too.

Set boundaries for your wild Indian's happy haunting grounds, including only streets with which he is familiar and homes of families whom he knows, and review with him pedestrian safety rules, especially if you live in a suburban area that is sans sidewalks. On his own reservation, your war-painted brave won't have to cope with unfamiliar traffic hazards or unfriendly dogs, and you'll avoid the possibility (remote but real) that he be given nonedible or even dangerous "treats" by strangers.

Depending on your neighborhood, a parent may have to shadow along behind your Bride of Frankenstein or little green man from Mars if he's younger than age seven. He can ring the doorbells and collect loot by himself, of course, but he'll be safer and feel more secure if his father is lurking somewhere out there in the bushes with the other fathers.

A preschooler will be happier and safer going treating in late afternoon, before the skeletons begin to dance on the lawns and the banshees start to howl in the dark. Then he can share the fun by staying up, in costume, to dispense treats from the security of your front door.

But most toddlers tend to be terrified of masks and monsters, even in the daylight and even if you explain carefully beforehand what Halloween is all about. If you have a two- or three-year-old, you'll probably want to have him suppered and asleep before he sees the werewolves at your door.

46. OCTOBER AND THE PROBLEMS OF A SCHOOL-AGE CHILD

It's early October and Susie, age seven, has been in tears at least twice a day for the past two weeks. Steve, six, dawdles so with dressing that he's missed the school bus five times in three weeks despite his mother's impatient prodding. Billy, nine, is so tense he can't stomach breakfast on school mornings although he eats well on Saturdays and Sundays.

The distress signals these youngsters are sending out are common in late September and October, as the initial excitement and novelty of a new school year wear off and the routine grind begins. Difficulties with kindergarten children usually occur early in September; once the initial adjustment is over, the year goes smoothly. But first-, second- and third-grade problems are most apparent after school has been in session a few weeks. The sooner they are identified and corrected, the less serious they are.

In a few youngsters, school-morning tensions, headache, queasiness, irritable behavior and rebellion about going to school may indicate a specific learning disability or over-placement in a grade. But most fears and anxieties connected with school have a simpler cause and a more direct solution.

285

One of the most common causes of early-fall school problems—and easiest to overlook—is simply lack of sufficient sleep. School's start means a sudden shift from unscheduled, leisurely mornings to a 6:30 or 7 A.M. alarm, and a busy, all-day pace. Yet youngsters often rebel against a return to school-night bedtime hours, especially with the lure of new-season television programs.

Add to the shortage of sleep the stresses of trying to learn the ways of a new teacher, to meet the demands of a new grade, to make new friends, and the result is often crabbiness, touchiness, discouragement and tears. Fatigue can also lower resistance to the new assortment of viruses and bacteria brought to school by classmates returning from summer vacations.

It should help to enforce a reasonable bedtime, explaining why to your child. Maneuvering a quiet time into your child's day helps, too. A rest-and-snack break right after school or a rest-and-read time just before dinner may make it easier for him to get through the day on an even emotional keel.

You should check out, too, what your child is eating and when, especially if he stays at school all day. Just because your school serves a nourishing hot lunch doesn't necessarily mean it's doing your offspring any good. Often finicky eaters don't like what's on the menus at school and find ways—usually by trading—to subsist on rolls or potato chips. Occasionally, lunch lines are so long that children don't have time to finish what they're served. Or they bolt through their food to have more time for outdoor play. Sometimes a first- or second-grader is so overwhelmed by the din and congestion of a crowded lunchroom that he can only pick at his food. Or if a teacher tries to insist he clean his plate, he may rebel with an upset stomach. Older boys and girls occasionally sign up for so many noontime extracurricular activities that they haven't time to eat. Pre-teen girls may deliberately skip eating to lose weight.

Bringing a first- or second-grader home to eat once or twice a week helps in some cases, if the school lunch period is long enough. Sending a bag lunch along with a fussy eater may also work; a cold meal a child will eat does him more good than a hot lunch he leaves on a tray.

Sometimes a child has a specific reason for dreading school, a concrete basis for his worry and tension. Hopefully, you already have such a good relationship with your child that he'll feel free to tell you what troubles him with a little loving questioning. But many youngsters hate to admit to a parent that they feel fearful, stupid or inadequate. So it may take much patience and love and some casual comments about things that bothered you or Daddy or a friend when you were a child before you unearth the difficulty.

Occasionally, for a five- or six-year-old, the problem is a big, barking dog on the way to school. Some psychologists see symbolic meanings in a child's fear of dogs. But most mailmen will tell you there's nothing symbolic about some of the dogs they encounter.

You can help, perhaps, by working out an alternate route to school. Or, by asking the dog's owner to keep the animal fenced or leashed just before and after school hours. Or, with the owner's cooperation, you may be able to help your child make friends with the animal.

Often the cause of school fears is older boys who bully smaller children—on the way to school, on the playground, at the bus stop, even on the bus. In a few schools this has occasionally come to outright extortion of lunch money or payments for "protection." Usually, however, it's pushing, snowballing, taunting, teasing, or snatching books or clothing. But it's enough to make a young child sick with fear and shame.

You can work, of course, to strengthen your youngster against such bullying. But it's expecting too much for a first-grader to cope unassisted with a ten- or twelve-year-old bully. In some school districts mothers take turns supervising children at bus stops; in others, an expanded corps of patrol boys helps. You may need to resort to organized action through your parent-teacher association.

If your child is in a school where the youngsters in each grade are juggled anew between two or more classes each year, he may be discouraged and unhappy about the problem of making new friends. You can encourage him to take the initiative in inviting new classmates to your home and arranging some playtime with friends from last year's class, whom he now sees infrequently.

Other social problems with classmates are often a major source of fears and unhappiness about school, especially for a youngster who isn't dressed the way the other children are or who lacks the athletic skills considered essential in his particular class. Many budding school phobias have been nipped by a parent who privately coached a third-grader in how to jump rope or a fifth-grader how to hit a baseball.

Could your youngster be so overloaded with out-of-school activities that he's too tired or too pressured to do well in school? Some youngsters—usually abetted by eager mothers—sign up for so many dancing classes, music lessons, after-school sports, religious school and other activities that they're exhausted before they have time to start their homework. A school problem, especially in early fall, should be the impetus for an immediate evaluation of out-of-school activities. Only a parent can protect a youngster's right for some time every day in which to relax, to be free of having his performance graded, to do nothing if he wishes.

It's possible that your child may simply be discouraged or scared by a big increase in the academic demands of school. This may occur particularly in the first few months of first, fourth, sixth and seventh grades, when classwork usually becomes noticeably harder after September's review. Should this be the case, it often helps just to reassure your youngster that his feelings of discouragement are normal and that you have confidence he will be able to handle the new challenge just as he always has in the past.

Sometimes when a child begins to think he can't do the work in class, he may turn his energies from studying to thinking up ways to avoid even trying to work. Here, your strategy is to plan with his teacher how to get him the help he needs to catch up and succeed. He may need drill at home, extra review, even a bit of tutoring. Besides the academic boost, this strategy will, hopefully, help your child to look objectively at his problems and get busy solving them instead of evading them.

It's also possible that it's the teacher who is triggering your child's problems at school. Not every teacher in every one of the thousands of school systems is ideal. Many have been poorly trained. Some have overwhelming personal problems. A few should never have become teachers at all. Almost every teacher finds three to five children in every class with whom he or she can't get along, one leading educator declares. And even a top-notch teacher may use different methods than those you'd prescribe as best for your youngster.

The unhappy effects of a poor child–teacher relationship can upset your family the whole school year—and slow your youngster down for far longer. But short of moving to a new district, there's not much chance of getting your child out of the teacher's classroom. And the chances of changing the teacher are roughly similar to changing the weather. Almost always, your strategy will have to be to help your child get along with the teacher.

First, you should analyze precisely what it is about the teacher that is disturbing your child. Is she, perhaps, much more strict and demanding than anyone he's had before? Then, your best move is to encourage and strengthen your youngster so he can meet these stepped-up demands. You can help him see this rigorous scholastic training as comparable to tough—and sometimes bruising—athletic training. And you can point out how much easier future schooling will be after he's had this experience. Perhaps you can help him establish more efficient study habits or develop enough self-discipline to buckle down to homework faster. Certainly he will need your praise and pride in the efforts he does make to adjust to stiffer standards.

If this doesn't ease the problem, then it's a good idea to request an appointment with the teacher for a conference. You can explain that your child is having difficulty and is tense and upset and ask what you can do to relieve his anxieties.

You may simply discover that the teacher isn't the kind who praises good work as often as your child's former teachers—and thinks he's doing just fine. Or she may suggest a tutor, some extra drill at home or even volunteer to work with him a little after school.

You may also discover that your youngster dislikes his teacher because she is often caustic or critical. Or because she seldom smiles. Or because she ridicules the children. Then it may help to tell your offspring about the famous football coach who said he made it a policy never to smile at players because they tried harder when he didn't.

In this case, you can suggest to your child, his teacher's attitude may just be her way of trying to help him learn more. And you can try to give him enough self-confidence and emotional security so that sarcasm and criticism don't upset him so much.

If you are sure that the teacher is at fault in your child's case —and this can be difficult to determine, even if you are objective—you can help your child get through the year in much the same way you'd support your husband if he were stuck with a difficult boss. You can see that your child has friends to play with after school and as many successful personal relationships with adults as possible. You can provide opportunity for rough-and-tumble physical play to help work off his tensions. You can show him great love and affection. You can be understanding if he takes some of the emotional tension built up in school out on you at home. Then you can teach him to discharge these pent-up feelings in better ways—in physical activity, in talks to an understanding listener, or even, with some youngsters, in creative writing, music or art.

You can also teach your child that one of the most important lessons he'll ever have to learn in life is how to get along with all kinds of people and that even though this year is difficult, it will be valuable to him.

You must, however, remain on as friendly and cooperative a basis with the teacher as possible. Otherwise the situation will become even more hostile and your child will bear the brunt of it.

Some parents make the mistake of assuming the teacher is always at fault in school problems, of rushing angrily to a child's defense whatever the situation. But others err in the other direction by failing to realize that a few teachers can be mean, unfair or emotionally disturbed—just like a few adults in other walks of life. The children assigned to these teachers need their parents' calmest, wisest help; they have no other refuge.

There are many different kinds of physical problems that can also cause school difficulties, emotional upsets, tensions and anxieties—such as undetected visual abnormalities, hearing loss, specific learning disabilities, hyperactivity, chronic infections and allergies. If you can't pinpoint a reason for your youngster's difficulties in school or if his problems have been long-standing—or just to be on the safe side—you should have a competent physician check out these possibilities too.

47. How to Help a Child with Reading Problems

"My daughter still can't read the easy-to-read books we bought her months ago," worries a Michigan mother. "Shouldn't she do better than this after six months in first grade? Or is this normal?"

"I keep hearing about four-year-olds who can read," writes a Kansas parent. "But my son's first-grade teacher keeps saying the class needs more reading readiness, that boys should wait until they are six and a half or seven even to start learning to read. I'm sure Nicky is bored in school and that's why he's becoming a behavior problem."

"Robbie has yet to read a book voluntarily for pleasure and he's almost eight," complains a Florida father. "If you ask him about a word, he says, 'We haven't had that yet,' or looks out the window and makes a wild guess. What's wrong?"

It's no wonder these parents are confused. For how, what, who, where and when to teach reading are still the most explosive issues in education today—after decades of controversy and research.

Traditional theories about reading readiness and the optimum age for starting reading instruction are being revised on the basis of careful, new research. There is now sound evidence that children do not need a mental age of six or six and a half to learn to read, that vision is adequate for reading in normal children by about twelve months of age and that a prolonged period of reading readiness isn't necessary. Millions of children younger than age six have learned to read—or have made a strong start in reading—before they entered first grade, to their own great pleasure and with lasting benefit, according to careful research. And these youngsters who learned to read early and easily—some of them taught by a slightly older sister or brother who liked to play school—are not necessarily brighter than average. Most of them merely benefitted from a relaxed and happy opportunity to learn to read in their own home, at their own pace, with the help of someone who took time to answer their questions and give them some information about words and sounds.

Today there are many promising new ideas and methods for teaching reading that are in various stages of experiment and development. There is new hardware (teaching machines and audiovisual equipment) and software (programs for such equipment). There are successful new phonetic and linguistic reading programs; better ways of diagnosing and treating children with learning difficulties; preschools that teach reading easily and happily. For specific children, or classrooms, or even entire school systems, these innovations in the timing and way of teaching reading have shown that the reading levels of a majority of children can be raised significantly and reading problems can be cut sharply.

But these new programs are only beginning to make significant dents in the overall reading problems in the United States. Estimates of the percentages of children in this country who do not read at a level proportionate to their intelligence still range from 30 to 50 percent. And obviously this retardation in reading carries over into all school activities that require the use of written language.

Today reading problems are found among children of every

intellectual level. (Bright youngsters tend to be more retarded in proportion to their abilities than average or below-average children.) There are reading problems in well-financed suburban school districts among offspring of well-educated parents, as well as among youngsters from illiterate homes in low-income areas. (However, culturally deprived children who are generally deficient in verbal English have special difficulties when they start learning to read in school, and the proportion of children from low socio-economic backgrounds who have learning problems is higher than among other children for many complex reasons.)

There is no single cause for reading problems—and no single remedy. Reading specialists have listed more than two hundred separate reasons why children may not learn to read easily and well, dozens of which are found among youngsters from good homes who have at least average intelligence. So you'll need to check out several possibilities before you know how to go about helping—or getting help for—a youngster who isn't reading as happily and well as he should for his age, grade and intelligence.

As a guide, here are some factors to consider, with the aid of your child's teacher and doctor. Some of these problems are easy to detect and correct; others are much more complex to diagnose and complicated to treat:

Is your youngster being taught by an efficient, logical method? Probably the most common cause of slowness in learning to read well is poor teaching methods—those that force youngsters to guess at words from their general outline and context rather than to decode them phonetically as written-down speech. This is also the easiest cause of reading difficulty to detect and to remedy, provided help comes before a child loses interest in learning to read and becomes convinced that he cannot ever succeed.

You can't always tell how much phonics instruction a first-, second- or third-grader is getting by asking the teacher. Since research has shown that a knowledge of phonics is essential in learning to read, most teachers—and publishers of reading materials—are quick to say they do include phonics among other "word-attack skills." But often the phonics is too little and too late, and teachers who were not trained in phonetic teaching methods in college sometimes do an inadequate job of presenting these concepts.

You can tell quickly, however, whether your child has some working knowledge about phonics just by copying this list of words in the size of lettering he is accustomed to and asking him to read it to you: mat, mate, meat, boat, bat, bait, bit, bite, hat, hate, got, goat, pit, spit, spot, pots, stop, post, toast and toad. Then ask him to explain to you how he knows how to pronounce these words. Third, you can ask him to write to your dictation this list of words: spun, vet, rob, cup, lump, skit, match, pet, pat, put.

An average first-grader in a class where reading instruction begins with phonics is expected to be able to read most one-syllable words with a long or short vowel sound after about eight weeks of instruction—by the first or second week of November. He also knows why a vowel sound should be long or short. By late winter of first grade, he should also be able to write most of the words that follow this regular pattern. This gives him an enormous lead over youngsters who learn by the look-say method, for they are expected to memorize only 150 to 300 words during the entire first-grade year. Because they do not have adequate tools to decode most new words they encounter, they are still restricted to easy-read books with limited vocabulary and content far below their level of interest and comprehension.

If your child is not getting good instruction, what can you do about it?

1. You can wait and see. A substantial percentage of children—more girls than boys—do manage to keep memorizing word by word until they are eventually taught enough phonics

to become independent readers. Or subconsciously they figure out enough phonetic principles by themselves to read well. This is difficult to do during first grade because most look-say word lists contain many phonetically irregular words and make such deduction difficult. Some youngsters who learn better by visual means than through auditory perception may do quite well with a look-say method, but children whose most efficient means of learning is auditory will probably encounter greater-than-usual difficulty with a look-say program.

By the end of third grade, most youngsters will probably be exposed to some kind of phonetic instruction. You can help by encouraging your youngster to make use of these techniques instead of guessing when he encounters a word he doesn't know.

If a child is still having marked reading problems by the end of third grade, most school systems will refer him to a remedial-reading teacher. Remedial-reading instruction is usually based on phonics. If he hasn't developed too many feelings of discouragement and inferiority by this time, and if he doesn't have a specific learning disability, he'll probably learn to read adequately with this training. But he may not catch up with other youngsters who learned to read easily and enthusiastically years earlier.

2. You can teach your child phonetic skills yourself, as millions of parents have. Good, simple materials are widely available for this purpose, and unless parents have had similar training themselves, they may not realize how much these strategies aid the learning-to-read process. If you show these phonetic techniques to your child with the attitude that "here are a few simple secrets to help you decode written words" and not with a "sit here and learn this or else" stance, the experience can be a happy one for you and your child. And it won't interfere with whatever learning-to-read method his school is using.

You should also check out several other basic reasons why

your child may not be learning to read as well as he should. For example:

Does your child need glasses? You can't rule out this possibility just because your youngster hasn't complained about his eyes or because he's passed an in-school vision screening. The usual visual screening given in first grade picks up many youngsters with eye problems—but not all of them. A child who is lagging in reading should have a complete examination by a specialist who not only checks each eye separately but evaluates their functioning together.

Even if his vision is normal, could your youngster have a perceptual problem? Some children with reading problems can see normally with each eye separately but have difficulty fusing two images into one in the brain. Neither eye may be clearly dominant. Such a youngster may "see" the first word in a sentence, then the fourth word, then a word from the line below or above. He often reverses digits in arithmetic, too. Or, he may have a distorted view of spatial relationships or difficulty in visual tracking from left to right along a line of print.

Problems involving visual perception arise in the brain or the nerve pathways leading to the brain from the eyes, not in the eyes themselves. Although not all these difficulties are clearly understood as yet, many can be diagnosed by means of tests now available, and often youngsters with such problems can be markedly helped by special educational techniques and by perceptual training.

Can your youngster hear normally? It's surprising how often parents and teachers fail to notice slight hearing impairment in young children. Some boys and girls can hear normally except for certain tones or in some auditory ranges. Although they seem to get along adequately in school, they have to depend on a combination of guessing, lipreading and faking to make up for what they can't hear, and they miss or misunderstand enough to develop learning problems. Other youngsters have hearing loss that fluctuates with ear and throat infections or with allergy and is easy to overlook. (One good clue to occasional hearing loss: Does your child sometimes turn the TV up to a higher than usual level?)

Frequently, special placement within a classroom, or careful medical care for a respiratory infection, is enough to clear up reading problems based on minor hearing loss. But no evaluation of a reading difficulty is complete without a thorough check on hearing.

Is your child up to par physically? Allergies, anemia, low-grade infection, malnutrition—there are many physical problems that can be easily overlooked, yet are troublesome enough to keep a child from putting his energies into learning to read. Your doctor should be aware that your youngster is having difficulty in school and should make sure there are no physical reasons.

Could your child be so bright that he is bored with the Oh-Sally-see-Spot stupidities typical of many classrooms and doesn't even try? Many six-year-olds are so skilled at getting complex information from television, radio, movies and other sources that they see no reason to make an effort to master the inanities of the usual look-say primers. If this should be the case with your youngster, you may be able to persuade the teacher to enrich his curriculum and give him more challenge. You can also help by continuing to read books and newspapers to him at his interest level, so he'll become more aware of the mental riches to be gained from reading. Many of the suggestions in Chapter 42 are also useful in this situation.

Could your child be too immature for the grade in which his chronological age places him? Children differ markedly in their growth and developmental patterns. A few youngsters, particularly boys who are among the youngest in the class, may benefit from being transferred to a lower grade. Chapter 49 discusses this possibility at greater length.

Could your youngster have missed some essential teaching because he was ill or because of a change in school? In this case, your youngster's teacher may be able to pinpoint gaps in his knowledge that can be corrected with a little help at home or from a tutor.

Could your child have lacked enough sensory stimulation in the early years of his life to nourish his eagerness to learn and to help his brain develop? "Culturally deprived" children are found not only in slums but in homes in every socio-economic level where parents do not understand the great needs of small children for mental stimulation or where a youngster has usually been left with uneducated or uncommunicative household help. Spending more time with your child in reading to him, talking with him, taking him on minitrips and sharing his innate eagerness to learn may overcome part of this deficit.

Could your youngster's reading problems be due to a specific learning disability or minimal brain dysfunction? Minimal brain dysfunction is a broad term that covers learning problems and behavioral difficulties which stem from minor injury to the brain or other parts of the central nervous system, or from what seems to be a lag or immaturity or difference in neurological development. The term "specific learning disability" is often used interchangeably with minimal brain dysfunction and is usually preferred by parents' groups and educators.

There are many causes of minimal brain dysfunction: injury before, during or after birth; infectious diseases with high fever in early childhood; unknown factors affecting an unborn baby during pregnancy; and possibly, in some cases, inherited factors. No two children with minimal brain dysfunction are alike. And the precise connection between a possible injury or immaturity and the child's learning problems is usually difficult or impossible to establish.

But the more doctors, psychologists and educators study minimal brain dysfunction, the more it seems to account for a substantial percentage of chronic learning problems. Between 5 and 20 percent of all children in the average classroom have learning disabilities, experts in this field now estimate. One study shows that minimal brain dysfunction can be detected in 70 percent of all children referred to child-guidance clinics for any reason.

Symptoms often associated with learning problems of this kind include hyperactivity, awkwardness, poor coordination, impulsiveness, short attention span, emotional instability, immature development, perceptual disabilities and inability to use language as well as others of the same age. But the symptoms of minimal brain dysfunction vary enormously. One key characteristic is a marked difference between various abilities of a youngster. He may talk like a six-year-old, but have the coordination of a three-year-old. Or he may do well in math, but poorly in reading. Or his writing may be surprisingly awkward for his intelligence. Many children with learning disabilities score average or better than average on I.Q. and achievement tests, but the subscores on these measures will be markedly inconsistent.

If your youngster has some of these symptoms, if there is marked discrepancy in his abilities, or if the cause of his reading trouble isn't obvious, then he should have a complete neurologic workup, ideally by a pediatric neurologist or physician with experience in these problems, or in a special medical clinic.

A diagnosis of minimal brain dysfunction is useful, for special educational techniques are available which can help most of these youngsters considerably. Medications can also be effective in some cases, particularly when hyperactivity is involved. Most parents are relieved to know that a physical factor, for which remedies are available, is responsible for their children's difficulty, and that they are not causing his problems in some subtle psychological way.

Increasingly, school systems are adding specialists in learning disabilities to the staff, and hospitals, particularly those connected with medical schools, are establishing clinics where minimal brain dysfunction can be diagnosed and treatment prescribed. Most communities now have organizations of parents and teachers concerned with helping children with learning disabilities. Information about such groups can be obtained by writing to the national office of the Association for Children with Learning Disabilities, 5225 Grace Street, Pittsburgh, Pennsylvania 15236.

Is your youngster so worried about something connected with school that he can't concentrate on learning? A child who frequently is bullied or teased or unable to compete with his classmates on the playground may become so tense that he can't learn. You should also seek professional help if your youngster seems to have an emotional problem for which the cause is not obvious or which cannot be eased within a reasonable length of time.

Along with all of these specific suggestions for finding help for a child with difficulties in reading, you can use the strategies listed in Chapter 42 to help keep your offspring interested in reading and learning at home and for making his learning a pleasant, happy experience.

48. I.Q. Tests: Advantages and Limitations

I.Q. tests have been banned in the primary grades in a few metropolitan school systems in recent years, the result of festering tensions between educators and parents. Parents often worry lest I.Q. scores be used to penalize, rather than help, their children or made the basis for educational decisions to the exclusion of other measures of ability and learning. And minority groups often charge that the tests are not fair to children who do not come from white middle-class homes.

The nagging questions persist everywhere I.Q. tests are given: Just how good are the tests? Precisely what do they measure? Are they unfair to the child who is not of middle-class, English-speaking background or who tenses up in testing situations or who isn't feeling well on test day? Are I.Q.'s used inaccurately to shunt children off into slow academic tracks, or do they prejudice teachers against low scorers?

Originally I.Q. tests were intended to measure "intelligence," which was considered a fixed and unchanging quality that could be separated from experience, achievement and other aspects of human behavior. By giving a child an I.Q.

test, it was assumed, accurate predictions could be made about the kind of schooling from which he would profit most and the level of occupation he could seek as an adult.

Today, however, it's known that "intelligence" is not a fixed quality. It changes, sometimes considerably, as a result of environmental stimulation and physical changes in the brain itself.

An I.Q. test compares how well a youngster does on a given set of mental tasks on a specific day with the performance of a large group of youngsters used to standardize the test. How high he scores depends not only on his innate intelligence, but also, to some extent, on his past experiences and learning.

If the child's background is somewhat similar to that of the children used in standardizing the test, his score will be a more accurate indication of his abilities than if his environment has been quite different.

In recent years, many new forms of I.Q. tests have been devised which are called "culture-free" or "culture-fair" in efforts not to penalize children from other than middle-class, English-speaking backgrounds. But it seems almost impossible to devise tests that don't reflect in some way a youngster's past opportunities to learn and the impact of his environment on his mind.

Despite the fact that tests never can be completely "culture-free," they are still useful in predicting success in school and identifying youngsters who will need special help, proponents argue. To blame the test for giving a lower score to a child from a culturally different or culturally deprived home is like condemning a scale for indicating that a youngster is under-nourished, one educator has pointed out. Like the scale, which shows a child's need for extra food, the I.Q. test can help identify the youngster who needs extra help to succeed in school because of his different background.

Originally, I.Q. was determined by a mathematical formula in which a child's performance on a test was expressed in terms of "mental age." The mental age was divided by the young-ster's chronological age and multiplied by 100. Some more recent I.Q. tests now use a standard deviation method of expressing I.Q. test scores, again with 100 as average. Scores then are based on the percentage of children who score above and below this norm. Differences in scoring mean that a youngster could rate 20 to 30 points higher on one I.Q. test than on another published by a different testing company.

Whichever scoring method is used, test publishers empha-size that a child's score should not be considered a precise measurement. Instead, it indicates that his theoretical, "true" score is probably within about 10 points higher or lower than the number.

Because I.Q. testing usually is done at pivotal points in the lives of children, and because many educational decisions hang on the scores, it's important for parents to understand the advantages and limitations of I.Q. measurements.

Advantage: I.Q. tests do a good job in measuring how well children can perform a given set of mental tasks in comparison with a large group of youngsters used to standardize the test. Because questions are closely related to the kinds of intelli-gence and learning required in school, I.Q. tests can be useful predictors of success in school.

Limitation: Because I.Q. tests do an effective job in measur-ing scholastic aptitude, it's easy for teachers and parents to forget that the tests only evaluate a few of many factors that make up "intelligence."

Advantage: The I.Q. test is one of the few tools yet devel-oped for measuring an aspect of human behavior. It can be useful in balancing out prejudice by teachers and in lessening reliance on human fallibility in assessing children's abilities and potential.

Limitation: Because I.Q.'s are numerical, it's difficult to re-member that they are imprecise. A child's score could vary by 30 points or more, depending on how hard he tried on a test, how well he felt that day, his experience at test-taking, his anxiety about the testing situation and which publisher's test was being used.

Advantage: I.Q.'s can add one more dimension to our understanding of children. They can help evaluate why Tommy daydreams in class (he may be bright and bored instead of lazy or slow) and whether Debbie needs more educational challenge or David is being pressured beyond his abilities to perform.

Limitation: A teacher or parents, especially if not fully aware of the limitations of I.Q. tests, may find it almost impossible to avoid seeing "142" instead of "Tommy" or "83" instead of "Jennifer."

Advantage: I.Q. tests can be valuable in helping schools—and parents—make educational plans for children. This can be particularly important in the case of slow learners or gifted pupils who will not make optimum progress in regular classrooms.

Limitation: Too often, low I.Q.'s have led to low expectations by a teacher. Then the I.Q. may become a self-fulfilling prophecy, although a child's poor performance may have been due not to lack of ability but to a difference in cultural background, failure to take enough interest in the test to try hard, temporary emotional upset or mild illness. No major decisions should ever be made about any child on the basis of a single I.Q. test, particularly if it is given in a group situation.

If I.Q. tests are used by schools within the framework of their limitations and for the specific purposes for which they are valid, then they can be a valuable tool—among many others—for educators. And within these same qualifications, I.Q. test results can also be helpful to parents, particularly in deciding whether a youngster might be being pushed too hard in school or whether he might need more enrichment and stimulation.

School administrators and teachers used to withhold the

results of I.Q. tests from parents on the grounds that such information might somehow be harmful to the child—that parents would brag about him too much if his scores were high, or think of him as dumb, to his detriment, if his I.Q. were low.

But the Family Educational Rights and Privacy Act, passed by Congress late in 1974, has given parents the legal right to see the school records, including test scores, of their children. Supporters of the legislation hope school administrators will take the time to help parents understand the meaning of test scores in a child's records and what use the school is making of such data. What is important is making sure that the school does not make far-reaching decisions about a child's education and future based on the flimsy information provided by an I.Q. test, especially one given in a group situation, and particularly if the score is low.

49. Should Your Child Repeat—or Skip—a Grade in School?

From the moment the teacher telephoned David's mother to come in for an extra conference, Mrs. Canfield knew what she was going to say: David hadn't done well in second grade and should repeat. Did Mrs. Canfield concur? Should she agree that her son should be flunked?

Even without the emotional turmoil associated with flunking, it's difficult to decide when a child should repeat a grade, to predict how much he'll actually learn the second time around, to know whether the embarrassment of being left back will hurt him more than the day-to-day failure to keep up with the rest of his class. The answer varies, of course, from child to child. Before an decision is made, several factors need to be carefully weighed.

Hopefully the school will have results of I.Q. and achievement tests to share with David's parents. If not, it will be well worth the Canfields' time and expense to have such testing done at the nearest university or family service agency. Everyone helping David should remember that individual testing gives more accurate results than group tests and that no far-

307

reaching decisions should be based upon a single test, which is often an inaccurate predictor.

David should also have a complete physical checkup before a decision about next year is made. The doctor should be told about the boy's academic difficulties and asked specifically about physical problems which could contribute.

Many children who fail in school have auditory or visual problems which aren't picked up in routine group ear and eye tests in school. Partial hearing loss is particularly hard to detect because many youngsters become adept at getting by with a combination of lipreading and guessing and may not even be aware themselves how much they are missing. Even if a child fails to hear only a few tones, this can distort his understanding of words and make reading more difficult. A few youngsters have a hearing loss that comes and goes with respiratory infections or allergies, yet is enough of a handicap to trip them up in school.

If an easily correctable physical problem is discovered, David should probably be promoted with his class. A summer to relax and grow, plus next fall's reviewing of subject matter, will probably be all he needs to catch up with his contemporaries again. Or, with his teacher's recommendation, some summer schooling or individual tutoring may help to fill in any academic gaps before September.

The Canfields also need to ask themselves other questions: Has David always been somewhat immature for his age? Has he always had to hustle hard to keep up, even on the playground? Is he among the youngest in the class? Does he seem to play better with children somewhat younger than his classmates? Boys tend to lag behind girls physically and academically all through elementary school. The stresses on the most immature boys in each class are great. If this is David's situation, repeating a year now may give him just the breather he needs to catch up with his classmates and to do well every succeeding year.

Has David been feeling over his head academically ever since he started school? Is he so discouraged by the grinding failure to succeed in class that he's stopped trying? If so, his relief at having a year to catch up may be far greater than the trauma of flunking.

Have emotional problems been bothering David this last year? Has he changed schools? Been upset by a death or long illness in the family? Has he missed a considerable amount of schoolwork because of his own illness or a series of colds and infections? With this kind of obvious—and temporary—problem behind him, a summer's growth and a fresh start in the fall should be all David needs to get back in step academically.

Is David's greatest difficulty in reading? Does his school use archaic instruction methods or techniques by which David finds it hard to learn? A summer's individual tutoring with a different reading method may be more helpful to him than repeating a year of the same work.

If there's a wide discrepancy between David's evident ability and his performance in school, if he's highly distractible, overactive, clumsy and a behavior problem in class, the Canfields should investigate the possibility that he has a specific learning disability or a perceptual handicap. A youngster of normal or above average intelligence who shows any of a wide variety of symptoms of a learning disability should have a complete examination by a pediatric neurologist or other expert in learning disabilities before any decision is made about grade placement. Often the academic problem can be best overcome by drug treatment and/or special educational techniques. Repeating a year in school in the same kind of learning situation that proved unsuccessful in the past won't help David much next year. Instead, he needs a specific educational prescription tailored to take advantage of ways in which he can learn most effectively and successfully despite his handicap.

Using medication to treat hyperactivity has recently become controversial. But careful research shows that a youngster usually responds rapidly and well to medication if his hyper-activity has a neurological basis, however slight, and is not due solely to emotional problems. The most successful of these drugs is methylphenidate, with amphetamines a second choice. Although these drugs are stimulants, they have a calming effect on hyperactive children, helping them to concentrate and learn without so much purposeless distraction. Because they are stimulants, they are not effective in youngsters with emotional problems, but instead make them much worse. Such medication must be prescribed by a physician who monitors the child's reactions carefully, ideally working with his teacher as well as with his parents.

How do David's I.Q. and academic achievement tests compare with those of his classmates? In some suburban areas, I.Q. scores may average 15 or more points higher than national medians, putting a slightly below average youngster at considerable disadvantage. (For a child with learning disabilities, it's important to look carefully at subtest scores, not just total I.Q., and to consider other evidence of intelligence and ability as well as I.Q.). Less than average ability, especially if combined with immaturity, may indicate that David would be more successful if he takes an extra year in his present grade.

If David does repeat second grade, will he have the same teacher? Unless the Canfields are sure she understands David's difficulties and knows how to help him, keeping him back a year may just mean an unsuccessful rerun of the last nine months.

Some research does indicate that a failing child makes more progress if he's promoted with his class than if he repeats a grade. But the hazards of attempting third grade without an adequate grasp of second-grade skills are obvious. If David constantly feels defeated, discouraged and insecure in class now, the one big disappointment of knowing he isn't going to pass may be easier for him to take than the daily, grinding failure he experiences now. If a second-grade placement next September would mean some small daily successes, they may soon outweigh the failure he'll feel this spring. And if he usually plays with younger children, repeating a year may not necessarily be uncomfortable for him socially.

Whatever the Canfields decide, however, David will need their abundant love and encouraging support.

The difficult problem of flunking can usually be avoided in less rigid schools which do not insist that all children progress through the same work at the same speed. If children are grouped according to ability within each grade, the slower learners can benefit from a teacher and teaching methods especially geared to them. They have a better chance of keeping up to grade level than in a heterogeneous class where they encounter frustrating competition and get only a fraction of the teacher's time.

Ungraded elementary schools make it even easier for the youngster in temporary academic trouble. He simply spends a few extra weeks at the level where he is having difficulty— without gambling a year of his education on the decision as to whether he should repeat an entire grade.

SKIPPING

When—if ever—should a child skip a grade in school? Can skipping ease the frustrations of the bright youngster who is bored in class? Or will it just create different problems later on? What factors need to be considered before a youngster is double-promoted?

In today's educational climate, skipping has become far rarer than flunking. (About 6 percent of youngsters in the United States are a year or more ahead of their normal grade placement.) Yet experts who study gifted children consider acceleration one of the best—and easiest—ways for a school system to help a bright youngster find interest and challenge in the classroom.

In schools which do not group pupils according to their

mental abilities, double promotion may be the only realistic way of helping an unusually intelligent child partially escape lock-step education geared to the average.

A highly gifted youngster may be three to five years ahead, in mental age, of his classmates in elementary school. Studies show that he already knows one-half to three-fourths of all that is to be taught during a given school year, and therefore wastes a large part of his time in the classroom. In terms of his innate ability, the brighter the child, the more likely he is to be relatively retarded in educational achievement, studies show.

Concern lest double promotion put a child out of his depth emotionally or socially has been a major brake on the use of skipping to help bright children. But surveys and studies show that gifted youngsters, as a group, are more advanced physically, socially and emotionally than their chronological equals, and that after double promotion they are usually indistinguishable from classmates a year older.

Research indicates that children who skip a grade do better throughout their school careers, generally, than youngsters of equal ability who remain with their own same-age classmates. In-depth studies made of accelerated students after high-school graduation show that they equal their older classmates in all phases of social adjustment and personal evaluations and that both they and their parents consider skipping to have been beneficial.

What factors need to be weighed in considering whether a child should be double-promoted? The major ones are:

How high is the youngster's I.Q.? Skipping should not be considered unless the I.Q. is at least 125, several experts advise. A youngster with an I.Q. of 150 or higher should be double-promoted at least once, and even then he will be scholastically ahead of most of his classmates, these researchers point out.

Exactly how old is the youngster? A child whose birthday comes soon after a school cutoff deadline is only slightly younger than pupils a year ahead of him in school. He may have much more in common with them, if he is advanced in mental age, than in a class in which he is one of the oldest, as well as one of the brightest, youngsters.

Does the child usually play with older children and feel at ease with them?

Is he bored much of the time in school now? Is he getting by without putting forth any effort to learn and slipping into sloppy study habits?

Will the teacher he will have in the advanced grade be sympathetic and understanding? Will she be willing to help him fill in any gaps in his education and help him over any initial hurdles?

How mature is the youngster physically? Did his parents and grandparents tend to have an early-adolescent growth spurt? A boy who is apt to be small physically and mature late during the teen years may experience some social difficulties during the junior high school years if he is double-promoted in the early elementary grades.

A bright girl who already seems large for her age and whose family history suggests she may mature early is usually a good candidate for double promotion. In fact, one study suggests that girls who are physically and socially advanced for their age should be double-promoted even though their classwork is only average because they will soon catch up and have a happier adjustment to school.

How competitive is the high school in your area? Sometimes a child who is double-promoted because he is bored in a grade school where youngsters are not grouped by ability finds the academic pace difficult in high school, where bright students are shifted into honors tracks and competition is much more keen. Occasionally a parent who thought double promotion was a good solution for his bright offspring at the age of seven or eight comes to regret the decision a few years later when the student does not rank quite as high in high school as the parent had anticipated.

Does the school system offer better alternatives? A good program of ability grouping, combined with advanced work in junior high school and advanced college-placement courses in high school, may be a better solution to challenging gifted students, for it avoids possible hazards of gaps in the education and too-young entrance to college.

Neither repeating nor skipping a grade in elementary school is an ideal answer to the problems of a child who does not fit in easily with his chronological grade level. The youngster who is flunked must inevitably repeat some material he already knows; the one who is double-promoted always misses a few pieces of essential learning that must be acquired in some other way. Both children face adjustments to fitting in socially with new classmates.

Nongraded primary classes, independent learning, flexible class grouping and a dozen other educational innovations come much closer to meeting the needs of all children—including those who fall above or below the norms—than does traditional classroom organization. All parents—and particularly those whose children are not average—should look for opportunities to encourage the adoption of these more flexible plans.

50. RAT RACE, JUNIOR GRADE

In the beginning, it didn't seem like pressure, but opportunity.

Debbie really should keep up her piano lessons; her teacher said so. Ballet would be wonderful for helping her conquer pre-adolescent awkwardness. Surely you couldn't argue against a ten-year-old's wanting to join the Girl Scouts. Or against orthodontia; that just involves 15 minutes once a week, unless you count the wait in the dentist's office.

Sally, next door, urged Debbie into signing up for those swimming lessons on Saturdays in the high-school pool ("These are free, Mommy; you said we couldn't afford those tennis lessons at the indoor courts"). Then there's Sunday school. A bit of homework. A chore or two to do around the house. A pet to care for. The piano to practice.

Suddenly ten-year-old Debbie is scheduled from breakfast to bedtime. So is Debbie's mother, who is either chauffeuring or telephoning about the day's car-pool complexities, or reminding Debbie to practice or to remember her leotard or to feed the parakeets or just to hurry-you'll-be-late. And life is filled not so much with opportunity as it is with pressure. There is no time to invite Barbara over just to play. Or to experiment with a new cookie recipe. Or read a book that isn't required for school. Or just do nothing.

"But Debbie isn't being challenged enough in school," explains Debbie's mother as she sets the clock for her daughter's piano practice. "If I didn't keep after her she'd just sit in front of the TV and do nothing. I want her to have every advantage."

Some youngsters—usually bright, high-energy types for whom school offers little challenge—thrive on after-school extracurricular activities. A few others with special aptitudes or interests will discover lifetime pleasure or even career opportunities in ballet or music or competitive sports. But for others, the trap of too many wonderful, worthwhile, enriching activities can snap shut on most of the after-school freedom, leaving them caught in a rat race, junior grade.

"I wish I'd catch a cold," sighed an eleven-year-old wearily. "It's the only way I think I'll get a day off."

A parent should be extra-cautious about signing a youngster up for out-of-school activities if: he has a low level of energy; he's a perfectionist who won't be satisfied just to enjoy an activity but will push himself to excel and brood if he isn't best at everything: he's in an honors track at school and loaded with homework; he's already under considerable pressure at school to keep up with his class. And if he's an unusually creative and independent child, what he may need most is opportunity to think and work by himself on projects of his own choosing without the constant groupism that school and most outside activities require.

What extracurricular activities are most important for a school-age child? It's wise to leave as much of the choice up to your youngster as possible. One mother talked the situation over with her sixth-grader along these lines:

"First, you must do as well in school as you can. That means getting your homework done—carefully and on time. It means going to school every day rested and ready to do your best.

"You'll also have to save two afternoons a month for the orthodontist, and go to Sunday school. After that, the activities and lessons you sign up for are your choice, subject to our approval and the cost.

"You can't possibly do all the exciting activities open to you," the mother explained. "In selecting, remember these extracurriculars have two purposes. One is to make your life happier and richer. So you should choose those you enjoy. The other purpose is to give you a chance to explore new fields and try new things so you'll know what really interests you and what you can do well. Then, when the time comes in high school to pick a college or a career, you will have a better idea of what you want to do and where your abilities lie.

"At your age, it's not a disgrace to try something—organized football or piano or art—and later drop it because you find you aren't interested or good at it. You have still learned something valuable about yourself, and enough about that activity to appreciate those who do it well. You must give it enough time, thought and effort so that it's a fair trial, however."

You can help your child by talking over objectively with him the advantages of any extracurricular activity you feel he does need, such as after-school sports or Junior Great Books. If he signs up with the understanding he won't be labeled a failure if he isn't doing well or is overloaded, you'll have a better chance of gaining his enthusiastic participation than if you simply issue orders. If he plans his own extracurricular activities on the basis of his own interests and curiosities, he'll achieve more and feel less pressure. And as an adult he won't sometimes think, "I wish I'd had a chance to try . . ."

51. THE CAR AS MULTIPURPOSE
THERAPEUTIC DEVICE

Chauffeuring is the curse of the suburban-class mother, according to a current myth. From behind the wheel of the family car, the theory goes, mothers not only drive their offspring to school, athletic events, pediatrician and orthodontist —they also drive their children to physical unfitness, ulcers and overdependency.

But this theory, like so many, underestimates the ingenuity of mothers. For, rather than permitting the car to turn into a traveling trap, many mothers have discovered how to use the family hardtop or wagon as a multipurpose educational and therapeutic device (as pedagogical parlance puts it). For example:

The car as dining-room table: Back in the pre-TV era, family conversation reportedly flourished around the dining-room table, as parents fed their offspring manners along with the pot roast and mashed potatoes.

Now that the evening meal is too frequently served in front of the TV, with conversation fitted into the commercial spots, the automobile has become the best available setting for family talk.

318

"I discovered on a cross-country drive to California that my children would actually listen to me reading aloud in the car, when they'd never sit still for it any other time," a mother commented. "Now I save magazine articles, newspaper clippings, jokes—anything I want my youngsters to know about—for times we're all in the car."

The car as wiretap: If you want to find out how your child is doing in school, what he thinks of his teachers and what his friends are really like, your best strategy is to volunteer to drive his car pool and then keep quiet.

You aren't actually eavesdropping, because you're sitting there in plain sight. But the passengers will treat you like some sort of gadget attached to the steering wheel. You will learn that your child got a D in the math test, why the music teacher quit, and that the reason your offspring has shut himself up in his room after school for two days has nothing to do with you, but with a blond seventh-grade cheerleader who has been ignoring him.

The car as couch: A car has three conversational advantages that the dining-room table, living room and bedside lack: Parent and child do not have to look directly at each other when they talk. Neither can walk out on the conversation. And because the parent is—in theory, at least—giving her chief attention to driving, the talk has a casualness that an eyeball-to-eyeball confrontation does not. So it's easier to make points on touchy subjects like sex education, report cards and behavior.

That the automobile can be a therapeutic milieu for parent and child has not been lost on psychologists and psychiatrists. "Sometimes I think the ride to and from the child-guidance clinic does as much good as anything that happens during the appointment," a psychiatrist once commented.

52. How Well Do You Know Children?

How well can you diagnose a youngster's problem? Can you unravel these six incidents and deduce why the children acted as they did?

1. A nursery-school teacher enters a playroom in time to see three-year-old Mark hit three-year-old Andy with a block. She separates the boys, sending Mark outdoors to play and suggesting to the weeping Andy that he fingerpaint. When Mark's mother comes to pick up her son after the morning session is over, the teacher tells her:

(a) Mark is really taking out on Andy the anger he feels at his mother for having recently had a new baby.

(b) Mark is symbolically hurting his new little sister whom he is afraid to hit because he fears his father's anger.

(c) Mark is still feeling insecure and emotionally upset because his father was hospitalized for two days several weeks earlier.

2. At age two, Richie cries himself into exhaustion at bedtime every night, often awakes screaming at 1 or 2 A.M., and

refuses to lie down in his crib until he has been rocked to sleep in his mother's weary arms. The underlying reason is:

(a) He is reflecting his mother's basic insecurities.

(b) He is spoiled and insisting on his own way.

(c) He's getting back at his mother for trying to toilet-train him.

3. Five-year-old Roger is the kindergarten cutup. He deliberately spills crayons, scribbles angrily on his reading-readiness book, refuses to put on his coat. Is he:

(a) Too immature emotionally for school?

(b) In need of extra attention from the teacher because his mother is preoccupied with a new baby?

(c) Showing that he has failed to resolve the Oedipus conflict?

4. Benjamin is five years old and still wets the bed occasionally at night. This is because:

(a) He is rebelling because his parents expect too much of him and were too rigid and pressuring when they toilet-trained him at the age of twenty-one months.

(b) He is subconsciously trying to drown his father.

(c) He is rebelling because his parents treat him too much like a baby and refuse to let him grow up.

5. Although Greg has an I.Q. well above average, he has been a problem all through first grade. He is easily distracted, full of mischief, unable to concentrate, fidgety, noisy, restless, "naughty." He has not learned to read at all, although he did memorize the words in his primer, and adults who talk with him are sure he is bright. Greg's problems are caused by:

(a) Marital conflicts between his parents, which make him feel insecure.

(b) An attempt to get the attention he feels he does not

322 · EFFECTIVE PARENTING

receive at home because he is a middle child whose older brother and younger sister take up most of his parents' time.

(c) Greg can already feel the subtle pressures his parents are putting on him because they want to make sure he gets into a top college.

6. Polly, seven, has been informed she must have her tonsils out in a few days. She doesn't seem unduly frightened. But she has slept an excessive amount, been listless and uninterested in play since the doctor told her about the surgery. This means:

(a) She is trying to escape from residual, unresolved childhood fears.

(b) She is trying to act like a baby to get more of her mother's attention so she can feel secure and protected.

(c) She feels the operation is a punishment for thinking "bad" thoughts about her parents.

Neighbors, teachers and amateur psychologists actually gave all of the answers listed to the parents of Mark, Richie, Roger, Benjamin, Greg and Polly. In a few situations, some of the answers might have been correct. For these six youngsters, however, none of them was right.

Mark hit Andy because Andy hit him first, in an attempt to force him to give up a tricycle it was Mark's turn to ride. Mark didn't need psychological help, but a few practical suggestions about how to deal with an aggressive playmate by more effective means than hitting back.

Rachel had unusually large tonsils and adenoids, which swelled with allergy or slight infection. Sometimes when she lay on her back in bed, they almost completely blocked her nasal passages, throwing her into the kind of panic an adult with a severe cold experiences occasionally when he wakes up suddenly feeling smothered. In Rachel's mind, this fright became associated with her crib, and she fought it until she slept from exhaustion. Removal of her tonsils and adenoids at an unusually early age solved the sleeping difficulty within two weeks.

Roger was color-blind to some degree, although no one realized it. He couldn't understand the distinctions in colors other children were making and reacted by fighting everything he could in kindergarten. No quick solution was possible, but Roger's behavior problems cleared up when an alert teacher, who knew how common color-blindness is among males, guessed his handicap and made allowances for it.

Medical examination detected that Benjamin had an unusually small bladder, which, coupled with his unusually sound sleeping pattern, made him a bed wetter. Medication and special training solved the problem in a few weeks after the situation was properly diagnosed.

Greg had a neurological problem, not an emotional one. A thorough examination by a pediatric neurologist revealed that he had minimal brain dysfunction. Special training in visual perception plus a specially structured classroom situation resulted in marked improvement both in Greg's behavior and in his reading skills.

A phone call to the doctor solved Polly's problem. The same day he decided on the surgery, the doctor prescribed antihistamine pills for the little girl, forgetting to tell her mother about possible side effects such as drowsiness. An adjustment in medication made her her alert, bright self again.

There are three morals to these case histories: Children differ, and similar problems do not necessarily have similar causes. It is more effective to look for physical causes and obvious reasons first. And a little knowledge of psychology can be a dangerous thing.

53. PARENT AS IMAGE MAKER

"You should enjoy learning that music," commented a mother as her eight-year-old struggled with a difficult piano assignment. "You always like to do hard things."

"I do?" asked Nicky.

"Don't you remember how hard it was to learn to ice-skate? But you kept at it until you could, no matter how often you fell. You learned to ride your bicycle the same determined way. And I remember how hard you struggled to roll over in your crib when you were a baby and to pull yourself up on the playpen bars and to walk by yourself."

"Oh, sure, I remember now," said Nicky, as he tackled the music again with renewed self-confidence.

Adults are forever putting children into categories, some beneficial, some unfortunate: "Linda always was awkward." "Marty never could spell." "Jack takes after his father—stubborn." "Nancy's always been a fussy eater." "Sarah just can't seem to make friends."

Children hear these labels with predictable results. Linda feels even more awkward, becomes even more clumsy. Marty decides there is no use trying to learn to spell. Jack takes pride in his obstinacy. Nancy feels she must live up to her reputation at every meal. Sarah's shyness grows worse.

Of all the image-makers in our society, none is more power-ful or more damaging than the adult who casually creates a derogatory image of a child, who pins an unhappy label on him, such as "slow learner," "unpopular," "naughty," "bad." Actually, the jeopardy to the child is triple.

First, a youngster finds it almost impossible not to believe the adult, even though he may have sounded off only in hasty exasperation. And the more a child sees himself as stupid or clumsy or disliked or naughty, the harder it is for him to be clever or coordinated or attractive or good.

Second, even though the labeling may have been done in momentary pique, the adult may almost unconsciously begin to look on the child as dumb or inept or unlovable or delin-quent. He expects the youngster to act in accord with the role in which he has cast him. And he tends to overlook evidence that doesn't fit the image.

An image created for a child also influences the attitude of other adults toward him. A youngster rarely lives down a repu-tation for being a troublemaker, or slow, acquired as early as first grade. And a neighbor who has heard a father speak dis-paragingly of his son for years isn't apt to hire the boy to do his summer yardwork or write an enthusiastic recommendation when it comes time to apply for college.

Yet image-making, done thoughtfully and lovingly, can be one of the most effective techniques of child rearing. If you work slowly and honestly at it, you can help your youngster build an image of himself as good, intelligent, truthful, trust-worthy and well liked, and he will find it difficult to act in any other way.

The strategy is to seize on those moments when you can honestly hang a happy, positive label on your offspring. It's no use calling him brave when he's just made a fuss in the dentist's office. Or to pretend he's dependable when you and he both know he just told you a fib.

In any small child's life there are moments when he has been helpful or courteous or hard-working or unafraid or thoughtful. If you comment on these actions appreciatively—and remind him later about them—you can do much to make them a permanent part of his character.

"It's such fun to go somewhere with you because you act so nicely." "I'm glad I can count on you." "I don't know what I would have done without your help today." "It's fine to have a boy who likes to try new things." Statements such as these help a child build a good image of himself and give him the self-confidence it takes to keep working at the long, difficult job of growing up.

54. The Number Two Child

Who Doesn't Try Harder

"I want to talk to you about Mary," a mother tells a fourth-grade teacher. "She is so convinced she can't do as well as her sister, Kim, is doing in fifth grade, she won't even try. How can I help her?"

"Johnny wants to do everything Chris does, and when he can't, he just gives up and calls himself 'stupid' and 'hopeless,' " says another parent. "But Chris is older, taller, better coordinated. How can I get Johnny to relax the competition with his brother?"

Martha won't practice the piano because she can't play as well as her older sister. Diane, ten, is sure her parents love Cindy, thirteen, better than they love her because Cindy won an eighth-grade essay contest. Jack cites a secondhand bike, a secondhand trumpet and a hand-me-down coat as proof his parents consider him a second-class child.

Most advice to parents about jealousy and competition between children centers on ways to protect the first youngster from feeling "dethroned" when a second baby is born. Mothers are urged to spend more time with the Number One child. Visitors are subtly reminded to bring a gift for the old baby as well as the new one. No one has paid much attention to the children who don't try harder because they are Number Two.

The second child does have a point. Parents are excited when a firstborn takes his first steps, starts kindergarten, loses his first tooth, is graduated from eighth grade. With a second child it's a rerun, even though the cast has changed.

Parents, with the best of intentions, usually pay more attention to a first child and his problems than to a second. They must learn how to be parents with the first child, and this takes time and practice. With the second, they know he'll eventually be toilet-trained, stop sucking his thumb and learn to ride his bike, so they relax and enjoy him more. But Second Child may sense the difference in attitude and attribute it not to experience but to lack of interest.

Parents also tend to expect more of a first child—and usually get it. He is urged to be a big boy, to take responsibility, to set a good example. A second child remains the family's baby, or eventually becomes a "middle child," without either the prerogatives of the eldest or the privileges of the youngest.

The difference does show. Research indicates that as a group, firstborn individuals make more of a mark in the world than second-born or later-born children. In proportion to their total number, firstborn people are overrepresented in groups such as gifted children, scholarship winners, professors, college students, medical students, high-ranking scientists and individuals listed in Who's Who, studies show.

What helps? Planning a family so there is more than a year's interval in ages tends to minimize some of the competition that is usually so hard on the second child. Being aware of the problem in itself can help.

But the key is emphasizing and valuing the differences between youngsters as individuals, and in not treating children identically, but trying to give each one precisely what he, as a person, needs.

If Marcia has piano lessons, that doesn't mean Linda must have them, too. She might do better with a flute, or ballet lessons, or on a swimming team. If Bill is a Little League batting star, look carefully at Brad's individual talents and interests before you encourage him to go and do likewise.

You should avoid comparing children, especially as a technique to jack up a younger one. If your second child insists on making discouraging comparisons anyway, it may help to remind him that the father and the mother in your family make vastly different contributions, yet both are loved and valued.

It helps, too, to encourage each child to appreciate the individual abilities and contributions of the other. It is difficult to be jealous of someone who loves and admires you, because the roots of jealousy lie in the fear of inadequacy.

55. Bullies and Tattletales

It took Billy's mother a long time to discover what was up-setting her usually cheerful, self-sufficient nine-year-old. He was obviously troubled. He poked at his breakfast, complaining of stomachaches. His lunchbox came home almost untouched. He was tense, jumpy, tired after school.

Finally, Billy told his mother. A gang of seventh- and eighth-graders were systematically tyrannizing younger boys at school. They spat on the smaller children on the playground, punched them at every opportunity, stole their jackets and tossed them away blocks from school.

Fourth- or fifth-graders caught in a washroom by older boys were forced to surrender noontime milk money before being freed. The washrooms were befouled by boys who drew targets on the walls and spit on them. Several children were dragged into a nearby clump of trees and stripped of some of their clothing.

"If I hit back at them when they pick on me and am caught fighting, I get a black mark on my report card," Billy told his mother. "The principal won't listen if you try to tell him the other guy started it. He just says it takes two to make a fight. But I'm tired of being a punching bag for big guys. And if you try to make them stop, they'll call me a tattletale and beat me up even worse."

Complaints about junior-grade blackboard jungles are increasing, even in high-income suburban school districts. Problems are usually worse in elementary schools extending through eighth grade than in areas with separate junior high schools.

"Mothers are afraid when their children leave home for school nowadays," one mother said bitterly. "When they get to the schoolyard, there is fighting. Bullies knock younger ones down on the sidewalk. I used to take my boy to and from school every day because of what I've seen on the playground," she added. "Lately, I've let him go alone and take the chance he'll come home without injury. But it's nerve-racking to me and to other mothers as well."

A parent can't brush off Billy's problem with a "Stand up for your own rights, son," or a "See that you don't get into trouble." A fourth-grader doesn't have much chance against two bullies who are three years older and 35 pounds heavier. He shouldn't have to fight to go to school without harassment.

Billy's mother should begin by talking over the situation with other parents and children. If Billy's complaints seem valid and he is not the only child being victimized, she should take up the matter with his teacher and principal. It will be more effective if another mother or two go with her.

Unless the situation improves, the next step would be through a parent-teacher organization or a complaint to the local school board. If the parent-teacher group is largely social or mostly ineffective, it's time to start working at bucking it up.

Lack of adult supervision outside the classroom is an important factor in the bullying problem, most parents conclude. In Billy's school, for example, youngsters have an hour lunch period, eat in 15 minutes and spend the rest of the time in unsupervised play outside. Student monitors are usually unable to control other youngsters in such a situation and teachers are often unavailable or busy. Parent-organization members could now volunteer to help, as they do in some school lunch programs. School districts employing women, active senior citizens or college students as crossing guards might expand the force to serve inside the schoolyard, too.

Being a personal bodyguard to an individual child usually isn't a good way to end bullying, however, and will probably expose him to a vicious form of teasing and derision. But there are a few steps a parent can take that may help a little. First, Billy's mother must assure her child of her understanding and support in what is a terrifying difficulty for him. She can also give him some insight into the unhappy reasons why a few boys can find nothing better to do than pick on smaller youngsters.

Billy's mother can work to build up his self-confidence, to encourage him to make friends in his own age group. She shouldn't insist that he look or act different from his class-mates in minor matters of dress and play. And she can help him develop the athletic skills his associates consider impor-tant. One mother, for example, solved a bullying problem by having her highly responsible sixth-grader taught judo. He only used his new skill once, but he was never bullied after that.

Ideally, all parents should teach their children respect for the rights of others. Ideally, all schools should cultivate an esprit de corps that makes rigid supervision unnecessary. But until then, Billy needs adult help to assure his right to attend school unmolested.

Some parents effectively strengthen a bully's power over a child by teaching him, directly or indirectly, not to be a "tattle-tale."

Most parents do teach their offspring that "one does not tell on someone else unless it is concerning something of enormous magnitude," commented a child psychologist. Backing this view are those who use verbs like "rat" and "squeal" and nouns like "stool pigeon" and "fink" to describe the reporting of misconduct. Or who say to a youngster, "Don't be a tattletale, Billy. It's your problem. You work it out. I don't want to hear about it."

"Ever since my boy was big enough to walk, I've taught him he shouldn't snitch on other kids," stormed one father.

But other mothers and fathers disagree. Usually, they believe, when a youngster reports cheating or petty pilfering to a parent or teacher, he's actually seeking reassurance that he has learned the rules correctly and that they apply to others, too. He's looking for reinforcement of what he's learned at home.

If you scold him for being a tattletale, what does he learn? That he is the only one to whom the rules apply? That right and wrong only matter when an adult is watching? Or that if you do get caught, it's the fault of the guy who ratted on you?

A no-snitch philosophy can boomerang to protect the bully and the delinquent. It can deny both the witnessing child and the young transgressor the help of adults when it could do the most good. It can make a child insecure in his own concepts of honesty, of fair play and of justice. And it forces a youngster to judge and to deal with situations beyond his ability without adult guidance.

Of course the child who tattles vindictively, or untruthfully, or merely to get attention, does exist. But tattling is a symptom of this youngster's problems, not the cause. There are far fewer of these youngsters than there are children who learn to get away with dishonesty behind the smoke screen of "Don't rat."

The adult who warns children not to come snitching to him is often the adult who just doesn't want to be bothered to take the necessary corrective action. He doesn't want to get involved.

Very few parents want a child to report all minor misdoings he encounters. But they should offer clear and helpful understanding help to the child who does feel the necessity for reporting.

If children are to grow up to be responsible, caring citizens, they must be taught that there is a law and order based on a moral code upon which they can count and that there are adults sufficiently responsible and interested to try to protect these values.

56. How to Help a Shy Child

"Is there any way I can help my child to be more popular with other youngsters?" a mother worries. "He doesn't seem to have any close friends and often has to play by himself."

There are several strategies a parent can try which usually help a youngster to get along better with his playmates. But they must be used with great tact and subtlety or they may make matters worse.

First, it helps to consider whether a child really suffers from a problem. Sometimes a youngster may simply have a quiet kind of temperament and several strong, individual interests. He may be quite content to play by himself more than most small-fry, yet get along happily with others when they do come around.

If his mother's idea of happiness is a house full of noisy, gregarious, boisterous people, she may be worrying unnecessarily. She may be able to suggest ways her offspring can share some of his interests with a friend or two. But she should be careful about trying to impose her image of an ideal child on a youngster who is happy being himself.

When a child really does need help getting along with other children, some of these steps may be appropriate:

A major study of popularity among children shows that the basic element is not an individual's possessions, I.Q. or physical appearance—but his energy. More rest, better nutrition or a less turbulent home life might give a youngster more energy to devote to activities with others.

Most children play best with others who have approximately the same interests and skills. This usually means youngsters about the same age and the same sex. In neighborhoods where such likely playmates are scarce, it may help for a parent to arrange transportation to bring potential friends together after they have become acquainted at school, religious class or day camp.

If a youngster varies markedly from same-age acquaintances because of a difference in intelligence or abilities or interests, he may also need help in finding at least one similar friend. A gifted child, for example, usually enjoys playing with youngsters a year or two older than he is.

A youngster may be left out or may himself reject proffered friendships because he can't hold his own in games or sports. Often, some private coaching to help a child become adept at whatever sport or game is currently popular can help solve a shyness problem.

Children are cruelly quick to gang up against any youngster who deviates from an accepted standard of dress, appearance or behavior. Sometimes a parent makes a youngster the butt of teasing or indifference or rejection by insisting he wear shorter hair or dressier clothes than the prevailing neighborhood norms or that he follow markedly different rules.

It is necessary to enforce appropriate behavior and safety regulations. But whenever a parent makes a child deviate noticeably in looks or actions from other youngsters, she should have a good reason for it—and be able to explain that reason to her child.

Sometimes an unpopular child has habits or personality traits that turn away potential friends. He may need tactful lessons in sharing, in good sportsmanship, in controlling his temper, in cooperating with others or in overcoming a tendency to brag or bully or boss. Often talking to him casually about the feelings of other children is enough to improve his behavior and make him less self-centered.

57. Music Lessons Without Discord

Many mothers feel there's a Van Cliburn—or at least a little Liberace—in every child, just waiting the chance for music lessons. So they're tempted to sign him up for private piano lessons or group instrument instruction in school on the traditional grounds that this is one "advantage" that "good" parents offer their offspring. Too often, the results are a lot of bills and a lot of battles about practicing.

Despite considerable evidence from the Japanese Suzuki groups that music instruction should begin early in the preschool years, most music teachers in the United States advise waiting until a youngster is about eight years old to start formal lessons on the piano or other musical instrument. Unless a child shows clear and unusual music talent, most parents are told to wait until he can read fairly well, until he has conquered problems of adjusting to school and until he is old enough to take on some of the responsibility for practicing.

But there is much a parent can do to stimulate an interest in music to ready a child for formal lessons long before that age. Every youngster should have considerable opportunity to experience delight and satisfaction in listening to records, in experimenting with simple rhythm instruments, in singing and in musical play starting in the early preschool years. Some primary teachers show children how to play tunes on simple eight-note pipes or small autoharps, as readiness for formal training.

Once you've decided that your child is ready for music lessons—either from a private teacher or in a group at school—you're faced with the question of what instrument he should tackle. Ideally, a youngster should have an opportunity to experiment with many ways of making music, to discover whether he enjoys most blowing or bowing or fingering or drumming, whether he prefers a brass, a woodwind, drums or keyboard.

An excellent way to provide this kind of guidance is a talent exploration class, like those pioneered by the National Music Camp in Interlochen, Michigan. Here, youngsters are provided with several kinds of instruments and given enough instruction to play a simple tune on each one. Besides learning more about the sounds the instruments produce, children also discover something of the basic skills involved in playing—that drums need an innate sense of timing and rhythm; that it takes considerable practice and accuracy with fingering to produce pleasant sounds on a violin; that embouchure is important for woodwinds and brasses.

With this kind of preliminary experience, a youngster is much more likely to make an informed choice about his own musical instrument—and to stick to it through the dissonant learning stages.

A few schools also offer instrumental-exploration classes, sometimes as a project set up by parents' groups. What's much more likely is that the fourth- and fifth-graders are invited with their parents to a big assembly soon after school starts, at which time the local music store displays all the instruments. Youngsters are urged to select whichever one they like best and to sign up for lessons leading to participation in a fifth–sixth grade or junior-high band.

With no more guidance than a two-minute demonstration of each instrument from the stage, many youngsters do make inappropriate choices. At these buy-now-play-later assemblies, most boys pick a trumpet because they like the powerful tone or a clarinet because it seems easy or drums because they look exciting and sound simple to play. Girls most often choose a flute because "it's pretty." The results are a musically unbalanced school band—and a high dropout rate among the beginning musicians.

You can help your child make an intelligent, happy choice by suggesting he consider factors like these:

How much is the instrument in which he's interested needed in the school band or orchestra? A trumpet, flute or clarinet player has great competition. Drummers may be so numerous that they have to take turns at rehearsals and concerts. But a youngster who can play oboe, bass clarinet or French horn may be particularly welcomed. And bassoon or harp players may be highly prized.

Can your youngster make music on this instrument quickly enough to sustain his enthusiasm? Clarinets, saxophones, organ, drum and piano offer much quicker success than, for example, French horn, oboe or violin.

Can you afford to provide your child with a good-quality instrument of the kind he wants? Most music stores now offer parents a wide range of new, "rental-return," and used instruments of beginner, advanced and concert qualities, along with several kinds of rent-purchase plans. But some instruments are still beyond the budget of many families. (Most schools own the largest, most expensive instruments; if your offspring is interested, the band director may assign one to him by the year.)

Can you manage the chauffeuring some instruments require? Clarinets and flutes are rarely a problem, but some school buses rule out even French horns and saxophones, and without a station wagon, a string double bass or drums are almost impossible.

Will the instrument your child chooses be fun for him socially? Drum, trumpet, trombone, piano, clarinet and sax players often find great pleasure and even some profit in various kinds of combos, particularly during the early teen years. But there isn't much a youngster can do with a bassoon apart from a full band or orchestra.

Will your child become discouraged and lose interest if he chooses an instrument that rarely plays the melody and has few solo parts? Many youngsters tire of playing little but counterpoint on an instrument for which there is limited musical literature.

It's also important to consider whether your youngster has time and energy left over from the usual demands of school to take on music as an extracurricular activity. Band is one of the few extracurricular activities offered in many grade schools and as such provides some enrichment for bright youngsters who are insufficiently challenged in class, even if they have little innate music talent. Private music lessons can give many youngsters their only opportunity to work and learn at their own speed.

Once you've decided on lessons and chosen an instrument, how can you avoid hassles about practicing? Expert music teachers make these suggestions:

· Don't insist on an hour of practicing, especially at first. Ten minutes a day may be enough for the first three months your child is working on a new instrument, with fifteen minutes the next three months and a gradual increase up to about half an hour daily by the end of the first year.

· Encourage your youngster to choose a practice time that suits his temperament and doesn't interfere with other cherished activities. Some budding Bernsteins enjoy playing before breakfast; others concentrate better right after an after-school snack. Or perhaps practice time is most effective if it's divided into two short sessions.

· Your child needs a quiet time and place to practice, with no distractions or interruptions. It helps to let your youngster know you put real value on his music by protecting his practice from conflicting activities and not casually changing it for your convenience.

· Don't insist that your child stick to formal exercises during his practice period. If he wants to try picking out a tune or composing on his own or even just experimenting with his instrument, his practice time is still being used productively.

· Show that you enjoy the music your child is making and be enthusiastic about his progress. Let him see you enjoying other forms of music, too, even if it's just by listening.

Music lessons are optional in a child's life and their purpose is enjoyment—now as well as in the future. If the lessons lead to constant nagging about practicing or if your youngster hates every minute he is forced to spend playing, it's time to re-evaluate whether he should be trying to play an instrument at all. You don't need to stop lessons at the first sign of discouragement or lagging interest. Sometimes a change of teachers helps, or a different type of music, or even a vacation of a few months when your child feels particularly pressured. But there is no point in insisting on years of music lessons when your youngster gives little evidence of interest, ability or enjoyment. He may have other talents which should be explored. And there may be many other ways of using leisure that will give him greater rewards.

58. How to Plan Your Child's Summer

Summer's the season to give your child what he, as an individual, needs most, away from the ever-present groupness of his school classroom. It's a time to challenge the gifted and shore up the academic foundations of the slow; a time to relax and a time to seek a new horizon; a time to cultivate a child's talents and a time to let them lie fallow; a time to travel and a time for home; a time to hold a child close and a time to let him go.

Sunshine, exercise, play, freedom from routine and pressure, extra rest—all of these make summer a vital part of childhood. But with some thought and planning, you can use June, July and August for even greater lasting benefits for your youngster. For example:

If your child has been tired, tense, anxious—you can plan his summer as a respite, a relaxing of pressures and demands, a freedom from fear of failure. A summer with nothing to do but grow and unwind emotionally may well be all he needs to bloom by September.

You will have to make sure there will be friends his age in the neighborhood. And you will have to take time to see that he has books, hobby materials and some creative things to do.

The hazard of leaving such a child entirely to his own inclinations is that he finds it too easy to escape into the unrealities and inactivity of constant television.

If school doesn't challenge your youngster enough—you can investigate some of the fascinating new summer school classes now offered increasingly by public-school districts. In many communities, the emphasis of summer school has shifted from the remedial to talent exploration and challenge for the above average. A gifted, creative child may well be bursting with projects of his own that he hasn't time to tackle during the school year. If he wants to spend the summer building a tree house or a go-cart, experimenting with oil paints or chemicals, writing poetry or learning to play another musical instrument, you can see that he has time and materials and that he takes any necessary safety precautions.

If your child has a shaky academic foundation—you should check on the possibilities of remedial summer school. An hour or two a morning in the relaxed atmosphere of a small summer class may easily give him the knowledge and self-assurance he needs to breeze comfortably through the next school year. Most school districts now offer developmental summer classes for such students at small cost, although you usually have to provide transportation.

If you have just moved into an area—you can use the summer to ease the transition for your child. Summer school could help him not only catch up with unfamiliar math methods or a foreign language, but also make new friends quickly and feel at home before September's strains. Or you might find a local day camp that caters for his age group and would provide the friends he needs, if you are sure his academic credentials will permit a smooth transfer.

If he needs more skill in sports or a place to play with friends —you can probably find both in a good local day camp. It can also be an answer if your neighborhood is short of youngsters within your child's roaming limits.

Many park districts now offer excellent programs at minimum cost; some even provide inexpensive transportation. Community agencies often sponsor low-cost day camps. And in some localities you can choose special-interest day camps to give your youngster an introduction to French, local points of interest or an emphasis on a particular sport. (More details about choosing and checking out a day camp are in Chapter 59.)

If your youngster needs more opportunity to be himself—you can help him use summer as a search for identity. School sometimes doesn't give a child much chance to be more than a student. In summer, however, with your aid, he can experiment with other roles, try on a vocation for size, or at least come close enough to nonschool worlds to see what he might like, some day, to become.

The budding ballet dancer, for example, could spend a summer sampling the rigorous physical discipline required by the art. The might-be teacher could help out at a local day-care center. Summer can give a child time to experiment with a hobby that might lead to a career—or he might discover for himself that almost three months of insect collecting, mineral classifying, chemical mixing or studying snakes is enough for a lifetime.

Adventuresome summer school programs usually offer a far wider range of choices than rigid September-to-June curricula; any of several could provide a vocational sampling for your youngster. Specialized summer camps by the dozens give concentrated exposure to music, art, science, sports and theater, and can help a boy or girl decide whether his interest and talent are major or minor.

A child also needs time to think, to dream, to be free from the pressures of what adults tell him he ought to be doing, to let his own soul expand. It isn't easy to protect a bit of private life for a child in today's group-centered world. But summer is the time to try.

If your child is ready for a step toward independence—summer is the easiest time to provide it. School is a bridle for some children all of the time, and for all children some of the time. So summer should be at least one big step away from constant Mother-may-I and Raise-your-hand-before-you-say-anything.

For a child, independence may be only a sleepover night at Grandmother's. Or it can be a day camp or sleep-away camp. It could be a grass-cutting or baby-sitting job with its stepped-up sense of responsibility and economic independence. Or buying a new dress with a friend instead of a parent, or planning a family's dinner or painting a garage. Or almost any all-by-myself things a child wants to try and is reasonably safe in tackling.

The three-month summer school break in the compulsory lock-step and perpetual togetherness of school is the best chance a child has to be himself. But in this overprogrammed world, it still takes a parent's planning to make a worthwhile summer happen.

59. SHOULD YOUR CHILD GO TO DAY CAMP?

Day camps for children flower like dandelions every spring
—run by school systems, park districts, experienced educators,
churches, welfare organizations, private clubs, professional
camp directors, indigent widows and ambitious teen-agers.
Most summer day camps are well run and worthwhile. But
some are no better than group baby-sitting. And a few can be
downright dangerous.

Long before the bloom is on the forsythia and before you
can do more than guess what special needs your child will
have, come July, your mailbox will be full of brochures about
day camps and urgings to send in your deposit. But day camp
isn't always the best place for a child to spend the bulk of his
summer. The pros and cons shape up like this:

Day camp probably is a good idea for your child—
—if the day camp you choose can supply something your
child needs, such as a chance to develop athletic skills, friendly
contact with counselors, opportunity to use equipment you
can't supply, space to run in the sun and explore in the woods.

347

—if your child is constantly bound in by city living, without the freedom and fresh air of his own backyard.

—if most of his pals will be in camp or away during most of the summer so that he will constantly be dependent on you—or on television—for entertainment and something to do from June until September.

—if your youngster needs help in making friends, in developing self-confidence, and learning outdoor and sports skills, and you are convinced the camp counselors will help.

—if he's ready for the experience of getting away from home and being on his own a bit more than school provides.

—if you are frantically busy holding down a job away from home or tied down caring for younger children and can't spend as much time with him as he needs.

—if he's heard talk about camp from his friends and is bursting with eagerness to go.

—if you can find a good day camp reasonably near your home that you can afford.

Day camp may not be a good idea for your child—
—if he is the highly creative type of youngster who is bursting with projects of his own for which he never has time and full of impatience with the everlasting togetherness imposed by school.

—if your neighborhood is full of safe and sunny play space, and stay-home children of his age with whom he can plan his own fun.

—if you have time, energy and inclination to arrange a few special trips and treats for him, to stimulate his curiosity in the world around him and to make his vacation from school more than a continual round of television and whining about what he can do next.

—if you aren't completely satisfied that available day camps in your area meet your standards as to staff, facilities, sanitary regulations, equipment, program and basic philosophy. Day camps have sprung up like weeds in the fast-growing suburbs, and along with the many fine camps with responsible directors are makeshift operations run by untrained teen-agers, well-meaning incompetents and profiteers.

—if you have any doubts about the safety of the method of transportation that will get your child to camp every day.

—if you can't easily afford the rates (which are minimal in many community-sponsored day camps but can run quite high for eight weeks in a privately owned camp).

It isn't always easy to choose a good day camp, if you do decide your youngster will profit from such an experience. Fees are not always a good guide, because some of the best—sponsored by community recreation departments in city parks or by social or youth welfare organizations—may be among the lowest in price.

You can get a good idea about the summer day camp you're considering for your youngster by asking questions like these, based on standards set by the American Camping Association:

1. Does the camp have a varied program? Are activities geared to the needs and interests of campers? Is there time and opportunity for some individual activities as well as projects for small groups and for the entire camp?

2. Do campers have some leisure time for resting and for their own spontaneous fun?

3. Does the camp make use of its natural setting and natural resources? Does the program include campcraft skills and experiences?

4. Is the camp director at least twenty-five years old, with special training or education related to camping? Is he a college graduate, with at least two years of administrative or supervisory experience?

5. Are all the counselors at least eighteen years old, with camping experience? Do at least 20 percent of the staff members have college degrees?

6. Are there enough adult counselors to care for the campers? The American Camping Association calls for one counselor for every ten campers who are eight years old or older; one for every eight campers between the ages of six and eight; and one counselor for every six campers younger than six.

7. Does the camp hold a pre-opening training program for counselors, totaling at least 24 hours?

8. Is there adequate shelter for bad weather?

9. Does the camp have a definite system of health supervision? Does it require a health examination and preventative inoculations before admission? Is a physician on call and a registered or practical nurse or adult with an American Red Cross first aid certificate on the campsite? Is emergency transportation always available?

10. Does all waterfront or swimming-pool activity conform to American Red Cross standards or the equivalent?

11. Are fire-prevention measures adequate?

12. Are children grouped by ages, with provision for special interests at each level?

13. Does the camp comply with all local, county and state sanitation laws? Is storage of milk and perishable foods properly maintained? Are food preparation and dishwashing done according to accepted health and safety regulations? Is rubbish disposal adequate?

14. Are bathroom and handwashing facilities adequate? Clean?

15. If your child will ride a camp bus or station wagon, is the equipment safe? Does the camp have a program of driver safety education? Do the buses and station wagons have sufficient seating for each camper?

Unless you are satisfied with the answers to these questions, you'd be wise to make other summer plans for your child.

60. SUMMER SLEEP-AWAY CAMP

Time was when summer sleep-away camp came in only one style—living in a tent, swimming in a lake, taking turns at KP, hiding a snake in a counselor's bed and braiding a leather belt for your father in handicraft class.

Such conventional summer camps are probably still in the majority among the 13,000-plus camps ready to welcome more than five million youngsters each summer. But today, the concept of summer camping has widened to appeal to a vast range of special interests, talents, personalities and needs among youngsters.

If your offspring enjoys music, you can send him to a camp where he can perform with a symphony orchestra, learn modern jazz, sing with a choir or take courses in conducting, composition, orchestration, harp or accordion. There are camps where he can major in ceramics, sculpture, photography or oil painting.

If your youngster is intrigued with the performing arts, dozens of camps will let her specialize in ballet, modern dance, drama, makeup techniques, set design, choreography or musical comedy. There are camps that feature conversational French, German or Hebrew.

351

Boys and girls who need an academic boost before September don't have to forgo camping in the summer. Dozens of camps provide varying degrees of remedial reading, remedial math, how-to-study and tutoring programs, all combined with the usual swimming, campfire and recreational activities of the conventional camp.

For overweight girls, special reducing camps offer supervised diet and diet instruction along with charm-school courses which include, as one blurb burbled, "hair styling, speech improvement, modeling and social graces." (Most kids come home from camp with mosquito bites, sunburn, dirty fingernails and off-color jokes.)

Science camps for bright youngsters are on the increase. Boys and girls can study biology, chemistry, physics and meteorology in an outdoor setting. One camp lists "a study of mammalian physiology, using many modern research techniques in studying the rat with special emphasis on the study of endocrine, gastrointestinal, cardiac and renal physiology and hematology." (That's a vastly different approach to nature than putting a snake in a counselor's bed.)

Sports enthusiasts can choose among camps that specialize in tennis, baseball ("evening baseball films and critiques; daily instruction by nationally known players"), basketball, fishing, sailing or riding. For youngsters who want to keep on the move, travel camps of every variety cover the United States, Mexico, Canada, and even extend to Europe. For ecology buffs, special camps provide real opportunity to help restore a small space of environment or work on a real farm. For wilderness lovers, there are northern canoe trips and western mountain-climbing package programs.

But before you start sewing name tapes on 12 pairs of white socks or mailing off a deposit to Camp Lum-Bay-Go, there are at least a dozen factors you need to consider. Among them:

· Does your youngster really want to go to camp? Children spend so much of their time doing what adults insist they do that they should have some choice about vacations, if possible.

A boy or girl who is sent to camp without consultation, or under pressure, because his parents want him to lose weight, undergo some "discipline," become a better athlete, or keep out of their hair for two months isn't going to be very happy wherever he goes.

You can often spark enthusiasm for a camp by getting information and pictures for your child, encouraging him to talk to former campers or taking him to a pre-camp roundup. If your child is the kind who is hesitant about trying new things, it may be wise to arrange for him to go with his scout troop or a close friend, at least the first time.

· Is your youngster at least eight years old, preferably ten? Some residential camps take boys and girls as young as age six, but even eight-year-olds can have scarring attacks of homesickness in the best of camps. Ten- to thirteen-year-olds probably enjoy residential camping most. Teen-agers usually aren't enthusiastic unless the camp appeals strongly to a special interest or gives them counselor-in-training opportunities.

· Can you afford it? Private residential camps can cost as much as $800 to $1,500 for an eight-week summer, if you include special clothing, equipment, transportation and expenses for a visitors' day or two. These usually are excellent camps, with low camper-to-counselor ratios, abundant equipment, attractive campsites and often counselors with special skills. Most of these camps offer only four- or eight-week sessions.

Camps sponsored by organizations like Boy Scouts, Girl Scouts, YMCA, YWCA, Campfire Girls, settlement houses and churches usually cost only a small fraction of these fees and may offer scholarships or reduced rates. Often facilities and staff equal those in private camps because much of the cost is paid by the sponsoring agencies or by community-fund grants. But not all of these camps are suitable for every child, and you should investigate before enrolling your offspring. Many limit campers to one to two weeks.

· Has your youngster had experience being away from home overnight before? The independent, adventuresome type of child who has cheerfully slept over with friends since age six usually adjusts to camp with delight. But if yours is the kind who is reluctant to spend much time away from home and adapts slowly to new experiences, you should make sure he's had several happy overnight visits to friends and weekends with grandparents prior to camp.

· Are your expectations about camp realistic? A good summer camp can help develop a youngster's interest in athletics and make social contacts easier. It can give a youngster more self-confidence. But it won't transform a quiet chubby into a star Little Leaguer or turn a shy bookworm into a gregarious leader.

· Does the camp you're considering offer some activities in which your child is already interested? A sound choice gives a youngster a summer of great pleasure and a chance at career exploration; a poor decision may undermine his self-confidence and make him miserable.

· Have you checked out the safety standards and health procedures of the camp? Are you sure your youngster will be adequately supervised?

· Have you talked to parents of previous summer's campers? Such checking can provide an early warning system of possible problems at the camp.

· Does the camp's administration seem to spend an inordinate amount of time and money on recruiting new campers—costs which must be added on to fees charged for the youngsters to attend the private camps?

· Can you provide a good alternative to summer camp for your youngster? Organized, supervised group activity isn't always the best way for every child to spend the summer. Some youngsters need nothing more than a library card and free time, a bicycle and a buddy, or the challenge of finding and keeping neighborhood jobs. And camp is seldom a good substitute for family travel.

61. THE KEEPING OF CHRISTMAS

"Last Christmas our kids tore through an enormous stack of presents in five minutes," groused a suburban father. "Then they asked, 'Is that all we're getting?'

"My wife and I are fed up with Christmas and with our children's attitude," he complained. "It costs us more than we can afford. My wife becomes a nervous wreck getting ready. And it just seems to make our children more selfish and less satisfied."

There's no escaping Christmas in our society, whether you keep it as a holy day, celebrate it as a winter festival centered around the family, or try to explain to your children why you observe other religious occasions instead.

For too many small-fry, Christmas means nothing more than toy commercials on television, a hot and harried visit to a department-store Santa Claus, a shimmering metallic tree and a fight with a brother or sister about who gets the most gifts. It's also the season when full-blown cases of gimme-itis (an enlarged version of the normal "Gimme" which is part of every child) become epidemic. Christmas has grown into the best business-building gimmick of our time—and no matter what their religious faith, or lack of it, parents owe their children more at Christmas than letting them become targets for a commercial rip-off.

What can you do to help your children keep Christmas first of all as an experience of the spirit? Primarily, it's a matter of finding a still, small center of time, in the midst of all the shopping, wrapping, addressing, mailing, baking, partying, rushing, cleaning, decorating and fuss, to talk of meanings and of love. And it's finding a way to share your family's celebration with others outside your home.

If you celebrate Christmas as the birth of Christ, you can use Christmas to teach your children about your faith. As you wrap up presents, you can explain your gift-giving in terms of the Magi. You can talk about the life-everlasting symbolism of the Christmas evergreen as you hang up glittering baubles, and about the star of Bethlehem as you fasten your star on the topmost branch.

Preschoolers usually are intrigued with a crèche and enjoy re-enacting the story of the first Christmas. Putting the youngest child (when he is old enough) in charge of setting up and caring for the manger scene is a teaching tradition in many families. Advent calendars and Advent candles (to light each December Sunday) can also serve as excellent pegs for stories about the meaning of Christmas. And you can also share with your children the Christmas activities of your church: the young people's pageant, the midnight carol service (a memory-in-the-making well worth special planning for extra naps), and special projects for Christmas giving.

Even if you want to keep Christmas as a secular, not a sacred, holiday in your home, it is important to include your children in activities other than just receiving presents. It helps counteract the gimme-itis, for example, to encourage your children to contribute creatively to Christmas at your house in every way they can. Even a three-year-old can make simple decorations for the tree, cards to send to friends and gay decorations for your holiday dinner table, if you don't insist on perfection.

Three- and four-year-olds, particularly, like a tree of their own to trim and retrim with a handful of sturdy baubles, tinsels, pine cones, paper chains and Christmasy cutouts of colored paper. A table-sized, foldaway artificial tree is ideal and usually serves the secondary purpose of keeping small fingers off the fragile delights of the family fir.

You can help by making Christmas giving something children can do, too. If all of your Christmas gifts are store-bought and expensive, what's a seven-year-old to do with a 25-cent allowance and a gift list of eight? If you can show him that the presents which count most can be made with love and imagination, then you've opened the way for him to give, too, and not just to get.

You can fill your Christmas season with the nonmaterial things youngsters can equate with love and being loved: Cookie baking in a fragrant kitchen with all hands helping. Carol singing in a snowy twilight with hot chocolate afterwards. A picnic supper in the living room with carols and Christmas stories in the soft glow of the tree. Building a snow-family together after the season's first big snowfall. Quiet talks by Christmas-tree light when your children won't feel you're under pressure to be doing something else, somewhere else.

You can make some of these shared delights into your own December traditions, so that they become a kind of caulking that helps hold the framework of your family's life together. These are particularly important for parents in the mobile, executive-transfer generation whose children may never be able to remember a single place as their childhood "home."

Your traditions can be trivial or funny, sentimental, solemn or silly. But they should be your own. Your children will always remember the starlight nights you all went caroling. But they'll never even notice that the last few packages were still in store wrappings because you spent your time in better ways.

You can plan a family gift of love in which your children

can fully share, as they cannot participate in the check you send to a Christmas charity. Family discussions about what you can do can provide momentary hush in the holiday rush that provides meaning for all the rest.

For example, your family could build or choose together a toy for the playroom of your hospital's pediatric section. Or you can help your youngsters make some of the stuffed animals or dolls that many hospitals give to small homesick patients.

You could send a CARE package to a country about which your family has read. Or provide a piece of equipment, books, craft supplies or toys for the toddlers' room at your church, or your community's Head Start program for disadvantaged preschoolers, or a nearby day care center or home for mentally retarded children.

You could check on the needs of senior citizens at the nearest nursing home or retirement center. Perhaps your family can contribute an indoor garden, a parakeet, tropical fish, a large-print Bible, phonograph records, piano music, a magazine subscription. Or better, you can make a family gift of service. Youngsters can do many jobs oldsters appreciate: running errands, doing Christmas shopping, writing letters from dictation, reading aloud or pushing wheelchairs.

Whether you celebrate Christmas as a religious holy day or a humanist festival of family love, or whether your family observes the eight days of Hannukkah instead, you do need to keep the emphasis on giving instead of getting. Or your children's gimme-itis may well turn out to be chronic.

62. THANK YOU FOR THE BEAUTIFUL WHATEVERITIS

It's harder to receive than it is to give—especially if you're a parent opening a handmade present from your child on Christmas morning. Summoning up precisely the right words to say about a lopsided clay whateveritis or a papier-mâché somethingorother isn't always easy when your mind is already spinning with the logistics of Christmas dinner and the mental cataloging of thank-you notes owed to whom for what.

It's doubly difficult if you're not sure just what it is your child has created for you. A macaroni necklace is usually easy to identify. So is a car-key holder. But the rather concave piece of hardened, painted clay could be an ashtray. Or perhaps a dish for pins. The cut on the left side could be an abortive spout for a pitcher or maybe merely an accidental gouge. The askew square of woven material lovingly wrapped in hand-decorated paper might well be a pot holder. But sure as you say that that's what you truly hoped to get for Christmas, your child will inform you, between sobs, that it really is a dust cloth or a window wiper or an earring cushion.

Your moppet will be watching your initial reaction to his

359

gift intently. So it helps to have in mind a few noncommittal, appreciative phrases that will show your delight and admiration—and eventually produce enough clues to help you discover precisely what you've been given.

A good opener might be, "You always make such lovely things for me." Or, even just an "Oh, darling," if you can manage just the right tone and add a joyful hug. You also comment favorably on the design, the colors and the workmanship, or probe with "It's wonderful, honey; tell me just how you went about making it."

Another useful opener might be, "How did you ever know what I wanted?" With luck your child may reply, "You keep losing your keys, so I made you a dish to put them in," or, "I wanted to give you something you didn't have, so I made you a button-washing machine."

But be wary of overworking the ambiguities. One seven-year-old blurted angrily to her mother, "You always say something I made is 'interesting.' I think you really mean it's little-kid stuff. I hate that word 'interesting.'"

Once you've discovered what it is your child has so lovingly created for you, do use it. Even if it won't hold water, a clay dish can hold candy or parking-meter change or paper clips or buttons to be sewed on. A handwoven pot holder is always usable, especially if reinforced, unobtrusively, with a second one.

If your youngster's feelings are more important to you than your decor, you may decide that an abstract finger painting or a primitive ceramic does look fine in your traditional or early-American living room. Or you might display your gift in the kitchen on the grounds that "because I'm usually in the kitchen, I can enjoy it most there."

A macaroni necklace or a pipe-cleaner-and-felt ring can go to your most important parties (even if you leave it in the car after you've worn it proudly out your front door for your admiring young audience). Handmade candles can be saved for a special family occasion and used to celebrate a promotion, a good report card or a school election.

It is vastly important to appreciate and encourage your child's first impulses toward giving to others. But if you see with your heart the love with which these gifts are made and given—or remember that the 29-cent tie or the dime-store diamond pin may well have cost all the money your child possessed—you won't have to pretend when you say, "Thank you."

63. "Mommy, Is There Really a Santa Claus?"

In one way, Santa Claus is a lot like sex: Children are apt to be told more about these subjects by playmates than parents are ready for them to find out.

Many parents nowadays find it harder to cope with an unexpected, "Mommy, is there really a Santa Claus?" than with a "Mommy, where did I come from?" They fear that when a child discovers he has been myth-led about Santa Claus it may create a credibility gap that will make him distrust his parents about other matters, particularly the real meaning of Christmas itself.

Parents who are concerned about the Santa Claus problem may find these strategies useful in coping with the situation:

The subordinate Claus—The less a parent blows up the legend of the good Saint Nick, the less a child stands to lose when he begins to question the existence of the man in the red flannel suit.

So it helps to observe Christmas with an emphasis on the birth of Jesus, on mutual gift-giving and holiday preparations with all hands participating, rather than trying to make a youngster believe that it is Santa Claus who brings and decorates the tree and provides all the presents.

The myth-conception ploy—Most youngsters are quite clear about the difference between fantasy and reality by age six or seven, at least as far as witches, fairies, unicorns, dragons, ghosts and ghouls are concerned. A parent who talks about Santa Claus in the same tone of happy skepticism he uses for elves and trolls helps make it easy for a child to assign Santa eventually to the make-believing rather than the believing sector of Christmas.

This let's-pretend-for-fun attitude is also useful in answering a child's questions about Santa Claus in the years when he is still learning about the legend. If he asks, "How can Santa come down our chimney when it's so small?" a parent can reply along the lines of " He must be magic to do all the things the stories about him say he does," or "According to a wonderful story I heard . . ."

Some parents who feel uncomfortable telling a child even a benign untruth about a fantasy never do say to their youngster that Santa Claus exists. They answer "Is there really a Santa Claus?" questions with a casual and loving "No, dear, that's just one of the pretend things about Christmas," even from the early years of a child's life.

But this strategy won't necessarily eliminate the Santa Claus problem. The good saint's influence is so prevalent in our society that even with such parental handling, a child may pick up enough Santa lore from playmates, TV and other adults to convince himself of the whole reindeer-on-the-roof package. One mother who did take the pretend tack with her two youngsters found that one of them remained a contented skeptic all through his childhood. But the second, a congenital romanticist, caught enough of the Santa Claus contagion from playmates to be a firm believer until the age of seven. Then she announced angrily that if there was no Santa Claus she hated Christmas.

The reverse parry—Even when a child is bluntly told the truth about Santa Claus at the age most youngsters no longer believe, he may refuse to accept it unless he's ready. Some children deliberately block out a playmate's assertion that there is no Santa. Others almost seem to enjoy fooling themselves and happily tell parents, "I'm going to believe in Santa Claus one more Christmas."

To learn what a child wants to believe about Santa Claus, a parent can parry the "Is there really a Santa?" question with a loving "What do you think, honey?" If the youngster hopes to have his faith upheld, he'll probably reply something like "Johnny just said that to tease me; I know there's a Santa because he talked to me in the store and he brought me a sled last year."

But if a child is ready to give up the myth, he may answer, "Oh, I knew it was made-up stuff for little kids all along." A parent can then safely launch into a Yes-but-Virginia strategy.

The reverse-parry technique can also be useful in fielding such sticky questions as "How can Santa Claus make toys for all the children in the world?" One solemn four-year-old reassured her mother by answering her own question with, "Oh, his elves make them by the lots and not by the eaches."

Asking a child what he thinks about Santa can sometimes trigger a bit of a Ralph Nader attitude as the youngster begins looking for flaws in the corporeal Santa image. One grandmother still remembers her five-year-old sense of superiority when a department-store Santa used a pencil to write down her Christmas requests. "If he had been real, he would have remembered," she concluded.

Other children are disillusioned when a surrogate Santa can't remember their names from last year. More materialistic moppets may reason that because they didn't get all the presents they wanted, there isn't much point to the Santa business anyway.

The direct-access-to-the-supplier assurance—Often, a major cause of anxiety for a youngster who is facing up to the fact that there is no Santa Claus is whether he'll still get Christmas presents. Once he's convinced that the flow of holiday loot will continue unabated, the worst of the Santa Claus crisis is usually over.

Occasionally a particularly sensitive youngster will react with, "You mean you and Daddy have to pay for all that stuff?" and write a shorter-than-usual list of wanted gifts for a Christmas or two. But many children enjoy learning that the source of the annual windfall is much closer than the North Pole and subject to all the pressures they've learned to apply so skillfully to fathers and mothers.

The Yes-but-Virginia version—The key to the situation, of course, is to so order your Christmas celebration that your child begins to appreciate its true significance long before he outgrows Santa Claus. Before he is six or seven, he can be helped to understand the religious faith that is the foundation of Christmas. He can sample the addictive joy of giving instead of getting, if you encourage him to make Christmas gifts for others and are enthusiastic about his efforts. He can share in your Christmas remembrances for those less fortunate than your family.

One mother, whose son had learned there was no Santa Claus when he had caught his parents hiding presents, asked him a year or so later if the information had spoiled Christmas for him. "Heck, no," replied the eight-year-old. "I like it much better now that I know Christmas is really important. I couldn't figure out what all the fuss was before, if it was just an old guy with a white beard giving stuff to little kids."

Children who are helped to become participants in the celebration of Christmas rather than just spectators rarely miss Santa Claus very much or for very long. For they are able to say, "We have met the real Santa Claus and he is us."

64. BEATITUDES FOR PARENTS

Blessed are the parents who know when to say "No" for they shall not learn firsthand the progenitive powers of a pair of white mice.

Blessed are they who teach their children the relationship between effort and earnings, for they shall not have to support their grandchildren.

Blessed are the parents who do hunger and thirst after learning, for their children shall do likewise.

Blessed are they who do not attempt to tackle the new math, for they shall not fail.

Blessed are the parents who can laugh at themselves, for their children will laugh with them and not at them.

Blessed are you when you shall be called "stodgy" and "old-fashioned" and all manner of uncool adjectives. Rejoice and be assured that you are on the right track, for so have children persecuted their parents for generations and their opinions will change by the time they are old enough to pay taxes.

Blessed are the mothers who have not been warned out of toilet-training their two-year-olds, for they shall save money and time.

Blessed are those who can see the world with the freshness

and excitement of a small child, for they will always be young in heart.

Blessed are they who teach their children to understand and love each other, for they shall not get caught in the crossfire of sib-al war.

Blessed are they who have a colicky baby, for they will have a true appreciation of sleep for the rest of their lives.

Blessed are the parents who let a child do for himself whatever he is capable of doing, for they shall not be merely unpaid servants.

Blessed are the parents of babies who can wake up joyful and clear of eye at 5:45 a.m., for they will have to get up at that hour anyway.

Blessed are they who spend adequate time caring for their children during infancy and childhood, for they shall be spared many teen-age problems.

Blessed are they who do not expect more of their children than is appropriate for their level of maturity, for they shall not be disappointed.

Blessed are the parents who do not get involved in their children's spats with their playmates, for they shall not prolong such squabbles.

Blessed are the parents who take their children along with them often, for they shall see the world with fresh eyes.

Blessed are the father and mother who spend time together occasionally without their offspring, for they shall not go stir-crazy.

Blessed are they who listen to their children, for they in turn will be heard.

Blessed are the father and mother who have found successful creative outlets for their energies, for they will not need their children as status symbols or as justifications.

Blessed are the parents who do not pretend to be perfect, for their children will not be disillusioned.

Blessed are they who pay more attention to their own individual children and their specific needs and reactions than to abstract child-care theories, for they shall not be confused with the swings of the pendulum.

Blessed are they who can be a warm fire of encouragement for their childen, for their offspring will not stay away long from a hearth where they can warm their souls.

Blessed are they who enjoy their children, for they have found a new dimension of love and a reward for all their efforts.

Index